The Germanic Isle

This highly original book explains Hitler's view of Britain as both Nordic ally and role model, and shows that there was a surprising level of affection for Britain and British culture among ordinary Germans, from the discourses of the 1920s to the vigorous anti-British propaganda of the war years.

Despite Hitler's tactical duplicity at Munich, there is overwhelming evidence that one of the Nazis' fundamental objectives was to forge an alliance with Britain and to emulate the 'ruthlessness' of the British Empire in dealing with Eastern Europe. For the German public, admiration of Britain and enjoyment of its culture were enduring factors, even through Goebbels' frequent attacks. But both the Nazi leadership and ordinary Germans lacked first-hand knowledge of Britain, while independent sources were suppressed. Instinctively Hitler predicted that American pre-eminence would deprive the British Empire of great-power status and calculated that Britain would do anything to avoid this. This led in turn to an over-estimation of Britain's willingness to fall in with Germany and an under-estimation of Britain's determination to fight.

The book includes a number of unusual and striking illustrations, most of which will be unfamiliar to modern readers.

GERWIN STROBL is Lecturer in Modern History, Cardiff University.

The Germanic Isle

NAZI PERCEPTIONS OF BRITAIN

GERWIN STROBL

CAMBRIDGE
UNIVERSITY PRESS

PUBLISHED BY THE PRESS SYNDICATE OF THE UNIVERSITY OF CAMBRIDGE
The Pitt Building, Trumpington Street, Cambridge, United Kingdom

CAMBRIDGE UNIVERSITY PRESS
The Edinburgh Building, Cambridge CB2 2RU, UK   http://www.cup.cam.ac.uk
40 West 20th Street, New York, NY 10011-4211, USA   http://www.cup.org
10 Stamford Road, Oakleigh, Melbourne 3166, Australia
Ruiz de Alarcón 13, 28014 Madrid, Spain

First published 2000

Printed in the United Kingdom at the University Press, Cambridge

Typeface Joanna MT 11/13pt.   System QuarkXPress™   [SE]

A catalogue record for this book is available from the British Library

Library of Congress Cataloguing in Publication data
Strobl, Gerwin.
The Germanic Isle : Nazi Perceptions of Britain / Gerwin Strobl.
    p.   cm.
ISBN 0 521 78265 1 (hb)
1. Great Britain – Foreign public opinion, German.   2. Public opinion – Germany –
History – 20th century.   3. Great Britain – Foreign relations – 1936–1945.   4. Great
Britain – Foreign relations – Germany.   5. Germany – Foreign relations – Great Britain.
6. Germany – Foreign relations – 1933–1945.   7. Great Britain – Relations – Germany.
8. Germany – Relations – Great Britain.   I. Title.
DA47.2.S85   2000   327.43041'09'043 – dc21   99-086657

ISBN 0 521 78265 1 hardback

For Piers – *il miglior fabbro*

Contents

Illustrations

Acknowledgements

I am greatly indebted to Professor Michael Burleigh of Cardiff University for his advice and encouragement. I owe an equal debt of gratitude to my father, Professor Werner Strobl, whose ability to predict uncatalogued library holdings in the war-depleted collections of Germany and Austria proved invaluable. I would also like to thank Andrew Robinson of Eton College, at whose welcoming table some of the ideas in this book first started to take shape.

I am indebted to the Bayerische Staatsbibliothek, Munich, the British Film Institute, the British Newspaper Library at Colindale, the Friedrich-Wilhelm Murnau Stiftung, Wiesbaden, the German Historical Institute and the Studienbibliothek des Landes Oberösterreich for their helpfulness. Above all, I am grateful to Professor Jonathan Osmond and the School of History and Archaeology at Cardiff University for supporting and encouraging my research.

Introduction

The German image of Britain was a significant factor in the course of the Second World War. Among the enemies of the Third Reich Britain held a unique position. She alone fought Germany from the beginning of the war to its end, and did so, paradoxically, as the one country the Nazis had not sought to engage in conflict. Belief in a possible accommodation with Britain dominated German thinking in the thirties and resurfaced periodically throughout the war. Of the Nazis' many misjudgements none was more glaring and persistent than this. This is clear from events which punctuated and influenced the course of events from 1939 to 1945: Göring's last-minute efforts to avoid war, Hitler's repeated peace offers at a time of supreme Nazi self-confidence, the secret flight into the heart of the enemy camp by Rudolf Hess – an act unparalleled in modern warfare – and the hopes of the Nazi leadership even in their last months of power that the Allied coalition would break up.

The facts are well known; their background much less so. In the vast literature on the Third Reich there are surprisingly few works that examine its perceptions of Britain in any systematic way. Many of the accounts are very wide in scope and thus unable to focus specifically on Britain. Studies of Nazi foreign policy do scrutinise Anglo-German relations very closely but they concentrate, quite properly, on speeches, memoranda and diplomatic exchanges. Only rarely do they attempt to examine the underlying German assumptions. The same is true of the literature on Nazi propaganda. Biographies of the leading members of the regime, meanwhile, portray the views of individuals, and inevitably tend to do so in relative isolation. Intellectual history, finally, has largely neglected Nazi perceptions of Britain in favour of accounts of racial thought that inevitably directs the gaze eastwards towards the Reich's killing fields.

This study, then, aims to fill a gap. It seeks to place the views about Britain of prominent Nazi leaders within a wider context. The aim is not necessarily to prove specific influence but to establish patterns of thought common to Germans – both Nazi and non-Nazi – before and during the Third Reich. Such an approach carries undeniable methodological problems. A nation's perceptions are less easily traced than the policies of its government or the views of its leaders. But there are clues. The press provides an obvious starting point. In a country as large as pre-war Germany this itself poses challenges, however. Given the range of the German press, it is important to understand which publications were the most significant in influencing the regime's views. Newspapers and periodicals with liberal views, for instance, clearly had less impact on the Nazis than those of the various strands of the political right. Weeklies are given particular attention, since they are less concerned with day-to-day events than the press and can devote more systematic thought to the issues. For example, a widely read periodical such as Der Türmer is of particular relevance, due to its editorial policy of combining politics, philosophy and the arts. This reflects more accurately the workings of the human mind: it is around connections detected and parallels attempted that perceptions first take shape. Retracing such perceptions is not unlike viewing a pointillist picture: the individual dots remain baffling until a larger section of the canvas is examined.

More generally, in a country as proud of its Kultur as Germany, British culture substantially influenced overall perceptions of Britain. It is helpful, therefore, as a second focus, to understand the reading habits of the German public, the choice of plays in the country's vast network of publicly funded theatres, etc. The fact that the Nazi regime famously devoted great attention to controlling the arts after 1933 merely underlines their importance.

There is a third area that seems worth examining in detail. During the Weimar years, the teaching of English became a recognisable factor in German education as English supplanted French. Just as French thought and culture had entered Germany along with the French language, there is evidence that a similar process occurred in the case of English. Hence this study also considers the perceptions of Britain expressed in the publications of Germany's Anglisten – the teachers and professors of English. Their views were a significant influence, especially on younger

Germans who came to adulthood at the time of the Nazis. What is more, the Third Reich later relied substantially on the expertise of the *Anglisten* in its propaganda war. Combined, all this provides the background against which the development of Nazi thought in the party's own publications and the writings of its leadership is examined.

After 1933, the vast range of sources available during the Weimar years is rapidly impoverished: the flood of thought becomes a stagnant pool. Since the press was brought very rapidly under Nazi control, and books for a general readership were subject to strict censorship, academic publications are of particular interest. They enjoyed at least a measure of independence, and the topics covered thus allow one to chart the gradual nazification of German society. This process ends with the outbreak of war, which completes the intellectual *Gleichschaltung*.

The war years constrain the available sources. There is still technically a substantial range of newspaper titles, but the editorial content of individual papers is practically indistinguishable. None the less, some publications are of greater interest than others. The newspaper of the SS, for instance, often provides hints of internal party debate. *Das Reich*, was close to Goebbels, who regularly contributed articles. Since this was all essentially *propaganda* – not necessarily the same as perceptions – it needs to be supplemented by other sources. The leadership's private opinions, where these survive, are of obvious interest – not least because discrepancies with official propaganda regularly emerge.

As for the German public, individual diaries provide an invaluable starting point. Deliberately 'apolitical' periodicals, such as the *Berliner Illustrierte Zeitung*, are also useful. Their inevitably restricted choice of topics allows at least an indirect glimpse of their readership. The reports of Himmler's security services provide additional evidence: conversations overheard, letters transcribed, public reactions to events or their reporting in the papers and the cinema newsreels, etc. The result reveals a reassuring plurality of views, thus adding to the credibility of the sources. But discernible patterns in German perceptions do also emerge for the period investigated in this study.

A degree of caution is none the less indicated. History deals with facts, but needs to assess their relative importance. This book is an interpretation of the available evidence. Such evidence can never be complete, and the interpretation will need to be tried, evaluated and, where necessary, corrected. The diarist Viktor Klemperer provides in his wartime journals a graphic example of the difficulties facing the historian. Klemperer, a Jewish German, who survived because of his marriage to an 'Aryan' wife, records a conversation with a friendly stranger in 1943. When he observed that as a 'non-Aryan' restrictions were placed on his freedom of action, his interlocutor inquired without a trace of disingenuousness, 'What is a non-Aryan?'[1]

This was more than ten years after the Nazi Seizure of Power. For Klemperer, who had been professionally concerned with the intellectual traditions of European nations, it was an epiphany. It provoked in him fundamental questions which resound down the decades: what can safely be assumed about the extent of a nation's knowledge? What does this collection of individuals think? What does it feel? The challenges in understanding national perceptions and making assumptions about the impact of propaganda could scarcely be expressed more clearly than this. Yet this did not dissuade Klemperer from seeking to establish what the country around him thought and felt. For the alternative, as Klemperer knew, was to concede victory to the Nazis and leave uncontested the fallacy that the Führer expressed the thoughts and desires of the entire German nation.

I The view from Weimar: German perceptions of Britain before 1933

The origins of Nazi attitudes to Britain lie in the early years of the Weimar era. Unlike much of the National Socialist mindset, Nazi perceptions of Britain were not primarily shaped by the *Fronterlebnis* – the experience of fighting in the trenches of the Western Front or on the Russian plain. They were a post-war phenomenon: the result of a reassessment after Versailles of Germany's and Britain's respective places in the European order. Their gradual development is familiar enough. It is reflected in the transcripts of Hitler's early speeches in Munich. These records, produced by Bavarian constables on political surveillance duty, document a slow transformation of Hitler's thinking in the early 1920s.[1] The blind hatred of Britain, carried over from the trenches, is progressively attenuated. There are, quite simply, more pressing targets: Weimar democracy at home, and France and her eastern allies abroad. In the case of Britain, enmity thus softens to indifference, which in turn gives way to the first tentative suggestions of a possible future Anglo-German accord. By the time of Hitler's trial and imprisonment after the Munich *putsch*, the transformation is complete. *Mein Kampf* and its well-known advocacy of an alliance with Britain merely confirms the new outlook.[2]

That process is mirrored in the recorded response to Hitler's views among the emerging Nazi hierarchy: in the diaries of Joseph Goebbels or the journalism of Alfred Rosenberg, the party's main 'intellectuals'. Goebbels moves in the space of a few weeks in 1926 from independent thought, via a period of uncertainty ('Perhaps he's right?'), to the new orthodoxy ('His reasoning is compelling').[3] Rosenberg, too, has detected the strength of the prevailing wind, and reacts to it with his customary alacrity. While Goebbels still agonises, his perennial rival is already re-writing history: 'The Nazi party', Rosenberg declares in February 1926 in an article for the party newspaper, 'has always looked on the British Empire not merely as something that exists whether we like it or not but as a stabilising factor'.[4] Dissenting voices – both within the party and the wider nationalist constituency – thus did not ultimately matter: it was Hitler's views that carried the day. A study of the Third Reich's official position towards Britain might therefore content itself largely with an analysis of Hitler's thought on the subject, and older 'Hitler-centric' accounts have indeed followed that approach.[5]

There are, however, problems with this – and one does not have to go to the opposite extreme of dismissing Hitler as a mere cipher, pushed hither and yon by the contending factions in his party, to find fault with it. Two principal objections must be raised. The first is about how Hitler himself arrived at his conclusions. Any interpretation focusing narrowly on Hitler's personality runs the risk of implying that his views were somehow created in a vacuum. This is a rather unfortunate echo of the Nazis' own preferred account: that of the Führer wrestling with his soul in the loneliness of Landsberg prison and discovering deep inside himself Germany's road to salvation. This is not quite what happened. Hitler may have disliked the detailed briefings and lengthy memoranda of more orthodox politics, but he did seek information. Both *Mein Kampf* and the oracular pronouncements collected in the so-called *Table Talk* suggest a wide range of half-digested sources.[6]

The second problem with concentrating overmuch on Hitler's role is that it fails to explain why his views on Britain should have achieved such apparent resonance *outside* the party. Support for an alliance with Britain, as the example of Joseph Goebbels demonstrates, was by no means pre-ordained. The First World War cast a long shadow over Germany in the 1920s and 1930s, and the wartime mood of *Gott strafe England* – 'May God punish England' – did not form the most promising basis for a future alliance. Public enthusiasm after 1933 for Hitler's principal foreign-policy aim is therefore significant. And it cannot simply be explained away with references to his personal magnetism or the effectiveness of Nazi propaganda. For one thing, the new mood of anglophilia already existed in the earliest moments of the regime, before Goebbels and his ministry had properly got into their stride. Nor were the Nazis subsequently able to find similar support for other aspects of their foreign policy.

The Third Reich, for instance, bombarded its population over many years with glowing accounts of Germany's friendship with Italy.

The Rome–Berlin Axis was, moreover, specifically identified with the figure of Hitler.[7] Yet all the evidence suggests that this had little effect. The vast majority of Germans seem to have gone on disliking and distrusting their Italian allies; indeed, they appear to have found in the strategic disaster of Italy's desertion in 1943 the private satisfaction of having been proved right.[8] German anglophilia in the 1930s, and beyond, therefore cannot simply be explained by and through Hitler. It existed independently of him. The extraordinary welcome Prime Minister Chamberlain received in Munich proves that abundantly. By 1938 Hitler had largely abandoned the idea of immediate Anglo-German friendship.[9] The German public evidently had not.

The regime understood this perfectly. It is not for nothing that Chamberlain 'and his deceptive umbrella' became the object of an intense propaganda campaign after Munich to win over the crowds to the new anti-British course.[10] Readying the Reich for war clearly meant 're-educating' the German public about Britain. Significantly, no such endeavour was deemed necessary in the case of France or Poland, the other two prospective adversaries of 1939. And Britain remained the principal target of German domestic propaganda even after the Reich's strategic interests had shifted decisively elsewhere two years later. The vehemence of Nazi outbursts – Goebbels famously claimed, 'We hate the British from the depth of our soul' – was itself incongruous at a time when Stalin's Russia was Germany's main opponent on the battlefield. This struck some observers monitoring Nazi propaganda as remarkable even before the fighting had ceased. The authors of a 1944 study on the Reich's propaganda broadcasts specifically highlighted these points, and it is worth quoting their thoughts at length, since little written before or since has been more perceptive:

> Perhaps the Germans do not hate the British as much as the content of Nazi propaganda suggests . . . It may be interesting to note that Goebbels . . . has never found it necessary to proclaim, 'We hate the Bolsheviks from the depth of our soul.' One does not say what goes without saying, and one may, as a propagandist, sometimes have to make a statement of fact out of what is really an incitement.[11]

This was a shrewd – and a brave – observation to make in 1944: doubly so, since its authors had no access to the private thoughts of the Nazi leadership. After the war, and more particularly after the publication of

Hitler's *Table Talk* and of the *Goebbels Diaries*, the often startling gap between the leaders' public diatribes against Britain and their real opinion gradually became apparent. We now also know from the reports compiled by Himmler's internal security services that the German public remained largely unmoved by these incitements to hatred.[12] The Third Reich, in other words, had only limited success after 1938 in changing German perceptions of Britain. To understand why this should have been so, one must go back some twenty years earlier, to a time when the Nazi party was still insignificant, and Hitler's voice only one among many. And one must examine not just the political conditions of the period, but the emotional temperature of a German public living in the shadow of Versailles.

As the economic and political consequences of the imposed peace became apparent, Germany went into a state of shock. The sheer scale of the collapse in the nation's fortunes appeared overwhelming. With substantially reduced economic resources, mounting internal debt and almost open-ended Allied demands for reparations, the country lacked the means to regain even a modicum of stability. What is more, the network of controls and restrictions seemed designed to keep Germany at starvation level and so perhaps induce a break-up of the state. Beyond Germany's shrunken borders things seemed no less disheartening. The country lacked friends or prospective partners. Its pre-war allies had all but vanished from the maps of Europe and the Middle East. In their place, an iron ring of hostile nations, old and new, encircled Germany. Clearly, a return to the pre-war world of *Mitteleuropa* and the Central Powers was impossible even on a much reduced scale; that, of course, had been the intent of the various treaties signed on the outskirts of Paris. This left Germany with few choices in foreign affairs. Apart from cultivating ties with the handful of neutral countries on the fringes of Europe, some *modus vivendi* would have to be reached with former enemies in the Great War.

This was easiest with latecomers to the war, or countries which had only played a relatively minor role in it. The republics of Latin America were a case in point. Though technically in the enemy camp in the final stages of the war, they had largely remained free from the taint of being *deutschfeindlich* – 'Germanophobic' – which (together with its antonym – *deutschfreundlich*) became the main German criterion in the 1920s for distinguishing between the nations of the world. In the case of Latin America this solipsistic approach encouraged ties that would eventually stand the

Third Reich and its leadership in good stead – not least *after* the Reich's collapse. More generally, it encouraged trade links and a greater interest in Hispanic affairs both at a private level and as a government priority through the funding of university departments or research bodies such as the Ibero-Amerikanisches Institut in Hamburg. Efforts were also directed towards former enemies who had visibly broken with the politics of their wartime past. The two most prominent instances were Soviet Russia and Fascist Italy. If their respective forms of government made them each unpalatable to important sections of the German public, their potential usefulness as economic or political partners was none the less recognised. Both countries would later play pivotal roles in the Third Reich's bid for European dominance.

This still left the hard core of enemy nations to be considered. Here it is often overlooked that the treaty of Versailles, with which these countries were most closely associated, did not merely affect German national pride and economic health. It impinged on people's lives much more immediately. Take, for example, the case of a man living in Dresden whose family roots lay in the Prussian town of Bromberg. After Versailles he would have to think of his family's hometown as *abroad*. His wife, born in Königsberg – which remained German (for the time being) – was also affected: visiting her relations there now involved foreign travel (through the new Danzig Corridor). Friends of the family living in Danzig itself had become citizens of a third country: the Free City of Danzig, Polish-occupied and nominally under the supervision of the League of Nations. Maintaining personal ties thus required passports and three sets of currencies. Back in Dresden, where our man was professor of French, there were yet other signs of change. The city's university had traditionally attracted students from the nearby Sudetenland. These young people, German-speaking and Austrian by birth, culture and tradition, had at the stroke of a pen in St Germain become *Zwangs-Tschechoslowaken* – 'Czechoslovaks-under-duress'. As letters with exotic postmarks arrived from once-familiar places, the professor noted drily that these were exciting times for stamp collectors. Professional contacts brought further reminders of life in the new Europe; some of his colleagues from the Rhineland could only be contacted by letter because the French occupying authorities had restricted travel from one part of Germany to another. Colleagues from the lost lands had been affected more dramatically. Most of the academics teaching at Strasbourg University, for instance, had been summarily dismissed and quite literally frogmarched across the Rhine.

Their libraries and much of their personal property had been confiscated by the victors. One man, married to a woman from Alsace, had not just been separated from his books. He had not seen his wife for over a year because the French authorities, having deprived him of home, property and livelihood, had then also refused his wife permission to join her husband in Germany. These cases are neither hypothetical nor unique. They are recorded – with much more in a similar vein – in the diaries of Viktor Klemperer, the German Samuel Pepys of the period.[13]

Inevitably these experiences coloured German perceptions of the outside world. They led the fair-minded Professor Klemperer to remind himself of German conduct in Belgium and Poland during the war; but they led him also to quote from Homer's *Iliad* on the price of all hubris: 'the day will dawn that sees sacred Ilium fall'.[14] In the meantime, the sight of Ilium's provocative tricolour over the occupied town of Mannheim was to Klemperer 'like a physical blow', and on at least one occasion events drove this life-long admirer of French culture to wonder how it was 'that such sublime literature should have been produced by such a low and vile nation?'[15]

The general sense of national humiliation was frequently reinforced by personal indignities: being deprived of property, having to bribe or dodge occupying forces to cross the new internal frontiers, or simply being set upon by foreign soldiery.[16] Versailles did not discriminate between individual Germans according to their political views: it sought to punish the entire nation. The nationalist backlash therefore also went beyond its core constituency of disaffected officers and soldiers. If there is to modern eyes and ears something fevered and obsessive about the German reaction to Versailles, there is no mistaking the fact that the anger was often rooted in very personal grievances.

There seemed, moreover, no hope of redress. Dreams of the Fall of Ilium, or of the Flaming Sword of Justice descending on Allied heads seemed distant prospects in a disarmed and partially occupied republic. The catalogue of grievances did, however, have a more immediate effect: it encouraged the German people, individually and collectively, to distinguish between the main enemy countries. This was to have profound consequences for Anglo-German relations. The wartime hatred of 'perfidious Albion' began to wither, and it did so largely through being denied new nourishment. Britain, for whatever reason, seemed to be displaying less pettiness and spite than France or some of the new East European states in their treatment of the substantial German minorities which they had acquired. The sense that Britain was somehow different did not come at once. It was a gradual process and not without temporary setbacks. Nor, of course, was it a uniform process, affecting equally all regions and sections of society.

The causes for a change in the image one nation has of another are in any case rarely straightforward, cut-and-dried affairs. Public opinion is not solely shaped by the signing of treaties and conventions. It is often the small things that count: the spontaneous gesture as much as the carefully plotted diplomatic initiative. Where there is extensive personal contact between two nations, it will affect the collective perception. In the absence of much individual contact, and – with the exception of occupied Cologne – there was little of it between Germans and Britons in the early 1920s, specific well-published incidents can take on considerable symbolic significance. Wider European history proves the point. No one with memories of the Cold War, for instance, will have forgotten the deployment, for rhetorical effect, of Mr Khrushchev's shoe at the United Nations. That lively incident defined the essence of the Soviet Union for many who had been spared closer acquaintance with it.

It is probably fair to say that there were no moments of comparable drama in the history of Anglo-German relations during the Weimar years. In fact it was the absence of drama which eventually and as it were cumulatively produced an effect. Even the thorny issue of reparations did not seem able to puncture the calm politeness of British statesmen and emissaries. This did not go unnoticed. In July 1920, for instance, the German press reported that Prime Minister Lloyd George had inclined his head in the direction of the German delegation upon arrival at the Spa conference. That kind of reporting struck at least some German readers as 'humiliating'.[17] What made it humiliating was that it reflected all too accurately Germany's international standing. Much the same happened during the London conference on German reparations in the following year. The conference brought little cheer for Germany in diplomatic terms. Yet the press, once more, detected a silver lining. The German delegation had been allowed to move about freely in the streets of London and British officials and the public had displayed impeccable civility towards them. It would be easy to dismiss such reporting as poor journalism: an attempt to fill column inches in the absence of more substantial news. Certainly, it is evidence of the political naiveté of the young Weimar democracy and its belief that the Allies would see in it the democrats and not the Germans. Yet the German press was surely also right to detect a simple humanity and decency *at the personal level* that had been noticeably absent in France two years earlier. As such, these reports are revealing about the level of German expectations in the early 1920s.

In Munich, Hitler certainly thought so, as he inveighed against a state that regarded the barest civilities from foreign statesmen as a diplomatic triumph, and was ready to describe 'a kick in the pants' as being caused by a 'not intolerable boot'.[18] However hard it may be to gauge the exact effect of such press reports, Hitler's rage bears witness to their potency. A nation that has become accustomed to displays of enmity and contempt in foreign statesmen will eventually attach significance to their mere absence. Hitler's speeches and essays of the period, with their running commentary on events, are unintentionally revealing. The targets of his anger or sarcasm provide a glimpse of public opinion at the time: British 'tactfulness', 'moderation' and 'decency', hopes of British 'friendship' or 'succour' even, all amounted in Hitler's mind to a 'childlike and trusting *naiveté*' and a readiness to follow this British 'Pied Piper of Hamelin'.[19]

The notion of Britain being different gained credibility from other factors. And, paradoxically, it is Hitler once more who provides key evidence. It was Hitler's custom in many of his early speeches to set out in brief terms what he regarded as the nature of Germany's relations with the other European powers. These schematic exposés, designed to impress but not overtax his audience, invariably suggested that there were in the post-war world no obvious conflicts of interest between Germany and Britain. Above all, there were no rival territorial claims. This sanguine view might have occasioned some surprise in London at the time, not least in the Colonial Office. Yet, appearances notwithstanding, Hitler was right.

Germany had, of course, lost her colonies and most of these had gone to Britain or Britain's Dominions. But Germany's overseas empire had always been something of a minority interest. The colonial era had perhaps been too brief – less than forty years – to touch the Germans deeply. There continued to exist a colonial lobby which generated a level of noise wholly disproportionate to its numbers. Yet its tracts and meetings merely served to emphasise its remoteness from the common national experience. This put it more on a level with spiritualism and the raising of the dead than practical politics. It is significant that the influential Austrian travel writer Colin Ross could be entirely dismissive of the colonial lobby and its aims without apparently suffering a decline in sales. During the Weimar years Ross provided, through his books, a major source of information for middle-class Germans whose budgets would not permit overseas travel. It was therefore natural for him to comment on the subject of the colonies, and this he did in forthright terms. He did not regret the loss of Tanganyika or Togoland. If anything, he feared their return. By the late twenties, when a revision of the treaty of Versailles seemed increasingly likely, Ross expressed his alarm at the thought that Germany might eventually find herself encumbered with 'some worthless bit of Africa'.[20] German colonists, he argued, were encountering no noticeable difficulties in pursuing their commercial interests in most of the former colonies, and they could do so without incurring for the nation the costs of actual colonial government. The old colonial empire, by contrast, had simply been a drain on German resources. Ross went on to be much published in the Third Reich, and his writing may well have influenced a leadership rarely more than tepid about the return of the colonies.[21] Hitler, in fact, mentions Ross expressly in one of his wartime monologues as 'a more useful source of information than the [Foreign Office] diplomats'.[22]

In their attitudes to the lost colonies the contrast between the generation that grew up under the Kaiser and that which reached maturity in the Weimar years is often striking. A diary entry by Joseph Goebbels, then just in his forties, provides a telling example. It records in tones of disbelief that the ageing Foreign Minister von Neurath had attempted to negotiate with the Japanese about the return of a few token South Sea atolls. 'Poor old Neurath', writes Goebbels, and the condescension seems to owe as much to Neurath's quixotic quest as to the fact of his dismissal from the cabinet that morning.[23] It is one of the many ironies of Anglo-German relations that Whitehall at this time should have been agonising about how best to satisfy Germany's apparent colonial ambitions.

One other potential boil on the face of Anglo-German rapprochement, the fate of the Kaiser's fleet, had also quickly been lanced. The German Navy succeeded in scuttling much of it at Scapa Flow before the ordered handover. This display of the German equivalent of the 'Dunkirk spirit', under the very gun turrets of the Royal Navy, brought a rare moment of joy amid the post-war gloom. If Versailles to German eyes seemed like a brigands' charter, here at least the brigands had been cheated of their prize. And if, as the Allies claimed, the surrender of the fleet was in the interest of disarmament, why then they would have no grounds to complain. Britain's relatively calm response to the Scapa Flow affair further defused the situation and, again, provided a distinct contrast to French posturing.

Britain's way of implementing other treaty provisions also tended to reduce rather than exacerbate German resentment. This was particularly the case with British forces stationed on the Rhine. Unlike its French counterpart, the British Army had not been dispatched in pursuit of secret territorial ambitions, and conducted itself accordingly. This put the presence of the two Allies on a different footing from the outset. Historically, France had rarely been content with her acquisition of Alsace and Lorraine. Successive generations of French rulers – Bourbon, Napoleonic and republican – had made little secret of their designs on the entire left bank of the Rhine. The great medieval cities of Cologne, Mainz and Trier, and the coronation churches of Aachen, Worms and Speyer – Germany's historical heartland – had all shared periods of undesired French rule. For a short while under Napoleon, France even achieved the geographical feat of a common frontier with Denmark. Under the terms of Versailles, the Saar with its valuable industrial and mineral resources became in effect a French colony (and would do so again after 1945). France's so-called *Mission Rhenane* had been as much a constant in European politics as Germany's own *Drang nach Osten*. And it is not irrelevant here that Britain had repeatedly been instrumental in checking French expansionism. Germans were reminded of this not just in the schoolroom. Beethoven's musical tribute to the Duke of Wellington or Haydn's *Nelson Mass* were a lasting testimony to British help and German gratitude. Indeed, the very tune which in 1922 was adopted as Germany's national anthem revealed a connection with Britain. Haydn had composed it in imitation of 'God Save the King' as part of the (Habsburg) patriotic endeavour against Napoleon. During the French occupation of Vienna in 1809, the aged Haydn – then close to death – was carried to his piano each day to allow him to play 'God Save our Emperor Franz' as a personal act of defiance.[24]

Nor had Britain's past assistance been limited to the war against Napoleon. A century earlier the Duke of Marlborough had halted French armies at Blenheim – a good hundred miles *east* of the Rhine. In the Third Reich Marlborough would duly become the subject of a biographical novel celebrating the age when 'Britain's might' was thrown against 'rapacious' France, thus saving Europe 'from the French jackboot'.[25] (The family connection with Churchill added a mischievous piquancy in 1939 to such reminiscences.) There existed, in other words, a wider memory of European history which was itself a factor in the political and emotional equations. It allowed the German public to give Britain at least the benefit of the doubt, just as it made them instantly suspicious of French motives.

This perception of differing Allied intentions was in fact perfectly accurate. History had already repeated itself at Versailles: once again a French Prime Minister had attempted to sever the Rhineland from Germany, and like his predecessors he had been thwarted in this by the voice of Great Britain. The German public knew nothing of this, nor were they familiar with Clemenceau's characteristic remark that having secured the right to occupy the area for fifteen years, France would find an excuse for holding on to it afterwards; but the fact that French intentions in the early twenties were both hostile and dishonest was plain enough to see. Equally plain was the fact that Britain's own position *was* different.[26]

This was as much in evidence on the streets of Rhenish towns as at diplomatic conferences. At the level of the individual soldier, French antipathy frequently translated into an undisguised relish of the role of occupier, and of the opportunities it afforded for private acts of revenge. Tales of women and children forced with riding crops from pavements into muddy streets or being subjected to other petty humiliations tended to emanate predominantly from the French and Belgian zones. They were rooted no doubt in these nations' wartime memories but did little to win over German civilians to the post-war order. British occupation, while not without friction, was a more restrained affair.[27]

The British zone covered only a very small part of Germany. Most Germans, therefore, were not personally affected by it. Intriguingly, one prominent member of the Nazi leadership was. In 1919 Joseph Goebbels attempted during the university vacation to get from Heidelberg to his hometown of Rheydt. He was travelling without the necessary papers and was promptly stopped by a British soldier. An earlier attempt to cross the demarcation line had already failed. On this second occasion, a sum of money was gingerly offered – and accepted; the 'Tommy' smiled, attempted a word or two of German, and young Goebbels continued his progress unimpeded.[28]

Whatever the outcome of this particular Anglo-German encounter, the wider experience of the occupation does not appear to have left much bitterness in the Rhineland. In the well-documented case of Cologne, at least, the British were given a warm send-off. No British serviceman, it seems, could enter a public house on the eve of evacuation without experiencing exuberant Rhenish hospitality up to – and often beyond – closing time.[29] If the prospect of a city free at last from occupation may have helped loosen the corks that night, there are also intriguing details about the arrival of British forces in December 1918. British soldiers billeted in requisitioned houses or rooms were often astonished by the friendly reception that awaited them. Many of them were given Christmas presents by their involuntary 'landlords' – all of six weeks after the armistice, and at a time when malnutrition brought about in part by the British blockade was very much in evidence in the city.[30] (It is tempting to speculate what the reception of *German* soldiers would have been like in Britain under comparable circumstances.)

Some of the friendliness stemmed no doubt from sheer relief that at least the occupying army was not French. Not being French in fact constituted one of Britain's chief virtues as far as the ordinary German was concerned. Political events were soon to reinforce that perception. The Ruhr crisis of 1923, when France unilaterally occupied additional German lands to press her reparation payments, proved another accidental milestone in Anglo-German relations. At an official level, it revealed tensions between London and Paris which could only be beneficial to Germany's position. On the ground, British forces became the main obstacle to French attempts to break up the German republic and create a satellite state in the Rhineland. In retrospect, one can detect parallels between the atmosphere in Cologne in 1923 and that in Berlin a quarter of a century later during the Allied airlift.[31] Unlike 1948, however, German hopes of sustained British support were quickly dashed in the twenties. Yet even the ensuing disappointment could not entirely obscure the fact that Britain and France had *not* acted in unison against Germany. Ultimately, this also suggested an outlet for popular anti-French sentiment. Germany lacked entirely the means to retaliate economically, politically or by force of arms. Passive resistance had likewise failed in the face of overwhelming French force. That did, however, leave as a target France's well-known cultural sensitivities.

There were precedents. In the eighteenth century political impotence had spurred on a cultural revival directed against the dominance of French in the aristocracy's culture and manners. Culture became an obvious vehicle for individual patriotic sentiment both during the wars against Napoleon, known in Germany as the Wars of Liberation, and during the invasion scare of 1840. In 1923 Germany's secret weapon against French bullying was even more imaginative: it was the enthusiastic embrace of the English language. English finally replaced French in the curriculum of most German schools.[32]

The gradual eclipse of French had started during the war with a reluctance to learn or speak it. Victor Klemperer, who for professional reasons was highly conscious of Germany's linguistic preferences, refers by way of illustration to the example of a society lady in Dresden. French had been banished from her salon at the outbreak of the war (Italian followed suit in 1915).[33] Versailles had done little to make her change her mind. If rejecting French had been one possible reaction, taking up English became another. Before the war English had been a minority interest. With the exception of a small North German and Prussian elite that traditionally displayed its anglophilia by sending its sons to Oxford, few Germans had even a passing acquaintance with it. Many members of the *Bildungsbürgertum* – the educated middle classes – would have found it easier to conduct a conversation in Latin, or even Greek.

The growing interest in English after 1919 is therefore significant. In part it was simply a recognition of a changed world. Schoolmasters and academics tended to allude to this at first with revealing defensiveness. The emphasis was on the usefulness of the language – which contrasts tellingly with the traditional German ideal of knowledge as an end in itself. Support for this view came in the form of various government exhortations about the need to acquaint young Germans with the wider post-war world.[34] Such pronouncements, however, barely disguised the underlying anti-French agenda. After the occupation of the Ruhr this became even more blatant. Supplanting French officially with 'the more useful' English was, after all, a much more studied insult than merely neglecting it in the manner of Victor Klemperer's society acquaintance.[35]

The France of Versailles had sought to marginalise Germany in Europe – even to the extent of re-routing international express trains (the continent's most famous *grande ligne*, the 'Orient Express', for instance, had mutated into the 'Venice–Simplon–Orient' to spare French travellers the sight of German signs on railway platforms). After the invasion of the Ruhr, Germany took pleasure in demonstrating that France could be sidelined with equal ease. The Klemperer diaries of the 1920s provide among other things a record of a French specialist's worries about the double encroachment of English and Spanish on his profession: on limited government resources, on declining library provision and student numbers.[36] But the diaries also provide something else: they chart, if perhaps unintentionally, a corresponding erosion of the earlier anti-British animus.

At the first post-war meeting in 1920 of Germany's *Neuphilologen* – the country's experts in foreign languages and letters – politics had still interfered substantially with the meeting's agenda. Men and women teaching another country's language and culture might be expected to have a regard for that nation – if only as part of their *déformation professionelle*. This proved not to be the case in 1920. Some slight ambivalence about France might perhaps have been expected, and Klemperer does indeed note that 'professors of French seem to feel the need to apologise for teaching that language'. But the *Anglisten* – the professors of English – hardly fared any better. An attempt to restore the revoked membership of their organisation to an Oxford don of German extraction, who during the war had ventured some mild criticism of Germany in *The Times*, was voted down amid tumultuous scenes. All that could be agreed upon in the interest of international reconciliation was to delete from the minutes all reference to the unseemly row. There were calls, it is true, for increased provision of English in German universities; but one might agree with Klemperer's verdict that this was little more than enlightened self-interest: a case of professional men eyeing government funds. A remark by an eminent *Anglist* at Leipzig University captures the spirit of the meeting more accurately: 'what we need', he suggested, 'is a textbook . . . highlighting the problems of British colonial rule'. This observation, notes Klemperer, was much applauded.[37]

Against such a background the widespread adoption of English as Germany's first foreign language does seem significant. After the Ruhr Crisis teaching (and learning) English in schools had almost acquired patriotic overtones, rendering it more acceptable to those sections of German society otherwise suspicious of foreign influence. But, as the eclipse of French suggests, a language and the country where it is spoken tend to be associated at some level. It is difficult, therefore, to see in the embrace of the English language anything other than a mellowing of German attitudes towards Britain.

There is admittedly the obvious complication of the United States, whose growing international stature in the 1920s no doubt also played a role. Yet it was British (and not American) English that was taught, and the men and women – mostly men – who taught it looked quite definitely to Britain and not America.[38] Professor Förster of Leipzig, the advocate in 1920 of broadcasting Britain's colonial difficulties, had none the less referred to the British Empire as the most important argument in favour of the English language. America had figured nowhere in his plea. The US was quite simply beyond his professional horizons. The width of the Atlantic mattered in the 1920s. Weimar linguists experienced genuine difficulties in financing even occasional visits abroad. America was unreachable. (There was probably also an element of linguistic disdain involved. German encyclopaedias liked to point out that a substantial proportion of Americans were recent immigrants: the patois of this ethnic cocktail could only very loosely be described as English.)[39] All of this facilitated a cheerful equation of English with England – Germans habitually refer to Britain as 'England' in any case. This probably also helped insulate the teaching of English from the pronounced anti-Americanism of right-wing nationalists.

It is with this in mind that one must consider the wider post-war revolution in culture and leisure, which again was largely synonymous with the medium of the English language. Here the American influence was more pronounced and identifiable in the vocabulary of show business, sports and popular music. And here right-wing resistance was certainly noticeable. Even so, a whole range of English words entered the German language and it became 'fashionable' (itself an addition to the German vocabulary) to pepper one's conversation with occasional English expressions. Even leading Nazis were not immune to this fad. Goebbels, for instance, proves capable of writing in his diaries 'Nur Mut, old boy' ('Chin up, old boy').[40]

The sheer scale of Weimar Germany's enthusiasm for the English language did provoke some unease in nationalist quarters. The magazine *Der Türmer*, for instance, a publication that combined sweeping cultural pretensions with the narrowest nationalism, published an article in 1927 decrying the *Englische Sprachwut* – the 'mania for the English Language'.[41] Everywhere the author looked he claimed to see people reading copies of *A Thousand Words of English* or subscribing to English language clubs and societies. Such behaviour, he thought, was an unpleasant reminder of the Frenchified excesses of an earlier age. It argued a deplorable lack of 'national consciousness'. How should foreigners be encouraged to take German seriously as an international language if Germany herself was so ready to use English? The significance of this piece lies not in the nature of its argument – references to imperilled 'Germandom' are the stock-in-trade of Weimar nationalists – but in the unintentional acknowledgement of the popularity of all things English.

If individual linguistic endeavour did not perhaps progress very far, as *Der Türmer* rather acidly suggested, there was another field where Germans engaged more systematically with British culture and civilisation: that of literature. Weimar Germany was famously open to foreign influence – or so, at least, we are told. Certainly, a very wide selection of works were translated. Common sense, however, suggests that these would not have reached all sections of Germany's readers and theatre audiences equally. Soviet literature or Fascist Italian letters, or indeed anything that came out of France, automatically offended the political sensitivities of large sections of society. The only way many Germans would have come across them is through hostile reviews or barbed remarks in their respective newspapers of choice. British books and plays did not suffer this fate to nearly the same extent, for the reasons outlined earlier. The entries of titles in the *Deutsches Bücherverzeichnis* – the German register of books in print – document the considerable presence in 1920s' Germany of English literature in translation.

Much of this is due to a single genre of writing: detective fiction. However trivial its subject matter, its impact was considerable. No history of the twentieth century should under-estimate the influence of the mystery novel in disseminating favourable views about the British way of life. This is less of a contradiction than it might seem: murder in the detective story only serves to bring out the best in the Island Breed, as they put aside their secateurs or knitting needles to capture the villains through an appealing combination of Anglo-Saxon common sense (a phrase often left untranslated in German) and sheer pluck. The working-class hero of *Berlin Alexanderplatz*, Alfred Döblin's panoramic novel about Germany in the twenties, finds the words 'Conan Doyle's Collected Works' echoing in his mind as he drifts through Berlin. This struck the great Weimar journalist Erich Mühsam as especially convincing and authentic.[42]

Both Nazi Germany and its Italian ally would later feel uneasy about the great appeal of the detective story on their subjects. Goebbels eventually judged it necessary to institute a ban.[43] In the final six weeks before these restrictions were introduced in October 1939 no fewer than forty-two new detective stories had been published. In the assessment of the confidential SD report, these tales had acted as propaganda popularising 'British institutions and the British way of life'. Since the imposition of the ban, the report goes on to say, only two detective stories have appeared, and these have featured 'German police instead of Scotland Yard'.[44] This must have been welcome news to Himmler, who as Chief of German Police appears to have taken professional exception at the public's 'undignified and obsessive admiration . . . for Scotland Yard and English detectives'. (Already in January of that year the SS newspaper *Das Schwarze Korps* had run a series of articles about Himmler's force under the heading of 'Surpassing Scotland Yard'.)[45] The Nazis were, however, happy to exploit the public's taste for the regime's own ends: once the propaganda war got under way in earnest after the fall of France, the ministry's anti-British tracts imitated the loathed murder mysteries in their cover design and occasionally even in the choice of titles: *Britain's Trail of Blood*, etc.[46]

The popularity of English writing was, of course, not limited to detective fiction. The more literary authors, especially the 'big names' of the period, John Galsworthy, William Somerset Maugham, George Bernard Shaw, etc., also enjoyed considerable favour in print and on stage. Like the detective story, their appeal had an inevitable political dimension in the charged atmosphere of the Weimar Republic. Retrospective confirmation of this comes once again courtesy of the SS newspaper, in an article published late in the war. With the Allied invasion looming and much of Europe openly sympathising with Britain, the paper tries to explain the roots of such unwelcome anglophilia. It lays part of the blame on English novels and plays. With their elegant critique of British society these, it thinks, 'have proved of considerable value to Britain in her foreign affairs'.[47] The paper continues: 'abroad, the British thus appear more human; indeed by accusing themselves of hypocrisy, they manage to portray themselves as stern judges of their own weaknesses'.

To the SS journalist in 1944 this seemed little more than evidence of Anglo-Saxon cunning. But such paranoia is revealing. It gives an indication of the disarming effect the gentler form of English satire must have had on audiences originally hostile to, or ambivalent about, Britain. The drawing-room exchanges of Galsworthy's Forsytes, or of the stage characters of Oscar Wilde or Somerset Maugham, evidently encouraged an entire generation of suspicious German patriots to unbend. (As for the wordy wit of Bernard Shaw, it seems in retrospect expressly designed to appeal to their tastes.)[48]

The relatively narrow range of English plays performed in Germany was important too. Shakespeare apart, nothing predating the 1890s tended to be produced.[49] German theatregoers were exposed to none of the violence of the Elizabethan or Jacobean stage and remained ignorant of the astonishing bawdiness of Restoration England. By comparison, the plays of Wilde, Shaw, Galsworthy and Somerset Maugham, of Frederick Lonsdale and Jerome K. Jerome (to say nothing of that great German favourite *Charley's Aunt*) were, for all their ironic instinct, a safe and reassuring world. If the theatre is said to provide a temporary escape from reality, nothing in the turbulent world of Weimar Germany achieved this more successfully than the English drawing-room comedy. In this it provided a striking contrast to the contemporary German stage of Brecht, Kaiser and Piscator. Indeed, the domestic assault on middle-class sensibilities had started long before Weimar with scenes of sexual experimentation in Wedekind, the violence of the expressionists, or Gerhard Hauptmann's unrelenting images of poverty and destitution. Hitler, ever the mirror of petty-bourgeois Germany and its siege mentality in the 1920s, has nothing but rage and scorn for modern German drama: 'the offerings of the stage were of such a nature that it would have been more profitable for the nation to keep away from them entirely'.[50] And he was quite prepared to point to the contrast in this respect between Britain and Germany. 'The Führer condemns Wedekind', Goebbels records in his diary in 1937, 'but he thinks highly of Shaw.'[51]

These ostensibly *moral* objections to modern German drama – theatrical modernism and the spread of syphilis were closely connected in Hitler's mind – are not as trivial as they might seem.[52] It is surely significant that Hitler should have praised a foreign dramatist while dismissing out of hand an entire generation of German authors. Praising the foreign was not after all standard nationalist practice. If, moreover, Hitler identifies in *Mein Kampf* degenerate art as a symptom of the sickness that has gripped the German *Volk* – and the chapter 'A Reckoning' is a lengthy tirade on that theme – then his endorsement of a British author becomes doubly significant.[53]

Such Nazi approbation was not limited to Shaw, nor was it only voiced in the privacy of the Führer's dining-room. After the annexation of Austria, the major German theatres transferred several productions to Vienna in an effort to reassure the Austrians that the *Anschluß* would not endanger artistic standards. Apart from the classics, three modern authors were chosen to represent the Third Reich's cultural ambitions: two were well-known Nazi dramatists, the third was William Somerset Maugham.[54] Goebbels, meanwhile, had identified *Cavalcade* as exemplary and requested a German version of it.[55]

Noel Coward and Somerset Maugham make for unlikely Nazi heroes. Their personal views and private habits were conspicuously at variance with the Third Reich's preferences. Had the regime known even a little about some of the British authors it so admired, the list of proscribed plays would have lengthened rapidly. What this reveals yet again is that the Nazis inherited from the Weimar Republic a tendency to look favourably on all things British, and that such favourable Nazi views were often the result of misunderstanding or simple ignorance. Nor was such ignorance confined to the Nazis. Most Germans in the 1920s and 1930s had an extremely circumscribed knowledge of Britain. Often this did not extend much beyond a handful of topographical names like Avon, Eton or Kent which, because of their brevity, recur perennially in German cross-word puzzles.[56]

This widespread ignorance had been exacerbated by the country's recent history. Almost five years of wartime siege, followed by Germany's economic collapse, had severely limited the scope for foreign travel of an entire generation. The Klemperer diaries of the 1920s, that rich source of the minutiae of Weimar life, again provide graphic detail. Nothing is more revealing than the eager quizzing of foreign visitors or German business travellers about their impressions of 'abroad'. When travel resumed for a few brief years between Hyperinflation and the Great Depression, it tended to be limited to short distances in central Europe and parts of the Mediterranean. Klemperer himself, with his academic contacts and pro-fessorial salary, was able to visit several southern destinations by travelling steerage on cargo ships. Britain remained for him a land of misty fascina-tion as he tried to guess the outline of Beachy Head while gliding up and down the Channel.[57]

The insularity of the Nazi leadership and their almost total ignor-ance of Britain has routinely featured in accounts of the Third Reich. The leadership were not alone in this. The titles of German books about Britain published in the 1920s and 1930s speak for themselves: *The Unfamiliar Island*, *The Unfamiliar Country*, *How the English do Things*, *John Bull at Home: the Englishman's Day-to-day Life: how he Lives, Entertains Himself, Dresses; what he Learns, Does, Earns and Spends*, etc.[58] Nor is it an accident that one of the most popular children's books of the inter-war years, Erich Kästner's *Das fliegende Klassenzimmer*, has as its central conceit a flying schoolroom in which German boys are able to visit foreign shores during geography classes. Germany felt marooned in the 1920s and 1930s. The near obsession of West Germans with travel after the Second World War probably has its origins here. More impor-tantly, the enforced isolation had political repercussions in the thirties. National Socialism as an ideology was perhaps only ever viable in a society that so signally lacked the means to test political assertions against per-sonal impressions of the wider world.

Against this background of isolation and ignorance, Weimar Germany's interest in what it thought it could glean from British novels and plays assumes obvious importance. Nor does it seem an accident that

Kulturkunde – the belief that a nation's culture held the key to understanding its character – should have exercised such dominance on German intellectual life and academic practice of the period.[59] Literature, quite simply, had few rivals as sources of information. Television, that great post-war conduit of the British way of life did not yet exist; the BBC's radio broadcasts attracted only limited audiences in Germany, since London was only calling in English during the Weimar years. As for the cinema, perhaps the most important medium between the wars, British films remained on the margins. They were generally overshadowed by Hollywood, and indeed by the German cinema itself, then, at the height of its glory and outshining at times its American rival.

In its quest for information about Britain, Germany was thus largely limited to the bookshelf and the stage. And that in turn meant inspecting the contents of upper-middle-class drawing-rooms in London and the Home Counties, as portrayed by a handful of middle-aged male writers. Two things need to be borne in mind here: one involves British literature itself, the other the issue of translation. In the first decades of the century, artistic innovation in British literature was most noticeable in poetry. But poetry, notoriously, does not translate. The conservative German public, which ultimately sealed the fate of the Weimar Republic, therefore did not encounter a British modernism that it might have found as unpalatable as the home-grown variety. The plays that reached them, on the other hand, had all been subjected in Britain to the Lord Chamberlain's vigilance and were thus guaranteed not to alarm or offend. Among the novelists another kind of pre-censorship was in operation. Publishing houses tend to prefer the commercial safety of established names – especially in turbulent days. This effect is even more pronounced when literature is published in translation. Seen from today, the inter-war novel is the era of experimentation and left-wing writing, the age of Joyce and Virginia Woolf, of Orwell, Priestley and Greene. With the partial exception of Joyce and Priestley, none of them were known at all well even to the small number of readers who might have been able to read them in English.[60]

Instead, Germany heard the more established voices of older writers. And these, not unnaturally, viewed the transformations of the post-war world with some unease. Nothing, of course, could have struck a more resonant chord in German hearts, particularly as it seemed to suggest that in spite of past disagreement common ground did exist between Britain and Germany. This favourable impression was complemented – or at any rate not disturbed – by other cultural evidence. Weimar Germany, it should be remembered, was the setting of extraordinary innovation in every artistic sphere: in architecture and design as much as in painting, music or dance. And what was so richly pouring forth from the country's creative minds was almost uniformly loathed by right-wing Germans. They detected in it subterranean links with the objects of all their other hatreds: with the political left at home, and the forces of degeneracy abroad; with 'negroid' America, the Russia of the formalists and commissars, the Paris of cubism and Clemenceau, and, above all, 'world Jewry' in its myriad shapes and guises.

That there existed in the minds of the German right no clear dividing line between politics and culture may seem a familiar point. But this needs to be borne in mind also in discussing German views of Britain. If the period of 1933–45 has aptly been called 'the revolt of the losers', that revolt was not confined to politics and the military. Hand in hand with the overthrow of Versailles went a dizzy insurrection against artistic modernism in all its forms. The Third Reich was energised from top to bottom by people who wanted to whistle a recognisable tune after a concert, who liked to be able to tell from a distance whether a painting was hung the right way up or not, and who longed for the return in architecture of pointed roofs, vernacular ruralism, and the doric order. It was, therefore, not irrelevant that Britain appeared to have held aloof from the perceived cultural pandemonium of the twenties.

Literature apart, the country of George V was conspicuous in the inter-war period for making no perceptible impact on any artistic field. There was no British Bauhaus, no Gropius, Grosz, Schönberg or Weill, nor even a Max Reinhardt or Fritz Lang. London was simply not in the same league as Berlin, Paris or New York – or even Stockholm, Brussels or Barcelona. Those in Germany who loathed anything modern were happy to mistake failure for judgement. In the middle of the war Hitler would still privately pay tribute to British 'common sense' in this regard: 'It is one of the strengths of the British that they provide their people with stuff that doesn't go over people's heads. In Germany practically everything healthy had been dismissed as kitsch by those filthy Jews.'[61]

This perception of Aryan 'healthiness' was bolstered by the official reaction in Britain to examples of artistic modernism. The fate of Joyce's *Ulysses* – widely known (by title at least) as a *succès de scandale* – was instructive. The book had promptly been banned and its importation into Britain rendered one liable to arrest at Dover. Likewise, when a London gallery exhibited paintings by D. H. Lawrence in 1929, it was raided by the Metropolitan Police. This readiness on the part of the British authorities to resort to censorship, and threaten with prison or exile those slow to submit, contrasted favourably with Germany's legalistic regard for civic liberties. (Years later, when Weimar's freedom had been extinguished, Britain's record would become a useful propaganda tool for the Nazis. In 1936 the SS newspaper informed its readers with gleeful malice that in Britain the first thing that flashed up on cinema screens before each showing was a photograph of the 'censorship permit' issued by the British 'censorship authority'. There were rather obvious limits to 'free speech' in Britain, the paper concluded.)[62] In the Weimar years such state intervention for the greater good seemed immensely attractive to German conservatives. Wilhelm Dibelius, the leading conservative *Anglist* of the 1920s – who would later be singled out for praise by Alfred Rosenberg – duly pronounced the British people 'thoroughly healthy' in body and soul.[63]

It is against this broader canvas that reporting of political news must be considered. And the British news that reached Germany seemed distinctly familiar: an escalating national debt, currency crises, strikes and bankruptcies, the suspect superficial glitter of the mid-twenties, and later near-starvation in the Welsh coalfields and hunger marches in Jarrow. That this might have produced in the German working class an idea of national lives running in parallel seems an obvious point. But it is the reaction of the right that matters, and for two reasons. The left was in any case self-consciously internationalist, and therefore did not invest the British experience with special significance; moreover, its political power eroded rapidly in the late twenties. In the history of Anglo-German relations in the build-up to the Second World War, the left simply did not matter. The right did, and though it was clearly hostile at first, it gradually warmed to Britain, much as Hitler himself did.

Initially, reports of economic setbacks abroad had been received with undisguised *Schadenfreude*, as had details of Britain's mounting political problems with independence movements in various parts of the Empire. This was not simply Germanic gloating at the misfortunes of others. There existed a very wide consensus among Germans both during and after the First Word War that Britain's decision to go to war in 1914 had been wilful and unwarranted. British difficulties resulting from that war were therefore unlikely to elicit much sympathy. But there was more. President Wilson's Fourteen Points and their somewhat selective adoption at the Paris peace conferences had added another dimension to German perceptions of the Anglo-Saxon world. Britain's imperial difficulties were inevitably seen in the context of Allied rhetoric at Versailles and elsewhere. The vast demonstrations in India and Egypt against British rule, and the rapid breakdown of British authority in Ireland, now acted like balm on injured national pride. Coinciding with, or coming shortly after Versailles, where Germany had formally been pronounced incapable of colonial government, they had seemed a sublime case of poetic justice. Yet this perception of Britain richly reaping her reward had also drawn some of the poison. The bleak economic news reinforced that effect. Both countries, it seemed, had been weakened by the blood-letting, and Britain's gains as part of the peace settlement were revealed to be more apparent than real.

It is enlightening in this context to turn, once again, to the nationalists' favourite journal 'for Spirit and Soul': *Der Türmer*. In September 1925 its editorial pages inspected for the umpteenth time the post-war scene. The analysis started, like that of most Germans, from the assumption that Britain had played a pivotal role in the outbreak of war in 1914. Had it not been for Britain's *entente* with France, neither that country nor Russia would have felt able to declare war on the Central Powers; and in the absence of such readiness, Serbia would have accepted the Austrian ultimatum, designed to prevent any further act of terrorism in the Sarajevo mould. There would have been no war. War occurred only because Britain was determined to have a war. She sensed an opportunity to cripple the economy of her major trading rival. This perception of events was the standard right-wing account of the period. Hitler had been making much the same points in speech after speech in Bavaria. But it is *Der Türmer's* next thoughts, posed in a series of rhetorical questions, that are striking:

> Has the war brought . . . [any] material benefits? Have any amongst those who provoked it actually profited by it? To be sure, sundry territories have been acquired . . . But is there any European economy that is healthier today than before? . . . The economic blood-letting has been such that even the most ruthless plundering of the defeated nations has proved unable to make up for it . . . To talk of victors . . . is absurd.

And turning specifically to Britain, the editorial observes that the benefits of destroying German trade have in fact been reaped not by Britain but by America and Japan who, between them, inherited the lion's share of Germany's former overseas markets. Britain, on the other hand, had ended up losing her traditional central European market, which was now too impoverished to buy British products. And the article concludes: 'If twelve years ago they had known in London what they know now, there would have been no World War.'[64]

What is important here is not so much the echo of Keynes in some of the reasoning but the psychologically important break with the perception of victors versus losers. Versailles continued to loom large, but it had in a sense become disassociated from Britain. It was now simply a system invented and maintained by France and her East European allies, who had all benefited territorially and shared a pathological hatred of Germany. Britain, on the other hand, the land of 'common sense' and shrewd business acumen, would not indefinitely remain blind to reason. For an Anglo-German understanding was in the long run as beneficial to Britain as it was to Germany. The student of Hitler's emerging foreign-policy conception during the 1920s will recognise a familiar line of thought in this. But the point is that it was not limited to Hitler and the Nazis. It could, moreover, take forms that would have been anathema to genuine National Socialists.

Perhaps the most striking instance of this was a book published in 1927 by a man with a resonant family name: Wilhelm von Richthofen. The title of his opus was no less arresting: *Brito-Germania: Europe's Salvation*.[65] Its author perceived a 'sick Europe' for which there was only one remedy: Anglo-German political union. The combined resources of the two countries would quickly result in *imperium mundi* – world domination. If this sounds like an attempt to achieve in defeat what had eluded Germany on the battlefield, the book swiftly dispels such notions. Richthofen was under no illusions about the balance of power in any such Anglo-German venture. Germany would have to content herself with a subservient role. She would in effect assume Dominion status within the British Empire. If Churchill in 1940 briefly dreamt of re-uniting the crowns of Britain and France, there were Germans a decade or so earlier who wanted the Houses of Hanover and Saxe-Coburg-Gotha to renew the severed ties with their ancestral land.

Such schemes of political union were, admittedly, not limited to Britain. Rival projects of various European confederations existed. The Austrian Count Coudenhove-Kalergi and his Pan-Europa movement, for instance, sought to create out of the ashes of the Habsburg Empire a wider Catholic union. But these projects had found little support among right-wing – and mostly Protestant – German nationalists. (That Britain's own Protestantism was a factor in the country's popularity with the German right seems an obvious point: from Bismarck to Hitler there was not much love lost between 'Teutonism' and Rome.)[66]

A distaste for Catholicism does not in itself, however, provide adequate grounds for embracing political union with Britain. Von Richthofen's *Brito-Germania* might therefore be regarded as evidence only of personal eccentricity. What gives it wider relevance, apart from its unmistakably *völkisch* tone, is the fact that it should have received a noticeably warm review in *Der Türmer*. The reviewer did express slight doubts about the practicality of the venture but was clearly sympathetic to Richthofen's line of reasoning. 'Certainly, a degree of subservience to a fellow Germanic British nation would be preferable to servitude and creeping death at the hands of the French, or Bolshevik chaos instigated by Russia.'[67] Moreover, the long-term prospects for Germany were perhaps not so bad after all: Britain's manifest imperial difficulties would gradually help ameliorate Germany's position within *Brito-Germania*. Renewed German strength would eventually prove indispensable to the Colonial Office in London. In this regard Richthofen's reasoning does not seem so very far removed from Hitler's repeated offers some twelve years later to help defend the British Empire. German misjudgement of Britain's likely reaction to such offers was clearly not limited to the Führer's entourage.

Von Richthofen's affection for Britain was based on memories of his days as an undergraduate at Lincoln College, Oxford. This set him apart from most of his fellow Germans, whose growing anglophilia during the Weimar years was based strictly on second-hand knowledge. What little conservative Germans knew, however, seemed distinctly reassuring. If Britain shared the upheavals and sense of dislocation which the war had brought about, the country had nonetheless held itself better than most. When, for instance, in 1926 the left had attempted to bring the kingdom to its knees in what to conservative German eyes seemed like a re-run of events in Germany in November 1918, they were thwarted by a magnificent display of practical patriotism: public-spirited citizens took over strike-bound omnibuses, thereby crushing revolution in its infancy. The impressions of the General Strike loomed large in some German minds even thirteen years later, on the eve of the Second World War. To the writer of a study of intellectual trends and attitudes in post-(Great)war Britain, the reaction of British youth in 1926 provided a shining example of national health. It proved that the modish cosmopolitan cynicism of the twenties had only been skin-deep. 'In the moment of crisis, which always brings out the best in the British, the means and the aim seemed clear.'[68]

To German conservatives the monarchy itself was a powerful symbol of all that was healthy about Britain and diseased about Weimar. One catches the clearest sense of this – retrospectively – in the reporting of the cluster of royal events in the mid-thirties: George V's Silver Jubilee, his funeral a year later, and finally the coronation of George VI. The Nazis, by then in power, were decidedly hostile to kingship but their wooing of Britain gave German monarchists a final opportunity to show their true colours. The reporting for major papers, such as the *Berliner Illustrierte Zeitung*, brings out a warmth which genuinely Nazi journalists reserved for Mussolini (and which contrasts with the more dutiful reporting about the House of Savoy). The following thoughts on the death of George V would seem to suggest that conservative Germans detected a political lesson in the late king's life:

> No British monarch was ever closer to his people than George V. His sincerity, his sense of dedication and his simple habits made him approachable and exemplary to the common man . . . He was a ruler who was able to reconcile enemies and bridge divisions through his quiet dignity and strength of character.[69]

The fact that this encomium actually appeared on the anniversary of the *Machtergreifung*, one of the most hallowed days in the Nazi calendar, may well be significant. By then Germany had three years' experience in the art of reading (and writing) between the lines. Much the same effect can be observed in the meetings of bodies with British connections. Here monarchist hearts could be worn on ostensibly diplomatic sleeves. The German Shakespeare Society in Weimar, for instance, tended to combine its elaborate tributes to the House of Windsor with loyal toasts to its local royalty: the House of Saxony-Weimar. It is surely a last discreet expression of what German conservatives had been hoping to bring about by installing Hitler as Chancellor in 1933. The political dividends they had expected from a restoration become apparent in another instance of royal reporting in the mid-thirties: the descriptions of King George and Queen Mary's triumphant Jubilee progress through the impoverished East End of London. Here, surely, was Bismarck's dream, which had so signally eluded Germany: a quiescent working class.

In our own day the provocative claim has been made that, apart from the regime's anti-semitism, there was nothing about the Third Reich's government with which British conservatives might not have sympathised. Be that as it may, the converse is certainly true. Except for the puzzling acceptance of Jewry, there was little in the Britain of George V and Stanley Baldwin which German right-wingers – Nazi and non-Nazi – would have found uncongenial. The relative social cohesion in spite of vast differences in wealth seemed highly enviable. So, too, did the observance of convention, and the astonishing degree of conformity that resulted from it in all aspects of life. If Rupert Brooke saw regimented German violets and dreamt of 'the unofficial English rose', German visitors to Britain saw rows and rows of identical Georgian terraces, and mile upon mile of suburban street with identical houses, from which emerged identically dressed people on their way to city offices, and small boys and girls, in uniform no less, on their way to school. And such observers concluded, half-regretfully, that Germany, with its tradition of rugged individualism, would never stand for it.[70]

Above all, there was the emphasis on the rural life and the ambivalence about cities, even after two centuries of industrialisation. The sounds of the smithy and the sight of the ploughman coming over the crest of the hill, to which Baldwin was so partial, would have appealed just as strongly to the East Elbian Junker who kept a picture of the Kaiser in his study throughout the Weimar years, and to the Nazi elite who did not. The strength of this attraction can be sensed, even across the decades, in the memoirs of a man like the SS protégé Reinhard Spitzy, who came to London as Ribbentrop's assistant.[71] Spitzy had lived, in rapid succession, in Vienna, Rome and Paris, and had liked all three cities. But it was London – or rather, it was England – with which he truly fell in love; and England, if his memoirs are anything to go by, meant country house weekends, a succession of hunt balls and shoots, joyful hours in the saddle, and trysts among the briars with comely blonde maidens. To use his own favourite term for it: it was all 'so civilised'. 'Everything concerning race, class and *savoir-vivre* which we as idealists had always admired and considered worth striving for had been a way of life here for years past', he writes without apparent irony.[72] It was, to put it another way, the life to which the Nazis were hoping to become accustomed.

In the early thirties, when they were still being kept from power by President Hindenburg, an estate-owning Prussian conservative distrustful of social upstarts, this was but a dream. It was a dream, however, which in due course they would bring about: from Göring, who at Karinhall somehow managed to combine vulgarity with panache, to the egregious Arthur Kreiser and the Nazi-Palladianism of the 'country seat' he built for himself in occupied Poland. This fondness for the trappings of rural life would in turn give rise to misconceptions in both countries. A series of photographs throughout the thirties of British politicians and German leaders enjoying country pursuits either separately or in each other's company, as in the case of Lord Londonderry shooting with Göring, would suggest to the German public a reassuring symmetry in British and German national lives.[73] In Britain meanwhile, the magazine *Country Life* would select for a photograph of Hitler at the Berghof the caption 'A Countryman at Heart'.[74]

To sum up, Weimar Germany knew relatively little about Britain. But what little it knew – or thought it knew – it liked. That went especially for the political right, both Nazi and non-Nazi, who discovered to their initial surprise that Britain seemed a highly commendable country. That this Britain was largely a figment of a romantic imagination, produced in equal measure by the hankering of British conservatives after the vanishing feudal age and the wider desire of their German counterparts to return to pre-war certainties, will have become clear. This agreeable delusion was able to flourish because of Germany's enforced isolation. It rarely had to stand the test of personal contact between the two nations. When Britons and Germans did meet, they tended to do so *on German soil*. Circumstances thus conspired to preserve the romantic image: it was reinforced by the courtliness of British visitors and their obvious retrospective doubts about the wisdom of Versailles.

The German hosts, on the other hand, had frequently become predisposed to finding their British visitors admirable, and were happy to attribute occasional discordant notes to language problems or the famous British eccentricity about which they had read so much. Victor Klemperer, who professionally met more foreigners than most Germans and could be quite prickly on occasion, felt able to declare by the mid-thirties that 'All Englishmen and women we have ever met, we have found delightful.'[75] A decade or so earlier, his enthusiasm had been rather more muted.[76] Colin Ross, meanwhile, whose travel books so fascinated Hitler, had already made up his mind in the twenties. He was conscious of an 'extraordinary emotional proximity' towards the British: 'The members of no other nation are more approachable.' Whatever the merits or shortcomings of Britain as a nation state, he added, 'the individual Englishman is uncommonly decent and reliable'.[77] These sentiments are all the more striking since Klemperer and Ross – unusually – both regarded *Franco-*

German reconciliation to be of paramount importance. Yet even their hearts, clearly, tended another way.

If Klemperer met Britons in Germany at their most diplomatic and Colin Ross found them friendly and helpful as fellow white men in distant corners of the globe, encounters in Britain could prove more ambiguous. Germans who were able to visit England sometimes found the experience disturbing. A grammar school teacher travelling to London in 1927 to perfect his English provides a graphic example.[78] Everywhere he went, he found himself confronted with reproachful memories of the war. Monuments and plaques abounded. Outside the British Museum he encountered a tank on a plinth. In the boarding house in which he stayed each of the guests, separately, took him to task over the German atrocities in Belgium. At first he was all conciliation and regret. Eventually, however, his temper flared and he suggested that the Boers too, and the Punjabis of Amritsar, had tales to tell about the conduct of uninvited guests. (Apparently, this did at least assure him the sympathies of one interlocutor. The hotel's Irish maid seems to have felt that the activities of the Black and Tans were relevant to the discussion. The English, she duly informed him, 'are a nation of hypocrites and bullies', before adding that the Germans could always be sure of a friendly welcome in Ireland.)[79]

The significance of this intriguing tale is twofold. It emphasises the difference – hidden to most Germans at home – between German expectations and reality in the twenties. But it is also revealing about different perceptions of the war – and not just between Britain and Germany but also between the Weimar and Bonn republics. And that goes to the heart of Anglo-German relations. After 1945 (West) German attempts at reconciliation with the rest of Europe (or, at any rate with the continent's Western half) were based on sincere remorse about the Second World War and Germany's role in it. The very basis of West German politics was a repudiation of former German aims. This was not the case in the 1920s, at least not among German conservatives. There was regret about the war, certainly. Germany had suffered as grievously as Britain had in the slaughter. But there was no remorse. There seemed no cause for it. Germany, after all, was sure in her own mind that she had not sought conflict with Britain in 1914. The residents of that London boarding house were therefore quite mistaken to expect an apology from their German fellow guest. He was happy to express regret over the loss of life, and no doubt meant it. But an apology was not owing – least of all to Britain. This also explains his unease about what he considered to be ostentatious memorials to the war. The sight of the tank outside the British Museum, which to British eyes was merely a war memorial, inspired in him something of the feeling Hitler's legions would inspire in British eyes ten years later: the uncomfortable recognition of enduring hostility.

'The trouble with the Germans', it is periodically observed in Britain, is that 'they're always either at your feet or at your throat'. The trouble with Britain, most Germans would have responded in the 1920s, was that Britain never seemed to offer Germany a third option. What Germany wanted from the days of the Kaiser to the early years of the Third Reich was no more – and no less – than a position of equality. Chancellor Stresemann, the epitome of Weimar reconciliation, was happy to recognise at the Locarno Conference in the twenties that legitimate British interests extended as far as the Rhine. But, famously, he insisted also that, by the same token, German interests in the East encompassed the River Vistula. Hitler – the very antithesis of Stresemann – was no less ready during the Weimar years to accept British interests. Wilhelmine Germany, he suggested in *Mein Kampf*, had made a fatal mistake in pursuing colonial ambitions.[80] While these had never actually posed a threat to Britain they had nonetheless been perceived as such. Provided therefore that a newly powerful Germany made it unambiguously clear that she wished Britain no harm, then surely Britain would allow Germany a continental empire to balance Britain's own maritime empire. (The rights of the subject nations would in both cases have to give way to the more pressing interests of the two great powers.) What was common, therefore, to Stresemann and Hitler – and indeed to most of Germany – was the belief that Britain had not fought for Freedom in 1914 but for her own freedom, which was not quite the same thing. The 'Black and Tans' in Ireland and the fate of the Punjabi men, women and children massacred in Amritsar had proved that point beyond any doubt.

There remained, however, the hope that Britain would eventually realise she had misjudged German motives, and had gained nothing by destroying the ordered Edwardian world. Britain's increasing friendliness towards Germany as the twenties wore on and gave way to the thirties seemed to suggest that that moment might at last be on hand. When the Nazis took power the ground was thus more than prepared for the apparent Anglo-German *rapprochement* that marked the Third Reich's early years. And since it was based on a perception of equality, and of apparent British recognition of that equality, German expressions of anglophilia in those years were not a ruse but genuine sentiment.

It is again an incident at the personal level that is perhaps most telling. The story goes that at the Olympic Games in Berlin in 1936 the victorious British rowing eight were told at dinner by their hosts: 'If we weren't German, I think we should like to be British.' The visiting oarsmen took this as a typically plodding Teutonic pleasantry and replied with a plodding pleasantry of their own: if they hadn't been born British they thought they'd rather not have been born at all. Mutual incomprehension was thus complete. Britain, collectively and individually, failed to notice the ardour with which Germany, singly and nationally, was wooing her. The Germans, on the other hand, were so enamoured of a romantic image of Britain that they failed to recognise Britain's essential indifference to them. Such were the wider foundations upon which the Third Reich would attempt to construct its foreign policy.

2 'The Germanic isle': Britain and Nazi racial science

At the first Nuremberg rally after the Nazi seizure of power, in September 1933, the party ideologue Alfred Rosenberg delivered a speech on 'The Racial Basis of Foreign Policy'. In it he set out what he thought should be the guiding principles in the Third Reich's relations with other countries. He began by reminding his audience of the findings of *Rassenkunde* – Nazi racial science. Race, he insisted, was directly relevant to international relations: for 'without a deeper understanding of this issue it is impossible to understand the history of nations and thus their past foreign policy; nor can any future foreign policy be properly determined without reference to it'.[1]

Rosenberg's influence on foreign affairs was transitory: the failure of his mission to Britain in 1933, and a lack of charm so pronounced that even Nazis remarked upon it, soon ended his diplomatic ambitions. This does not, however, diminish the significance of his Nuremberg speech. For in emphasising the importance of race he was not alone. He was echoing the Führer's own stated convictions.[2] The existence of racial ties as the Nazis perceived them – or the perceived absence of such ties – could thus be expected to influence the Reich's foreign policy. Any political speech, any verbal assurance by members of the leadership, any solemn treaty even, that breached this fundamental principle could only be a temporary measure. The friendship treaty with Poland in 1934, and the various assurances to neighbouring countries that their borders would be respected, all ran counter to a racially orientated foreign policy. Not one of these promises was kept. Rosenberg's speech is evidence of the extraordinary shamelessness with which the Nazi leadership all but announced its acts of deception. By the same token, however, an Anglo-

German partnership could never just be a question of political expediency. Nazi ideology itself seemed to demand it.

An awareness of close ethnic ties linking Britain and Germany was neither recent nor limited to Alfred Rosenberg and the dubious Nazi 'racial experts' to whom he lent his ear. It was based on practical observation. The English language itself provided in vocabulary and grammar ample evidence of a close connection. This was particularly noticeable to North Germans, whose native patois seems sometimes closer to English than to standard High German. A journalist reporting for the SS newspaper from within the shadow of St Paul's Cathedral in London thus found that the very street names around him reminded him of his native Hamburg and its Fleete. 'There is', he exclaimed, 'so much here that seems familiar.'[3] In the great trading cities of Hamburg and Bremen, and along the North Sea coast where *Plattdeutsch* was spoken, a corresponding sense of kinship with the 'cousins beyond the sea' had traditionally existed, and had survived all political tensions.[4]

Language was important in less obvious ways too. Since the mid-nineteenth century, German philologists, and their Austrian and Swiss colleagues, had been conducting pioneering work into the history of European languages. It was a field they came to dominate.[5] Teaching practice at German universities reflected this. Students of any modern language would be expected to become acquainted not just with its present-day grammar but also its medieval structure and, wherever possible, its antecedents in antiquity.[6] German undergraduates would spend an astonishing amount of time tracing the history of individual words, diligently marking vowel shifts and the modification of consonants across the centuries. They would also attempt to trace back words beyond the written record to their putative common Indo-Aryan root.

This somewhat esoteric pursuit did have practical consequences: it provided a striking demonstration of the network of connections between the various European languages and the relative strengths of such ties. The notion of a Germanic family of nations was much more credible in linguistics than in recent history. Unsurprisingly, this linguistic evidence fired the imagination of nationalist minds. An encounter with scraps of extinct languages in the course of studying Old High German, or indeed Old English, could bring the vanished Teutonic nations of antiquity back to life. The Ostrogoths and Visigoths, the Lombards and Burgundians all reappeared after some thirteen centuries of linguistic extinction to haunt the language departments of German universities.[7] Through the universities' alumni, this effect also extended to the class-rooms of the country's *Gymnasien*, and thus also into many middle-class households. Historical linguistics was one of the springs that fed the Teutomania of the German right both before and after the First World War.[8]

In the case of English, it highlighted the close historical ties between Anglo-Saxon England and northern Germany. That connection had never been in doubt. Yet, in emotional terms, it had often been unable to rival the romantic allure of the vanished Teutons of old. Throughout the nineteenth century Germans had been encouraged by their poets and novelists (and successive generations of schoolmasters) to regard as their closest kin the Germanic nations that brought down the Roman Empire. What the alleged Ur-Germans had begun in 9 AD by defeating the Roman legions in the woods of Westphalia, their kinsmen had later completed on the shores of the Mediterranean.

The Goths in particular had engaged the German national imagination. From the poetry of Count von Platen at the beginning of the nineteenth century to the historical novels of Felix Dahn towards its end, their memory had been celebrated.[9] Part of the appeal was the Goths' romantic end: death in battle. This echoed perfectly the self-conscious heroism of nineteenth-century Germany. A solemn funeral of a fallen leader in the bed of a diverted river, or a gallant last stand against Roman treachery on the flanks of Mount Vesuvius seemed more inspirational than the survival of the Anglo-Saxons through trade and spinning cotton. In a sense, this Gothic obsession foreshadowed the Third Reich's own infatua-tion in the 1930s with a scarcely less mythical vision of Britain. Such flights of historical fancy could have far-reaching consequences. In the 1890s the discovery that the Gothic language had apparently survived in parts of the Crimean peninsula until the sixteenth century – almost a thousand years longer than had been thought – produced a sensation not just in German linguistic circles.[10] Its last ripples were still perceptible half a century later when the Third Reich decided to settle the Crimea with German colonists after the anticipated conquest of Russia: future genera-tions would again think of the peninsula as *Gotenland* – the 'Land of the Goths'.[11]

Imperial Germany's collapse at the end of the First World War had not necessarily dimmed the appeal of Teutonic antiquity, but it did encourage a reassessment of the Anglo-Saxons, for unlike the Goths and

Vandals, the English had survived, their empire was intact and had just helped inflict a traumatic defeat on Germany. It was much more difficult in 1919 than it had been a few years earlier to dismiss England as mere *Manchestertum*: a nation which, like the eponymous city, was motivated solely by economic gain. As late as 1915 the philosopher–historian Werner Sombart had felt able to characterise the English as a soulless race of tradesmen, wholly deficient in Germanic heroism.[12] Four and a half years of war and unbroken British resolve in the face of U-boats, poison gas, Zeppelins and Gotha bombers had challenged such assumptions. Germany ended the war certain of one thing only: that it had misjudged Britain.

It is important to stress this, since political realism was not otherwise a defining feature of the young Weimar Republic. As is well known, Germans – and in particular right-wing Germans – had considerable difficulty in accepting the fact of defeat. The trauma, the sense of humiliation, the apparent futility of so much individual sacrifice were simply too great. Like sections of the American public after Vietnam, half a century later, they preferred to think of their country as having somehow chosen not to win. The lack of self-delusion about Britain is therefore all the more remarkable. As early as 1922, a contributor to the standard reference work on the British Isles, the *Dibelius* handbook, felt able to declare that Germany 'had paid the price' for under-estimating Britain's 'toughness' and 'readiness for self-sacrifice'.[13] And the author was prepared to go further. The individual misjudgements on the part of German military leaders and politicians had in fact all been rooted in the same fundamental shortcoming: a complete 'ignorance of the British national character'.[14]

This view was not limited to academics. By 1924 Hitler had reached similar conclusions. The Wilhelmine view of Britain – the 'professorial view', as Hitler liked to call it – had been erroneous; the widespread 'parroting of phrases' about the 'mentality of shopkeepers' had clouded Germany's judgement and led it, fatally, to under-estimate Britain's resolve under fire.[15] In *Mein Kampf* he repeated these sentiments, adding for good measure, 'I remember well the look of astonishment on my comrades' faces when we faced the Tommy in person in Flanders.'[16] (What Hitler neglected to mention was that he himself had produced, in December 1914, a cartoon of a 'Tommy' politely allowing soldiers from other Allied armies to precede him on the way to the front line.)[17] Not everyone may thus have been entirely frank about their own past, but the break with 1914 was none the less unmistakable. And there was wide agreement also that it was imperative finally to make sense of the British – if only out of an instinct of national 'self-preservation'.[18]

Correcting earlier misconceptions was, however, only the most urgent task. German thoroughness demanded more. What was required was a proper theoretical explanation for Britain's fighting spirit in the Great War. The roots of the unexpected British heroism needed to be identified. Once again, historical linguistics seemed to provide the answer. The texts which they studied, after all, described a much older Britain: a feudal pre-industrial Britain, whose values seemed more able to explain events in Flanders than the writings of Adam Smith and David Ricardo did. But study of such texts also had a secondary effect: it reinforced the idea of underlying Germanic kinship. Books like Gustav Hübener's *England and the Moral Principles of Early European History* held up *Beowulf* as central evidence of Britain's ancient links with the continental Germanic tradition.[19]

To German readers the world described in the stanzas of *Beowulf* and in the surviving shorter Anglo-Saxon poetry was instantly recognisable. It was the world of their own ancient epics, of *Dietrich von Bern*, of *Wieland der Schmied* – whose name even appears in *Beowulf* – of *Hildebrand*, *Kudrun*, the great *Nibelungenlied* and countless others.[20] This world was, moreover, not just the preserve of an eccentric minority. It had been at the heart of German middle-class sensibility for over half a century. Modern prose and verse translations had kept it alive in schoolroom and drawing-room alike – to say nothing of the operatic stage and Richard Wagner, that other great font of Teutomania.[21]

This shared cultural ancestry – scarcely news in itself – now acquired for the *völkisch* right contemporary relevance in the way the Goths had in the decades of German unification. It made Germany's defeat in the Great War more comprehensible (and possibly more tolerable). It was one thing, after all, to concede a contest to a perceived equal, quite another to admit to having been stopped by the French. National self-respect was less threatened by acknowledging the power of the Royal Navy than by dwelling on the memories of Verdun. This may explain some of the logical twists in the nationalist mindset of the twenties. The flat denial of a German defeat in 1918 – 'unvanquished on the battlefield', in the famous phrase – was frequently combined with the observation that the British naval blockade had decided the outcome of the war.[22]

As the Weimar era progressed, the shared Germanic heritage began to acquire still further relevance. Old English verse now also conjured specifically the masculine world of war, valour and self-sacrifice, of the duty of vengeance and the bonds of fealty which the *völkisch* right, and National Socialism in particular, was trying to revive in Germany. As the Nazi party gained in strength and influence, that factor became more pronounced. Stressing Britain's Germanic inheritance began to assume political overtones in the 1930s which had been largely absent before. This is obviously most noticeable in education. The depiction of heroism in English literature from *Beowulf* to Shakespeare, for instance, could move Nazi ideologues to paroxysms of delight:

> The admiration of a man's strength is unmistakably Germanic . . . Only the best and most able can survive in the harshness of nature. This is why National Socialism advocates a masculine state and has decided to fight everything feminising and decadent.[23]

If Nazi ideology began to infect traditional academic disciplines, it was in turn affected by philological preoccupations. Germany had for decades been ready, through *Kulturkunde*, to examine a nation's literature in order to understand its national character. National Socialism went further and claimed to detect in literature and language signs of a nation's racial make-up. It is perhaps no accident that the man whom the Third Reich regarded as the founding father of German *Rassenkunde*, Hans F. K. Günther, had started out as an amateur linguist and literary critic. Before he took to measuring human crania and establishing an individual's racial background on the basis of the relative prominence of his lower back,[24] he too had felt the allure of historical linguistics: 'Those wanting to know what it is to live heroically . . . need to become expert in the structures of our languages. They have been called Indo-Aryan, being the languages of nations with Nordic blood.'[25] What the structures of Europe's languages revealed to the man who, in the Nazis' own words, 'had provided the intellectual basis for [our] struggle' was this:[26] Italian was the language of 'joy', French of 'pleasure', German of 'form and creation' and English of a 'ruthless act of will'.[27]

The manifest lunacy of Günther's various utterances should not blind one to their political effect. Weimar Germany had quickly identified him as a crank and denied him the academic career he craved. The Nazis, however, recognised in him a kindred spirit. They rewarded him with a newly created chair in social anthropology. It was a high-profile appointment: in fact, the very first academic appointment the party ever made in power; Hitler personally attended Günther's inaugural lecture at Jena University.[28] The newspaper of the Nazi Student

League duly urged all Nazi undergraduates in the Reich to try and spend one term at Jena in order to profit from Günther's racial expertise.[29] He was the first recipient too of the NSDAP Prize for Science (which, it was hoped, would rapidly supersede the Nobel Prize). Günther received this second signal honour at the 1935 Nuremberg rally from the hands of Alfred Rosenberg – the very man who, two years earlier, had explained to the same forum the link between *Rassenkunde* and Nazi foreign policy.

Given the calibre of Günther's political audience, it is worth taking a second look at his remark in 1920 about the English language. On closer inspection, it contains two significant words: 'will' and 'ruthless'. Both became important in what has aptly been called *lingua tertii imperii* – the argot of the Third Reich.[30] 'Will' (and its compounds) was one of the most hallowed words of National Socialism. Its place was, so to speak, at the heart of the Nazi belief system. Like 'honour' or 'might', it was chosen as the programmatic title of a Nuremberg rally. As for the adjective 'ruthless', with which Günther had combined 'will', this too became a key word in Hitler's vocabulary. Both men, moreover, use it in a sense that differs from ordinary German usage.

For Günther, as much as for Hitler, 'ruthlessness' was evidently a desirable quality: an essential precondition towards the achievement of historical greatness. What is more, Hitler – like Günther – links it specifically with Britain, as if to point a contrast with Germany. He uses it to describe British policy in the very essay in which he condemns past German illusions about Britain.[31] In *Mein Kampf* Britain is again repeatedly characterised in these terms: 'For no people has ever with greater brutality . . . prepared its economic conquests with the sword, and later ruthlessly defended them'; 'the determination for victory, the tenacity and ruthless pursuit of this struggle, remained unchanged'; or, on the subject of British propaganda in the First World War: 'as ruthless as it was brilliant'.[32]

The fact that something outside Germany should be described in what to Nazis was evidently emotive language is striking. Significantly, the word is not used later for the behaviour of Germany's other enemies, even where – objectively – it might have seemed appropriate. (The determination of the Red Army to avenge by any means the German rape of their country, for instance, never elicits the term 'ruthless'. Instead it was routinely described as 'bestial'.)[33] Only Britain – and the Third Reich itself – appear to have been 'ruthless' in Nazi eyes.

On more than one occasion, Hitler made that perceived link explicit. In 1942, during a fireside chat with his inner circle, he opined that the Reich was 'getting a better press in Britain these days. We are gradually being treated as social equals. [Wir werden langsam gesellschaftlich eben-bürtig]. That's because our conduct has become ruthless.'[34] The remark is instructive not just for its hint of Nazi class resentment. It reveals Hitler's views about what he evidently took to be the very core of the British character. This is confirmed by related remarks. A week earlier, his thoughts had gone back to an incident in the Spanish Civil War: the vicious German reprisal in 1937 for a Republican attack on the battleship *Deutschland*. That display of German ruthlessness had not just impressed the Spaniards, Hitler thought. 'After the bombardment of Almeria Britain was overcome by a wave of affection [for Germany]. It took Eden, Vansittart and their followers years to counteract it.'[35] The basis for this bizarre notion was probably the readi-ness of the governor of Gibraltar to bury the fallen of the *Deutschland* with full military honours.[36] But Hitler's wider reasoning – that the British as the orig-inal practitioners of gunboat diplomacy would recognise in the Third Reich an eager disciple and worthy partner – evidently had deeper roots.

Britain, Hitler always insisted, had won the war in 1918 because it was ready to starve Germany into submission. The thought of women and children dying did not appear to trouble anyone in London. That should not have come as a surprise to the world. (This, after all, was the country that ruled India with the help of regular famines;[37] that had reduced 8½ million Irishmen to a more manageable number of 4½ million, and had 'cynically starved to death 29,000 Boer women in concentration camps'.)[38] Wilhelmine Germany, on the other hand, had lacked the necessary ruthlessness to win. It had dithered, agonised, and had only ever done things by half. The result was not merely a lost war but open British contempt for Germany thereafter. In Hitler's eyes, Anglo-German relations were overshadowed by British memories not of the war but of the German collapse in 1918. The solution seemed obvious. Britain might yet be ready to consider Germany as a potential ally: but only if Germany presented a credible force. 'Of course no one in Britain will con-clude an alliance for the good of Germany', Hitler wrote in his unpub-lished *Second Book*, 'but only in the furtherance of British interests.'[39]

All of this may seem familiar enough, but it only makes sense if one recognises in it evidence of racial thinking. Britain's conduct past and present was racially determined. It was the expression of a national char-acter, which was itself rooted in Britain's racial origins. And these, as everyone in Germany knew, Britain shared with Germany. The difference was that Britain had remained true to its racial inheritance and Germany had not. Hitler, in other words, both rejected and re-affirmed the significance of the racial ties linking the two countries. He rejected firmly the older naïve assumption that Britain would determine its relations with Germany on the basis of its Saxon origins.

In this respect Hitler's views reflect a recognisable strand in German opinion during the 1920s and 1930s. There had been widespread recognition during the Weimar years that Germany's sense of kinship with Britain was not reciprocated. The *Anglisten*, in particular, had warned against exaggerated hopes in that regard. 'One is not free to choose one's relations', observed the author of a well-known book about contemporary Britain in 1929. It would be unwise to expect one's British cousins to act 'on a basis of the supposed moral obligations imposed by family ties'.[40] The nationalist writer Hans Grimm, whose 1927 book *Volk ohne Raum* (*Nation without Space*) was highly influential among the *völkisch* constituency, had also warned not to expect too much. In a series of essays in the mid-thirties Grimm sought to dispel illusions which he felt might do more harm than good. 'The English were always much less impressed by these ties [than we were]', he insisted in 1937.[41] Grimm had lived for several years both in Britain and South Africa, and was presumably speaking from personal experience. His sober assessment did not, however, translate into any perceptible coldness towards Britain. His motivation as a writer remained what he called 'our ancient German love of England'.[42] Other voices could be more ambiguous. Most German *Anglisten* during the Weimar years insisted that amid much obvious virtue there were also serious flaws in the British character. And these flaws – like the virtues – pointed to fundamental differences in outlook between Britons and Germans. While the Germans were a sentimental race, the British were the exact opposite: 'sober and cold', 'weighing up objects and people in the light of the possible profit to be derived from them'.[43]

There is no reason to believe that Hitler – or anyone else in the leadership – was familiar with these particular views: the professional journals of schoolmasters and academics did not constitute standard Nazi reading. The similarities in outlook are therefore all the more striking. Just as striking, however, are the differences. If many non-Nazis found these supposed flaws in the British character a matter of regret, and endeavoured to love Britain in spite of them, this was not true of Hitler. The Führer was drawn to Britain precisely *because* of them. The idea of Britain as a cold and calculating nation, always with an eye for the main chance, and a preference for fighting dirty, produced in him a profound sense of kinship. Even at the height of the war he could, privately, pay tribute to the British along these lines: 'They are of incomparable impertinence, but I do admire them.' And he looked forward to the day when Germany and Britain would be allies. Both countries would, in Hitler's revealing phrase, 'know exactly what to expect of the other'.[44] Fraternal feeling between Britain and the Third Reich would thus grow out of a shared lack of moral scruples. The British Empire, after all, had not been acquired – or maintained – by being nice to other races. Here was the decisive shift in Hitler's views about Britain; here also was where he had parted company in the early 1920s with most of his adopted countrymen.

In the immediate aftermath of the First World War German perceptions of the British Empire were coloured by their own experience as a defeated nation. 'The way the Entente powers talk of and to Germany', observed Viktor Klemperer, 'makes me as bitter as if I personally were being treated like a negro.'[45] 'It is reminiscent of the Congo', he had noted in his diary a year earlier.[46] To Hitler himself it seemed obvious that Britain's aim was to turn Germany into yet another British colony.[47] What, he asked in 1921, 'can one expect from the hands of slavers other than slavery?'[48] The fate of the colonial nations had become comprehensible.

The severe food shortages and the ensuing health crisis, which resulted from the British blockade, had illuminated yet other episodes in British history. The Irish famine was suddenly relevant, as were the periodic famines in other parts of the Empire. To preside over one such disaster, it seemed to post-First World War Germany, might be regarded as an act of carelessness, to keep presiding over them began to look like 'systematic devilry'.[49] Once Germany's fortunes improved again, in the midtwenties, the immediacy of these impressions receded. And as friendliness towards Britain grew, they were less and less talked about, in much the same way that one might choose to ignore the unsavoury private habits of an otherwise admired friend.

Not so in the case of Hitler: once the irritant of British hostility towards Germany began to diminish by 1923, the British Empire shone ever more brightly in his mind. By coincidence, Hitler's racial views began to clarify during the same period. And it may be noted that the word 'ruthless' also makes its first appearance at about this time.[50] From now on, the instinct to acquire the British Empire had been racial. An ambition for territorial expansion was simply part of the Anglo-Saxon genetic make-up.[51] The genius of the Anglo-Saxons, Hitler thought, lay, however, in the way they had exploited their racial qualities. The British Empire was 'the result of marrying the highest racial quality with the clearest political aims'.[52] And the 'audacity', the 'tenacity' and the essential 'ruthlessness' with which these aims were pursued had in the past been signally lacking in Germany. Even in 1941, with half of Europe enslaved, Hitler felt the Nazis 'still had a lot to learn there'.[53]

If one accepts the idea of a racially determined British ruthlessness to be at heart of Hitler's conception of Britain after about 1923, his bizarre pronouncements over the years do begin to make sense. Much the same goes for his foreign policy with its otherwise puzzling contradictions. The breach of the Anglo-German naval agreement of 1935, for instance, before the ink on it was properly dry, has long been seen as evidence of his essential duplicity. How else could the illegal naval build-up be squared with the Nazis' ostensible desire for an Anglo-German *rapprochement*?[54] There is merit in that argument: supping with Hitler did indeed require long spoons. But if, like Hitler, one is convinced of Britain's own ruthlessness, a covert naval build-up would be an effective insurance against later British hostility. Britain, after all, had been allied to Germany – or rather to individual German states – before. This had not stopped her from deserting these allies if British interests favoured a *renversement des alliances*. One of the most prominent victims of such an about-turn had been Hitler's chosen historical alter ego: Frederick the Great. The well-worn phrase of 'perfidious Albion' has recognisable roots in British policy towards the continent of Europe. Hitler's distinctive innovation was to regard past British actions not simply as evidence of Anglo-Saxon duplicity but as essentially Germanic ruthlessness.

This, of course, brings one back to Rosenberg's Nuremberg speech, and his insistence that *Rassenkunde* held the key to understanding 'the history of nations and thus their past foreign policy'. But, Rosenberg had added, racial science was also the compass that would help chart the course of the Third Reich's own future foreign policy. Once one accepts that there was an internal logic to Nazi reasoning, however grotesque its initial assumptions, everything else falls into place. The wooing of Britain in the early years of the regime was sincere, appearances notwithstanding. It was simply that, to employ Theodore Roosevelt's famous simile, speaking softly to the British was more likely to succeed if a big stick was perceptible in the background. This was after all how the British themselves had traditionally conducted their foreign policy. By the same token, the decision in 1938 to risk a confrontation over Czechoslovakia did not preclude a later settlement – just as Britain had repeatedly embraced countries she had opposed (and defeated) in earlier conflicts.[55] Even after September 1939 German policy towards Britain was not one-dimensional. It was never simply a case of what the classicists in the German Foreign Office would have called *oderint dum metuant* – let them hate us as long as they fear us. Intimidation – like the earlier charm offensive – was designed above all to overcome British indifference.

It is perhaps worth stressing again at this point that there existed a fundamental difference between Hitler and most traditional German thought on the subject of Britain. And that difference was rooted precisely in the perceived racial origin of (British) foreign policy. Unlike many of his adopted countrymen, Hitler never expected Britain to act out of a sense of shared Germanic origins. In world politics, he insisted in his *Second Book*, 'family ties play no part'.[56] Britain would only act out of self-interest. And she would only treat as an equal a nation that matched her own self-assurance and apparent absence of scruples. Whichever way one approaches Hitler's argument, one finds at its base the concept of British ruthlessness.

That this was based on a misreading of British history and an almost total ignorance of British political culture is essentially irrelevant. What mattered was that Hitler's views contained an internal logic and did seem able to explain British policy towards Germany during the inter-war years. If Britain did not break with France over the Ruhr in 1923, for instance, that was because the value of German friendship did not outweigh the advantages to Britain of a continued Anglo-French alliance.[57] Events after 1933 of course merely conspired to prove Hitler's point. Having refused to treat the disarmed Weimar Republic as an equal (rightly so in Hitler's mind), Britain promptly started to woo the more aggressive Third Reich. And the more threatening German conduct became, the more anxious Britain seemed to accommodate Germany.

The outbreak of war in 1939 did not really shatter this view either. It merely suggested an initial British miscalculation. Time would put that right. With German armies in control of the continent from the Atlantic to the Ukraine, Britain could not go on ignoring Germany indefinitely. Or, to put it in Hitler's own words, 'We're getting a better press . . . these days.' The corollary of this, however, was the constant need to keep earning that better press. The best way to maintain British respect now that it had been won, Hitler thought in 1942, might be to start 'stringing up' captured British officers. A minor blood bath, preferably of titled officers, would concentrate minds in London wonderfully.[58] It is an appropriately chilling reminder that Nazi *idées fixes* tended to have consequences.

All of which of course takes one back, yet again, to the alleged racial basis of British attitudes, and thus ultimately to the father of Nazi racial science: Hans Günther. The leading Nazis, it is worth remembering, had no first-hand knowledge of the Anglo-Saxon world. Günther's remark in 1920 about the English language and the supposed 'ruthlessness' it betrayed thus constitutes the bizarre beginning of the Nazi attempt to make sense of Britain. Günther may not actually have planted in Nazi minds the idea of British 'ruthlessness' – the First World War evidently saw to that – but he provided a pseudo-intellectual framework to explain it. A nation's potential for heroism was revealed in its language, which in turn was the expression of its 'racial soul'.[59] Through Günther, historical linguistics and an awareness of England's Anglo-Saxon past thus achieved fantastical consequences. That Günther's various aphorisms were based on a travesty of linguistic research did not diminish their effectiveness in the Third Reich. Hitler himself, after all, liked to indulge occasionally in a little after-dinner linguistics. The fact that he spoke no English did not prevent him from expatiating on its supposed limitations in expression or on the relative merits of its various pronunciations (Anthony Eden's aristocratic drawl sounded 'repellent', whereas Lloyd George's Welsh lilt was '*wunderbar*').[60] The curious way in which Nazi views about Britain took shape thus explains why they ultimately bore so little resemblance to reality.

The Nazi party had not engaged in any systematic thought about Britain during the Weimar years. It had been too preoccupied with domestic affairs and winning power to do so. Hitler's published views of the period – both in his speeches and in *Mein Kampf* – were distinctly sketchy. They related mainly to recent Anglo-German history, and were broad-brush affairs even by Hitler's standards. Essentially, there were just three basic themes: Britain's rivalry with Wilhelmine Germany, Britain's 'ruthlessness' in war and peace, and Britain's status as a possible future ally of the new Reich. (Much the same goes for his unpublished *Second Book*, and its chapter on Britain; the only new – and ominous – ingredient in it is an interest in Britain's treatment of subject races and its possible lessons for the Third Reich.)[61] Otherwise, the leadership had limited itself to occasional comments on the events of the day. Hitler, Goebbels and Rosenberg – the men most likely in the early years to comment about the world beyond Germany's borders – were not normally so self-effacing. They shared a marked urge to impress their audiences with the apparent breadth and depth of their knowledge. The transcripts of their public speeches run to a full shelf of volumes. In the case of Goebbels and Rosenberg there is also a substantial body of journalism. The relative silence about Britain is therefore suggestive. It cannot have been the pressures of party office alone that produced such reticence. Alfred Rosenberg found time to write the vast *Mythos des Zwanzigsten Jahrhunderts* – his famously unreadable *summa* of Western civilisation. Yet Britain merits only half a dozen entries in its index.

Such Nazi silence was not without consequences. After 1933, the new government's foreign-policy initiatives – including Rosenberg's own trip to London – made Britain an unavoidable topic of political discussion. Yet the details of an official Nazi view were still lacking. Anybody writing on the subject professionally – either as a journalist or academic – was therefore initially operating in a kind of ideological limbo. The only guiding principles available were the regime's obvious friendliness towards Britain and England's well-known Germanic origins. The racial angle was therefore an obvious starting point. This applied equally to genuine Nazis, 'fellow travellers' or the merely cautious.

Existing textbooks on *Rassenkunde* were duly ransacked for useful detail. And since H. F. K. Günther was the author of a whole series of racial primers, he would have proved influential even without his impressive party connections. The irony, of course, is that Günther had devoted no more systematic thought to Britain than his political masters had. All that was available was a series of *obiter dicta* as bizarre as any of the Führer's own insights. That Günther should none the less have been deferred to even by non-Nazi academics who not merely should have known better but did actually know better, owes more to the nature of Nazi rule than to any specific intellectual shortcomings on the part of the people involved.[62]

A readiness on the part of journalists and academics to echo uncritically the intellectual authority of the day is, after all, a frequent phenomenon even in a democracy. In a dictatorship that effect is vastly magnified. Free speech may not guarantee the exercise of free thought, but its absence is certain to rob independent minds of their audience. This was to have profound consequences for the Third Reich's perceptions of Britain. It was not easy in Hitler's Germany to challenge publicly the views propounded by a man of Hans Günther's official standing. The press would have been reluctant to risk the party's wrath. And in the case of Günther – or *Rassen*-Günther as he was widely known – the risk was real enough. A prominent SA man, for example, who had been rash enough to ridicule Günther's theories in print during the 1920s, promptly ran into difficulties after 1933. The fact that he was an *Alter Kämpfer* – a long-standing party member – did not prevent his removal from the civil service a mere nine months after the *Machtergreifung*.[63] Since honesty in print was thus practically impossible, this left as a public forum in which to voice discreet dissent only academic life. And given the extremely circumscribed German knowledge about Britain, universities did play a significant role in providing information. But they were not insulated from the political reality outside either. Evidence of even moderate independence of mind tended to arouse political suspicions. Careers – and livelihoods – were at stake. The threat was far from imaginary. Even established figures with international reputations were not safe. Professor Voßler of Munich, one of the most distinguished German philologists of the inter-war years, was pensioned off in 1937 simply because the tone of his work was too Catholic for Nazi tastes. He had, for a little too long, proved deaf to well-meaning hints. Representations on his behalf from abroad, and from Mussolini's Italy at that, did not save him.[64]

The fate of the English department at Hamburg University is even more instructive. Its head, Professor Wolff, adopted rigorous self-censorship after 1933 and never strayed from safe 'unpolitical' topics. This allowed the authorities to overlook his previously 'unmistakable liberal and democratic stance' and his 'semitophile tendencies'.[65] Judicious silence was, however, not enough for less established figures. Professor Marie Schütt – vulnerable as a woman in the masculine Reich – only survived by joining the party and driving away the spies among her students through the apparently unrelenting tedium of her lectures.[66] But it is the fate of the most vulnerable – the untenured academics – that is especially revealing. A Dr Buck tried throughout the early years of the regime to cling on to his job. His record as an outspoken critic of the Weimar Republic was not enough to save him, for though staunchly right-wing and no friend of democracy, he was evidently no Nazi. The National Socialist Student Union eventually succeeded in having him removed. The wording of their confidential report is of more than local interest:

Herr Dr Buck has not in any way actively contributed to the National Socialist cause. He approaches ideology from a purely intellectual basis. He thus lacks entirely a fighting spirit, and remains indifferent to the will and the feelings of the German Volk.[67]

The Hamburg Student Union's strictures against a 'purely intellectual' approach go to the heart of the Third Reich's problems with the outside world. National Socialism was, avowedly, an anti-intellectual ideology. It despised 'professorial' logic, disdained learning and rejected reason. It survived and flourished inside the Reich only because its leadership and its rank and file knew the terrain in which they operated. Outside Germany, or at least outside central Europe, it was a different matter. There, 'will' and 'fighting spirit' could not make up in the long term for the Nazis' fundamental lack of knowledge. Ignorance about Soviet Russia, its true military strength and the mettle of its people doomed Hitler's armies long before they reached Stalingrad. The propaganda of Joseph Goebbels – so effective at home – failed abroad because it knew nothing of the nations it was hoping to influence. Even the initial successes betrayed a cavalier approach. When General Dietl was ordered to conquer Norway, he famously went out and purchased a copy of *Baedeker*. In it, he found all he needed to succeed. But he was dealing purely with topography. In the case of Britain much more was involved, not least the psychology of its people, and the Nazi party had gradually sealed off all potential conduits of information about it.

The normal channels through which governments acquire knowledge about conditions abroad are, of course, the reports of embassies collated by the relevant sections in the Foreign Office. In this regard German practice traditionally had not differed from that of other countries. As is well known, this began to change after 1933. For of the various arms of government in the Third Reich, the Auswärtige Amt held out longest against nazification. Its often spirited defence of Wilhelmine tradition made it deeply suspect to a leadership already contemptuous of diplomatic custom. Hitler tried, wherever possible, to bypass it. Moreover, his detached style of government was incompatible with the dutiful perusal of civil service memoranda which forms the bedrock of more conventional administrations. The mechanics of Nazi government need not be rehearsed here. What matters is that Hitler looked to unconventional sources to keep him informed. Translations of articles in the foreign press covered day-to-day events. For more fundamental information he turned to books whose covers caught his eye. The impressions of travel writers provided a vivid enough picture of the wider world overseas and were more readable than Foreign Office prose.[68] A study about British rule in India, intended as bedside reading in his Ukrainian headquarters, so impressed him that copies of it were distributed to all the *Gauleiter* in the Reich.[69] Others in the leadership inevitably copied their master's approach. Goebbels derived much of his slender knowledge about British history from the work of just one Hamburg academic.[70] Rosenberg had read the Weimar *Anglist* Wilhelm Dibelius. This had immediately translated into a brief article in the party newspaper.[71] Ribbentrop, finally, did not trouble himself with individual books: he decided to acquire a whole research institution, the Deutsche Institut für Außenpolitische Forschung in Berlin. This guaranteed him access to information and, perhaps more importantly, it allowed him to control its output. (The cheque for 5,000 Reichsmarks, with which the acquisition was to have been put on a legal footing, incidentally, somehow never reached the payee.)[72]

Given such extraordinary reliance by the leadership on domestic academic sources, the Third Reich's anti-intellectual instincts and narrow racial dogma proved especially crippling. The problem was both exemplified and exacerbated by the party's admiration for *Rassen-*Günther. The root of the problem, however, was the Führer himself. Hitler favoured simple explanations with simple causes and simple effects. Like many of his acolytes among the so-called 'Old Fighters', he had not enjoyed his schooldays and had emerged from the experience with a distaste for intellectual complexity. Simplification, he decreed in *Mein Kampf*, should be the guiding principle of all future German education.[73] It was here that Günther excelled: he provided a simple message, and was able to deliver it with a learned flourish that did not fail to impress an audience more used to beer halls than lecture halls.

The message was that of the all-importance of race, which Günther had started preaching when the Nazi party was still in its infancy. The decorative flourish was, inevitably, his grounding in historical linguistics: 'For the racial soul has been revealed in the creative power of the Indo-Aryan languages.'[74] This ostensible vantage point between science and the humanities allowed Günther to pontificate on a wide range of disciplines: 'There exists among us a deplorable lack of knowledge about the racial structure of our nation . . . Nearly all scientific publications continue to confuse Race and Language, Race and Religion, Race and Citizenship.'[75] The attraction of such pronouncements to the Nazi party is obvious. For one thing, they accorded perfectly with Hitler's own beliefs. But since they came from a 'scientific' source outside the party, they carried added propaganda value. They lent National Socialism the appearance of logical rigour while simultaneously absolving it from any need for intellectual enquiry, since 'nearly all scientific publications' were in any case useless. It is not hard to see why Günther was awarded the NSDAP Prize for Science (nor, for that matter, why Germany's academic community should have been so aghast at his elevation to professorial status five years earlier).[76]

In the case of Britain, Günther's fundamental 'insight' meant that everything could and should be reduced to the alleged racial ties between Britain and Germany. The subject of Britain's racial background had, of course, been discussed before the Nazi Seizure of Power. Most Weimar *Anglisten* had touched upon it in one form or another. Prominence had specifically been given to the connection with northern Germany; and more than one author, impressed by Britain's dogged wartime persever-ance, had referred his readers to the stubbornness of the peasantry in Lower Saxony.[77] But such remarks had been balanced with details of other likely influences on the British national character: German academics were perfectly aware that English history had not ended with King Harold in a field near Hastings. This relatively balanced approach extended even to figures close to Nazi preoccupations. The editor of *Volk und Rasse*, one of the main journals of German *Rassenkunde*, had for instance produced a brief 'Racial Survey of the British Isles', which was published in a 1929 hand-book. As one would expect, it anticipates much of the Third Reich's think-ing. Yet, crucially, its author had emphasised the 'essentially fragmentary' and speculative nature of the piece. Such lack of certainty was noticeably lacking after the *Machtergreifung*.[78] Above all, there had been no shortage of voices that were unimpressed by racial links and breezily dismissive of the wider Nordic theories. And these voices had by no means all become more muted as the Weimar era drew to a close. To one prominent *Anglist* writing in 1929, the 'legendary Nordic types' constituted a small minor-ity in Britain and were far outnumbered by the 'darker oval-heads'. In the author's mind this was no bad thing, since such darker oval-heads had produced on the shores of the Mediterranean the foundations of Western civilisation; should any *Volk* miraculously have preserved its Nordic nature, he added, it would do well to dilute it with some Mediterranean imports.[79] At the beginning of the twenties it was possible to declare without much fear of ridicule or contradiction that 'The days are gone when people were taken in by the racial theory of the inventive Count Gobineau and that pseudo-Englishman Chamberlain.'[80] A decade or so later, Gobineau and Houston Stewart Chamberlain had in effect become state doctrine. Books or articles questioning their views now remained unpublished, and existing sources that dissented were either suppressed or declared irrelevant. They constituted what Günther had called 'unfocused and spineless dealing in knowledge'.[81] In Hitler's own words, they were the product of the 'mindless professorial view of history'.[82]

The scope for even cautious dissent was further reduced, since Günther had managed to explain away some of the more glaring contradictions in his racial theory. The twin poles of British national identity which had so fascinated Weimar – gallantry on the battlefield and trading acumen in boardroom and stock exchange – might have posed a problem. They could not both have the same ethnic source if heroism alone was deemed a Nordic quality. Günther's solution was to suggest a racial fault line between town and country: between Nordic farmsteads and the satanic mills of lesser races. This tied in conveniently with the Third Reich's well-known rural enthusiasms. The Nordic race, Günther explained, disliked city dwelling, which tended rapidly to damage its vitality.[83] The inhabitants of London or Manchester might originally have been of prime Nordic stock, but *Asphalt* – tarmac – debilitated. Besides, they had been joined in the nineteenth century by substantial numbers of immigrants from Eastern Europe. These recent arrivals were in many cases Jewish or of doubtful pedigree, and their presence on British soil threatened 'incalculable consequences' for Britain's racial future.[84]

The parameters of a British *Rassenkunde* had thus been set even before the Nazis seized power. And the simple theory of a racial divide fitted Nazi requirements perfectly. It provided an intellectual shortcut towards making sense of Britain. Above all, it proved able to account for all phases and permutations of British foreign policy. The First World War, Hitler always insisted, had been the result of Jewish agitation. Günther's racial taxonomy of urban Britons had furnished hard evidence supporting the Führer's more instinctive insight. And it tied in neatly with the belief – not limited to the Nazis – that what had prompted Britain's declaration of war in 1914 had been Manchester's envy of German industrial prowess. That view ultimately went back to the 1890s and Bismarck.

Asked about the poor state of Anglo-German relations, Bismarck was said to have pointed to the economy. The only way for Germany to regain popularity in Britain, he thought, would be to shut down German industry.[85] After 1919, Bismarck's alleged reasoning could be combined with the more strident anti-semitism of the inter-war years. Britain's role at Versailles was thus declared directly attributable to Jewish influence, and the provisions in the treaty about the transfer of German patents to Allied companies and the seizure of Germany's foreign assets 'proved' it. (Alfred Rosenberg was fond of pointing out that, on the eve of the Paris conferences, Lloyd George had been closeted with David Sassoon at Sassoon's country house: the Prime Minister of Great Britain had in effect been summoned by his Jewish masters to receive his marching orders.)[86]

Paranoia produces its own warped logic. Britain's initial wooing of the Third Reich after 1933 was thus not incompatible with the Nazis' conspiracy theories. It merely suggested a healthy resurgence of the Nordic majority. Günther and his acolytes, after all, estimated Britain to be between 55 and 60 per cent Nordic (with the rest dividing into 25–30 per cent *Westian* stock and only some 10 per cent representing the more problematic *Eastian* imports).[87] The British government's diplomatic restraint in the face of the Third Reich's escalating anti-semitic measures of the mid-thirties confirmed that impression. So did the spectacle of British Black Shirts rallying to the anti-Jewish cause. By 1938, and especially after the Munich agreement, events pointed, *per contra*, to a redoubling of Jewish efforts. But there remained always the hope that sooner or later the 'true' Britons would awake. Blood would eventually tell. To trained eyes, the first signs were already discernible. The SS newspaper *Das Schwarze Korps* reported in its final peacetime issue, on 31 August 1939, that 'the Tommies' had found new lyrics to go with a familiar tune:

> Onward Christian soldiers you have nought to fear.
> Isaac Hoare Belisha will lead you from the rear.
> Clad by Monty Burton fed on Lyons pies.
> Fight for Yiddish conquest while the Briton dies.
> Onward conscript army marching on to war.
> We are still the old mugs that we were before.[88]

Whether this remarkable ditty, and other evidence like it, actually convinced the German public is hard to tell. The leadership at least was always ready to be swayed. Some ten years earlier Hitler had pronounced the struggle between Aryans and Jews in Britain still 'undecided'. 'The Jewish invasion', he declared in his *Second Book*, 'is still encountering native British tradition. The Anglo-Saxon instincts are still sufficiently acute and alive to preclude outright Jewish victory . . . Should the Briton win through, a change in policy towards Germany is still possible.'[89] It was a belief to which Hitler clung with all his formidable tenacity. Even after the Battle of Britain he was confident of eventual political transformation on the other side of the Channel. Once the British people realised that the war against the Third Reich could not be won, he told his confidants in November 1941, Britain would experience an outbreak of anti-semitism on a scale and of an intensity 'unparalleled' in the annals of history.[90] A year later Hitler still firmly predicted that the British would 'sort out the Jews'.[91] Nazi perceptions of whether the Germanic or Jewish elements were in ascendance have aptly been called a 'barometer' of the state of Anglo-German relations.[92] They also made for a further loosening of logic: Hitler could thus describe the British as 'consisting of various racial components', only to pronounce them, before the same audience a few months later, a 'purely Germanic nation'.[93]

Such inconsistencies were by no means limited to Hitler. Contradictions, circular reasoning, selective evidence and outright error were not minor flaws in the Third Reich's intellectual underpinning, they were its very essence. And nowhere, perhaps, was this more obvious than in its racial theories. Nazi *Rassenkunde*, as even its supporters tacitly admitted, was not an exact science. The elaborate ancestral data of the *Ahnenpaß* – the Third Reich's genetic ID cards – gave the game away. It was evidently not possible to make definitive racial judgements solely on the basis of physical appearance. The Luftwaffe General Milch famously got around the problem of a Jewish father by the simple expedient of declaring his mother an adulteress and himself the fruit of Aryan loins. There was apparently nothing about the curvature of his spine that suggested otherwise. But the problems went beyond simple political expediency. *Rassenkunde* itself required the suspension of disbelief. No two experts agreed on the exact number of racial types allegedly inhabiting Europe. There was for a long time no common consensus even as to whether the Germans themselves formed one racial group or were in fact made up of several. Hitler, wisely perhaps, chose not to commit himself on this potentially explosive issue. (Himmler was less circumspect and championed Günther's Nordic cause.)[94]

To these general methodological weaknesses came an additional one specific to Britain: none of the leading experts actually had any first-hand knowledge of the object of their research. The straightened economic circumstances of the Weimar years had made foreign travel difficult. *Rassenkunde* – then still on the fringes of academic respectability (or outside it) – had not attracted the lavish funding it would receive in the Third Reich. After 1933 the difficulties were of a different order. Government funds were at last flowing freely but the newly fêted experts now lacked the time to travel. Research institutions had to be set up and constantly expanded as the regime's racial experiment gathered pace.[95] The professional gaze, moreover, was shifting eastwards in line with the Third Reich's perceptible ambitions. Racial analysis of Western Europe did not seem the stuff on which careers would be built. Günther's earlier efforts thus survived unchallenged and largely unchanged. They had been undertaken with a personal knowledge of only three countries: France, Norway and Sweden (and in the case of France the acquaintance was limited to a visit to Paris before 1914).[96] Unsurprisingly, Günther had not based his work on traditional anthropological methods. He had lacked the necessary data.

This had led him to extensive recycling of existing (foreign) literature, particularly the works of Madison Grant and Theodore L. Stoddard – who would deserve wider public recognition as America's intellectual contribution to the Nazi racial experiment.[97] There were also British authorities who indirectly contributed to Günther's racial survey, chief among them William Inge, the 'Gloomy Dean' of St Paul's.[98] But Günther also adopted more imaginative approaches to supplement his meagre data. History of art – paintings, drawings and sculpture – provided evidence of sorts. Where data was more abundant, as in the case of Germany, art was mainly used to prove the persistence of types across the centuries. In the Third Reich newspaper supplements frequently juxtaposed the faces of medieval statues or Dürer portraits with photos of modern Germans to underline the genetic continuity. Outside central Europe, however, art was often the only evidence readily available to deskbound Nazi anthropologists. Günther's racial study of Europe thus relied on a Victorian canvas of a guards officer to illustrate a perfect Nordic type.[99] Portraits of well-known Britons (Dickens, Byron, Tennyson, Sir Walter Scott, the Duke of Wellington, etc.) also featured prominently. These illustrations served a double purpose: they were intended to train the public's eye in the recognition of racial types, while providing clues along the way to Britain's probable racial composition.[100] Nazi racial analysis of Britain was therefore dependent on the illustrations available in the standard German encyclopaedias. Individual Britons were considered not because they were in any way representative but because their names happened to be familiar to Nazi racial experts. Günther's other evidence was no less idiosyncratic: Elizabethan sonnets extolling the beauty of fair maidens jostled with contemporary impressions about the number of blondes at a first night in a West End theatre.[101]

It is perhaps worth repeating here that this kind of evidence had earned Günther almost universal derision in Weimar Germany. No research institution was prepared to employ him. To the academic community he was not a scientist but a 'writer' – and the translation does not begin to convey the contemptuous flavour of the German term *Schriftsteller*.[102] At one point, he actually had to leave the country to find employment. All this was to change with the Nazis' first taste of (regional) power in 1930. Three years later, after the *Machtergreifung*, German universities were obliged to recant in much the same way as Galileo had been obliged to submit to a higher authority some three hundred years earlier. And just as seventeenth-century Catholic astronomers proceeded to calculate the immensely complicated orbits of planets revolving around the Earth, German *Anglisten* duly described a Nordic Britain. Literary critics detected Germanic themes with even greater readiness than before, while art historians were reassured by the Nordic brows of Elizabethan portraiture or the Georgian aristocrats of Gainsborough and his followers. (The *œuvres* of Hogarth or Gillray, on the other hand, were less encouraging: the gin-crazed syphilitics and bloated gluttons of the cartoons did not inspire feelings of kinship. Here a smattering of historical knowledge came to the viewers' rescue: these nightmarish creatures were evidently Celts.)[103]

This careful selection of paintings and drawings of course demonstrates one thing quite clearly: Nazi racial science did not approach its subject with an open mind. It discovered only what it intended to discover. In the case of Britain, it wished to find a Nordic nation, in much the same way that later on it wanted to find in Soviet Russia the racial dregs of Europe. In the East 'science' would demand colonial rule and genocide, in the West an alliance with a fellow-Nordic nation.[104]

Nazi celebrations of Germanic kinship with 'the English cousins' are therefore not all they seem. As we have seen, Britain's political, economic and military successes had left a deep impression among the German right after the First World War. That sense of reluctant admiration took hold amid profound and widespread German ignorance of British politics, national life and wider history. Britain's success, however, was not just in striking contrast to German decline, it also contradicted earlier Wilhelmine notions about Britain. By the early years of the Weimar Republic this contrast could no longer be ignored. There now existed what the Germans call an *Erklärungsbedarf* – a need for an explanation. Since the political right viewed the world increasingly in *völkisch* terms as the century progressed, that explanation was always likely to be cast in *völkisch* terms. Hans Günther's duly did so with his Nordic theory. Günther provided little actual detail about Britain, but crucially his work connected with an existing awareness of cultural and linguistic ties. This 'North German' connection had been substantially questioned in the intellectual mainstream of the Weimar Republic. Operating outside academic respectability, Günther was able to re-establish it, and adapt it for the needs of the *völkisch* right. The key was Britain's alleged 'ruthlessness', which according to Günther was rooted in the country's Germanic origins. Germany, on the other hand, had lost that vital part of its racial inheritance and needed to recover it. This accorded perfectly with Hitler's own political beliefs, which were taking shape at about the same time. This, in turn, would guarantee Günther a wide audience in the 1930s.

It is important to get the sequence of events right here. Among the *völkisch* constituency in Weimar Germany, the sense of kinship did not come first. The recognition of Britain's power and possible future usefulness to a new German Reich preceded it. This was not true of the German population at large; indeed, it runs counter to previous German perceptions. Yet it is unmistakably the case within the Nazi movement and its ideological mainstays. There is, moreover, no evidence anywhere in Günther's work of genuine warmth towards Britain. There is none either in *Mein Kampf* or the unpublished *Second Book*. There is merely a recognition of the reality of British power, and an envious desire to equal it.

Alfred Rosenberg's Nuremberg speech on foreign policy and its ostensible racial origins was thus both an accurate reflection of his master's thought and at the same time profoundly, if unintentionally, misleading. The German public, and a great many within the Nazi party itself, were promptly misled. They concluded that Anglo-German friendship was now not merely a policy aim but an ideological imperative. To Hitler, however, it meant copying, half openly and half by stealth, what he fancied was a racially determined British 'ruthlessness'. If the Third Reich were to become both powerful and unscrupulous in its dealings with lesser nations, then Britain would eventually recognise in it a continental alter ego. The German public's enthusiastic support for the regime's foreign policies after 1933 was thus based on a fundamental misunderstanding of Nazi intentions. It would take several years before the full extent of that error would become apparent.

3 'Empire builders': Britain as a paradigm for Nazi expansion

The precise basis of Hitler's admiration for Britain – the supposed British ruthlessness and absence of moral scruples – remained hidden through much of the 1930s. To have revealed it to the wider world might have invited unwelcome conclusions about the Third Reich's own intentions. *Mein Kampf* contained very little about Britain, and the *Second Book* with its references to the Anglo-Saxon 'genius' at territorial expansion was never published.[1] Hitler's public utterances after 1933 were also – deliberately – unenlightening in this regard. The fiction of a peace-loving government seeking only modest revisions to the terms of Versailles was crucial at first to the regime's survival. This demanded a degree of circumspection. Yet the leadership's fascination with the British Empire was no secret. The Empire had been the only British topic regularly touched upon by the party's intellectuals in their speeches and journalism during the Weimar years.

In part this was simply coverage of political events.[2] During the 1920s and 1930s Britain remained the dominant power in international relations; it would take a second war with Germany for that dominance to be broken. The fact that Britain possessed imperial interests and obligations was directly relevant to the various naval, credit or trade agreements which preoccupied international diplomacy between the wars. Lastly, the Empire presented a topic in its own right through the evolving status of the Dominions, and the increasing challenges to British rule in India, the Middle East and in East Asia.

But the roots of Nazi interest in the Empire clearly went deeper. This becomes obvious not just in the choice of topics raised but in the context in which they were discussed. Discussions of British imperial history often occurred in unlikely places. A piece that appeared in 1929 in the party newspaper *Der Angriff* provides a good example. *Der Angriff*, it is worth noting, offered only limited coverage of non-German topics. (The name of the paper – *The Attack* – gives a reasonable idea of its intellectual sophistication and the breadth of its horizons.) Yet, this paper not only ran a series of articles on British statesmen who had been instrumental in expanding the Empire, it even moved beyond mere historical outlines. For instance, it chose to acquaint its readers with details of the Battle of Plassey. As an editorial priority in 1929 this is surely striking.[3]

Nor was this an isolated case. After 1933, when Nazi influence extended beyond the party media, such articles were not uncommon in the Reich's press. As in the case of *Der Angriff*, they frequently highlighted episodes in British imperial history which had no obvious bearing on contemporary affairs.[4] Other nations – and other colonial empires – did not receive comparable attention.[5] The articles about Britain were thus clearly not random coverage: reporting about non-German topics was never coincidental in the Third Reich. The purpose was didactic – in line with the Propaganda Ministry's secondary brief, reflected in its title, to provide 'popular enlightenment'.

The suggested lessons from British history became more explicit as the regime gained in self-confidence. In the autumn of 1936, for instance, Germany's main illustrated weekly newspaper, the *Berliner Illustrierte Zeitung* discussed, at length, the Fashoda crisis of 1898. Memories of past Anglo-French discord were no doubt part of the attraction (and this particular instance was within living memory). The focus of the article was, however, firmly on Britain's handling of the crisis. This culminated in the thought that 'when the moment came, Britain seized the opportunity brutally'.[6] The link – in language alone – with Hitler's views about Britain is obvious. And the fact that this article appeared in the wake of German armies re-entering the Rhineland is surely no coincidence either. It suggests that for all the Nazi rhetoric about an 'unprecedented age', some party members saw the Third Reich following where other imperial powers had led.[7]

This would later become quite explicit: when the rump Czech state was occupied in March 1939, it was not annexed outright. Instead, a so-called Protectorate was proclaimed: an institution for which there was no real precedent in German history.[8] Allowing the Czechs all the trappings of independence, from postage stamps to presidential guard, was not just designed to facilitate collaboration. The fiction of Czech self-

1   *'An Indian ruler reviewing a guard of honour of the army occupying his country'*

government under the 'protection' of the Reich was intended above all for British eyes. For the new dispensation in Prague was a deliberate mirror image of Britain's own relations with the so-called Princely States in India. President Hacha, it was implied, would now receive avuncular guidance from Baron Neurath in much the same way that Indian maharajahs were assisted in governing their states by British Residents.[9] Creating such parallels was an act of conscious malice. Britain, it was hoped, could thus be shamed into silent acquiescence.[10] (When this hope proved elusive, Goebbels promptly charged Britain with 'hypocrisy':[11] or, as one newspaper put it in Shakespearean tones, 'hypocrisy, thy name is England'.)[12]

If the allusions to British imperial practice failed to bring the hoped-for benefits abroad, they were rather more useful domestically. The account in 1936 of the Fashoda crisis is a perfect illustration. The Nazi government's systematic breach of international agreements did not just provoke alarm abroad. It also caused concern at home. The quarrel was with the means rather than the objectives of the regime's foreign policy. Few Germans would have questioned their government's *moral* right to reoccupy the Rhineland, to recover Danzig and Memel, or to demand self-determination for the Sudetenland. Risking war in pursuit of such aims was another matter. And joy over the successful resolution of one crisis did not necessarily lessen anxieties at the onset of the next.[13] It is here that Britain's imperial record proved useful to Nazi propaganda.

British history, the regime suggested to its subjects, had demonstrated time and again that the use of force – or the threat of it – was the surest way of safeguarding national interests. And as Britain's international standing proved, this approach did not preclude diplomatic respectability. On the contrary, it was essential in securing and maintaining Great Power status. What had worked for Britain would now also work for the Third Reich. On reflection, it is striking how ingenious the apparently random choice of Fashoda was in 1936. Comparing the crises on the Rhine and the Nile made the Third Reich seem moderate. It had, after all, in the famous phrase, 'merely invaded its own front garden'. Events at Fashoda, on the other hand, had been an undisguised exercise in imperial expansion. Britain had had neither legal nor substantive moral rights in the Sudan. And if European claims were to be admitted, French claims on the Nile were no less credible than those of Britain. But British interests were at stake, and all other considerations duly took second place.[14]

This is a recognisable echo of Hitler's familiar pseudo-Darwinist views. Yet the significance of this article lies less in its content than in its ill-disguised objective: the attempt to influence public opinion in Germany by invoking the real or supposed British example. This was done in a spirit not of envy or resentment, but of frank admiration (even in 1939, amid deteriorating Anglo-German relations, the SS newspaper Das Schwarze Korps invited its readership to learn from Britain's road to worldwide influence).[15] If the Reich was to achieve a status comparable to that of Britain, it would have to equal Britain's single-minded pursuit of power.

This intention is even more evident in a second article on imperial history published by the Berliner Illustrierte Zeitung. This formed part of the same series of articles in the autumn of 1936. Before the paper turned to events at Fashoda, it had examined the beginnings of British India. Here, too, potential lessons were discovered. And it was, inevitably, the morally questionable exploits of India's first British rulers that provided the focus of interest. 'Men, such as Clive and Hastings', the paper observed, 'have often been called adventurers, desperados and murderers'. But this was to miss the point: 'they should be seen, fundamentally, as great statesmen who in all their actions were mindful only of the interests of their country'.[16]

The Third Reich's subsequent record makes such sentiments leap from the page. Whether they would have sounded quite as ominous to readers at the time is less certain. The article was after all concerned with India. Geography – or rather, ethnicity – is relevant here. It must be remembered that attitudes in Europe and North America towards non-whites differed from those of today. Normal moral judgement was routinely suspended where other races were involved. Paradoxically, this might have diminished the effect of this specific article. It is perfectly possible that German readers detected in it nothing of conceivable relevance to a country without dark-skinned subjects. Yet it is also clear that the author of the article, and the leadership of the Nazi party, thought otherwise.

This leads to a fundamental issue: if the German public did not generally envisage a colonial future for Germany, how and why did the British example seem relevant to them? Few, after all, can have foreseen even in the mid-thirties the regime's plans for a colonial empire in Russia; fewer still might have believed them possible. What, in other words, constituted the common ground between their perceptions of Britain and those of the regime?

That there existed, in the Weimar years, widespread German admiration for Britain has already been shown. Such admiration, reluctant at first but unmistakable, owed much to the combined shocks of defeat, internal chaos and international humiliation. The Great War and its aftermath had severely undermined the country's self-confidence. Germany did not simply move from the arrogance of the Kaiser to the hubris of Hitler. In between lay a period of grave self-doubt, which all the patriotic bluster of the Weimar right could never quite disguise. As the twenties wore on and the German republic (and most of continental Europe) moved uneasily from crisis to crisis, Britain's comparative stability stood out. The root of German admiration was therefore simply British power. And the most tangible expression of British power was the British Empire.

Put at its simplest, the Empire epitomised success to many German eyes, in much the same way that the new German republic embodied national failure. Perhaps inevitably, analyses of British policies and institutions – 'of how the English do things' in the words of one Weimar-era book – tended to be undertaken with more than half an eye on Germany itself.[17] The diarist Viktor Klemperer, for instance, records in 1920 a dinner-party conversation about British 'colonial methods'; his host, a prominent banker, promptly contrasted British success with

German failure.[18] This, Klemperer felt, complemented related observations by the great *Anglist* Wilhelm Dibelius: the British Empire, it will be remembered, had featured prominently at the Conference of Modern Linguists at Halle that year. What is interesting about this is not so much the topic as the tone. Neither Dibelius nor Klemperer were noticeably unpatriotic (Klemperer at one stage hoped he might still be fit enough to enlist in the coming war of revenge). The sentiments Klemperer recorded, and his own calm response to them, are therefore noteworthy: there was – less than two years after Versailles – a frank admission of German shortcomings in the former colonies, rather than complaints about their loss through Allied iniquity. 'The colonial crime of Versailles', as Nazi propaganda would later call it, did not prevent a cool assessment of Britain's success.[19]

Though the practicalities of colonial rule would in due course capture the imagination of the Nazi party (and, particularly, that of its leader), the colonies were for a long time purely a side issue. Not even Hitler at first was able to detect the direct relevance of British colonial methods to inter-war Germany. Instead, the focus of interest lay in the power that had created and now sustained the Empire. It was here that German observers hoped to derive lessons for Germany.

Wilhelm Dibelius, who perhaps more than any other *Anglist* shaped German perceptions of Britain after the Great War, detected useful lessons. He pointed particularly to the political arena. The British, it seemed to him, possessed as a nation a unique 'feel' for politics: a strong 'political instinct'.[20] This he contrasted with the situation in Germany both before and after 1918. Dibelius was influential not just in educational circles.[21] One catches clear echoes of his sentiments in Hitler's *Second Book*: 'If the Earth today holds a British Empire this is because there currently exists no nation more suited [to rule] by virtue of its general political characteristics and the average political intelligence [of its individual members]'.[22]

There is a distinct irony to Hitler's enthusiasm: Weimar *Anglisten* also regularly praised British 'common sense',[23] 'self-mastery' and personal 'restraint'.[24] Such inconsistencies are to be expected: Hitler, throughout his career, was adept at picking the plums out of any pudding and ignoring (ultimately to his cost) what he found less palatable. In spite of obvious contradictions between the *Anglisten* and the future Führer therefore, there existed some common ground between them: it lay in the belief that Germany could benefit from the British example.

There was agreement also as to what constituted the core of Britain's political culture: 'a strong urge at territorial expansion'; indeed, a desire for 'world domination'.[25] This was a commonplace in German studies about Britain in the 1920s.[26] In a sense, this was merely a reflection of Britain's international standing after the First World War and the sheer reach of her Empire. The view that an Englishman's first instinct upon stepping ashore in a foreign land was to plant the Union Jack on the nearest promontory was, after all, not limited to Germany. (The Third Reich was later able in its propaganda war to draw on a rich collection of non-German material, notably from French sources.)[27]

The Paris peace treaties had, of course, done little to discourage such views. It could hardly escape German notice that as the Ottoman Empire and Germany's own colonies were divided among the victors, Britain had selflessly shouldered a larger burden than any other power. It was therefore easy enough to identify the importance of empire to the British. Understandably, it was more difficult to agree on the specific lessons to be drawn from this. There was no suggestion that Germany could – or even should – copy Britain's relentless expansionism directly. Wilhelmine *Weltpolitik* was a thing of the past after 1918. This needs to be said in view of events two decades later. Yet British imperialism did not seem entirely irrelevant to the German experience post-Versailles. The history of the British Empire, after all, was the story of a small country achieving greatness through a combination of luck, skill and dogged determination. In its youth, the Empire had been threatened by larger powers only to survive; and in its maturity it had recovered, more than once, from severe reverses and substantial losses in men, land and treasure. This was a message not without its attraction for Weimar Germany.

The first practical advice Germany's *Anglisten* derived from British history, therefore, was not to abandon hope. The second was to lift Germany's sights above the immediate troubles besetting the nation. At least to one author, the thought of London was inspirational. The city's global reach through government departments, barges, warehouses and docks suggested the way forward: 'we need to aim for that larger perspective which can only be achieved by a nation that does not exhaust its energies in a dispute . . . over some border region'.[28]

Such robust good sense may seem unexpected. It might also lead one to conclude that Germany's *Anglisten* cannot have been very influential after 1933. Indeed, there is no denying that their professed 'Europeanism' – the belief in common European values – sits uneasily with the subsequent course of German history. Yet it would be wrong to dismiss the views of Weimar's academics and schoolmasters as irrelevant. For one thing, they possessed genuine knowledge about Britain at a time when few of their compatriots did. And as natural speakers and authors they were in a position to pass on some of that knowledge. Moreover, they had a recognisable influence on evolving Nazi perceptions during the Weimar years (in the case of Alfred Rosenberg's debt to Wilhelm Dibelius, it was even explicitly acknowledged).[29] What is more, after 1933, they contributed much of the detail to the official image of Britain. If Hitler provided a skeletal outline, so to speak, the experts added flesh, skin and colour, and breathed life into it. Later still, after 1939, not a few in the profession became active in the regime's propaganda war. Lastly, there is the thought that a substantial section of the Third Reich's population, particularly its more active younger members, would have received all or part of their education in the Weimar years. Their perceptions of Britain would clearly have been influenced by the opinions of their teachers and lecturers.

It might therefore be useful to consider briefly the underlying attitudes of these men (the profession was almost exclusively male). Since their published output is remarkably consistent in tone, a brief impressionistic glance will suffice. During a reception by Reich President Ebert for Germany's Modern Linguists in 1924, Viktor Klemperer was struck by the thought that the Social Democrat President was surrounded by members of a profession, 95 per cent of whom were supporters of various right-wing parties. The President, Klemperer relates, must have been aware of it too, for he expressed the diplomatic conviction that everyone present 'was united in wanting to help Germany'.[30] Four years earlier, at the conference of Modern Linguists in Halle, Iron Crosses were in evidence throughout the proceedings, and, as we have seen, attempts at postwar reconciliation had to be postponed amid a chorus of patriotic outrage. And there was Wilhelm Dibelius, who had made such an impression at Halle. In a possible allusion to the Duke of Wellington's views on the Battle of Waterloo and the playing fields of Eton, he observed that the war had been lost in the schoolrooms of Prussia[31] (the unspoken corollary of which presumably was the need to win the next one in the Reich's schools).

Taken together, these glimpses will go some way towards explaining the remarkable coherence the profession achieved in its pronouncements. This also helps explain the influence they would later achieve in the Third Reich. This is not to suggest that German schools and universities were uniformly Nazi in the twenties and early thirties. There was clearly much that separated many – even most – *Anglisten* from National Socialism. Yet the two groups shared a common frontier: they held very similar assumptions about Germany and the events of November 1918. And this resulted in other similarities, not least an interest in similar aspects of 'Britishness'. It bears repeating that most of what was said or written in Weimar Germany about Britain was intended also as an oblique comment on Germany itself.

To read eulogies on British 'will power', determination and toughness,[32] on British public schools specifically designed to educate rulers and teaching their pupils 'to lead [*führen* in German], and where they cannot lead to submit',[33] or to come across such British sentiments as 'my country, right or wrong',[34] is to see all too clearly in which direction Germany was heading. The intended destination, admittedly, may not have been National Socialism itself – the widespread respect for the intensity of British religious feeling would suggest it was not – but the overthrow of Weimar democracy was certainly desired. (Dibelius even contrived to distinguish a British parliamentary system rooted in native tradition with a democratic constitution both alien and damaging to Germany.)[35] Above all, the readiness of Germany's *Anglisten*, and indeed other intellectuals, to accept the existence of national types – *der Engländer*: 'the Englishman' vs. 'the German' or 'the Frenchman' – smoothed the path for National Socialism. This even went for obvious enemies of Nazi ideology. (In 1936, after he had been dismissed from his professorial chair as a 'non-Aryan', Viktor Klemperer felt that through his work on French thought and culture he too could not entirely escape blame.)[36]

After the Nazi Seizure of Power, the transition was therefore often relatively smooth. And as the regime set about reshaping Germany in a self-confident, heroic mould, the experts were not slow to detect parallels with Britain. These parallels were not unwelcome to the leadership; they were, after all, couched in flattering terms. The Third Reich in its early years was still only a second-rank power. Comparisons with the world's largest empire were therefore gratifying. What is more, they offered a welcome ideological rationale for the pursuit of Anglo-German *entente*. Cynical *Realpolitik* could thus be cloaked in the mantle of National Socialist idealism.

Perhaps the first sign of this was the attempt to interest the Nazi party in Oliver Cromwell. Among the *Anglisten*, 'the mighty Cromwell' had long been a source of fascination.[37] He had been known in Germany not least through Carlyle's biography (Carlyle, the admirer of Frederick the Great, was himself highly regarded both before and after 1933). Interest in Carlyle and Cromwell had grown noticeably after the First World War. This was clearly connected with the wider attempt in the early twenties to account for Britain's role in the war. As with other aspects of British imperialism, fascination and distaste were initially mixed. But it is from similarly mixed perceptions that Hitler moved to simple fascination. And it may be more than mere coincidence that the *Anglist* who first drew attention to Cromwell and Carlyle in the Weimar era would later emerge as a particularly fervent National Socialist. In 1920, he suggested that Carlyle's book *On Heroes, Hero-Worship and the Heroic in History* should be at the 'centre of the teaching of English to Germany's sixth-formers'.[38] What recommended the book particularly in his eyes was its supposed practical benefits to the modern reader: it offered a unique insight into British political thinking. Above all, it demonstrated the 'eternal maxim of British policy that might equals right'.[39]

It should be remembered that this was written in the immediate aftermath of Versailles. It was, however, not just Germany's own fate that suggested such thoughts in the early twenties: what was happening in, and to, Ireland recalled vividly the times of Cromwell. (At about this time, Viktor Klemperer noted a new readiness among his compatriots to identify with oppressed nations, since Germany was now acquainted with the effect on the powerless of 'the victor's ferocity'.)[40] All of this made Cromwell seem doubly relevant to German *Anglisten*: understanding past British policy might help predict future British conduct – not least towards Germany itself.

The idea that a nation's attitudes to others might remain unchanged across the centuries – as if engraved on its soul – would later become important in the Third Reich. In the 1920s, however, fears of enduring British hostility did gradually subside. This affected perceptions of the Empire – and thus, in turn, of Cromwell. German observers began to favour more nuanced interpretations. On the subject of colonial rule, they were increasingly willing to accept that coercion was not the only factor that held the British Empire together. The discussion of colonial methods referred to earlier, for instance, noted Britain's apparent ability to reconcile the captive nations to British rule.[41] The origins of Empire were likewise recognised as more complex. Dibelius even allowed for a degree of idealism and rejected simplistic condemnations of Britain's imperial expansion.[42] As so often, one catches indirect echoes of the contemporary debate in Hitler's own thought. Hitler, of course, by the mid-twenties, was very far from condemning British imperialism. But he rejected also the subtler accounts of it. The matter was altogether simpler, he thought, than the academics were suggesting. What had created the British Empire was not a Puritan mixture of missionary zeal and commercial self-interest or, as he put it, of 'subterfuge and swindling'.[43] It was the British 'will' to rule.[44]

German views of Cromwell are thus a useful gauge of wider assumptions about British imperialism. From the mid-twenties onwards, assessments of both were relatively balanced. The religious component in Cromwell's life – and in Empire – was freely acknowledged.[45] Yet there was also, following Carlyle, a continuing emphasis on the heroic. After 1933 this would provide an obvious link with National Socialism, both in its perceptions of Britain and of a wider Germanic heroism, which Hans Günther had first identified as the ancestral heritage of all true Indo-Europeans.

The Nazi *Machtergreifung* increased Cromwell's public prominence further, while predictably narrowing the range of historical interpretation. The early years of the regime were marked by a series of biographies, novels, essays and even plays about Cromwell.[46] One book, influential in party circles, anticipated the Seizure of Power by a few months: *Oliver Cromwell, A Struggle for Freedom and Dictatorship* was midway between a biography and a historical novel, and was clearly directed at a mass readership.[47] Its author, Heinrich Bauer, contributed regularly to Alfred Rosenberg's monthly journal, the *Nationalsozialistische Monatshefte*. There duly followed in that periodical a brief article for those seeking more concise enlightenment.[48]

Enlightenment was, in a sense, necessary. It is probably a fair assumption that many among the core constituency of National Socialism, especially those with more limited educational qualifications, would not have been familiar with Cromwell in 1933. 'After all, how much did we know of Oliver Cromwell even a decade ago?', as Bauer asks in a tone of revealing conciliation.[49] The title of his piece 'Cromwell and the German Revolution', however, explains why he thought this ought be remedied. Cromwell and Adolf Hitler – 'there exists no comparison more compelling' – were quite simply related phenomena.[50] Both men were possessed of an 'ardent will to destroy and to create'; both knew 'neither half-measures nor mercy';[51] both were manifestations of the same kind

2   *After-dinner thoughts:'The spirit of freedom in our two great democracies can never admit the absolute rule of a single individual'*

of 'national revolution', 'arising from deep down in the Germanic soul'; and in each case these Germanic revolutions had been victorious through the 'superhuman creative power of a single Man'.[52]

Such insights probably did not originate among the leadership itself. The leaders, for the most part, did not know enough about Britain and its history to be struck by such thoughts.[53] It was those with more detailed knowledge, both within the party and outside it, who thought they detected similarities. And, for reasons discussed below, they were anxious to publicise them. Such initially unsolicited information sometimes proved useful. The comparisons between Cromwell and Hitler, a recurring theme in the Third Reich's early years, may not have seemed particularly promising in propaganda terms.[54] Limited familiarity with Cromwell would have lessened the impact. But for specific audiences it could be relevant.

The title of Bauer's article 'Cromwell and the German Revolution' provides a clue about this. The term 'revolution' was initially dear to core sections of the Nazi party. Outside the party, however, it had a much more ambiguous ring to it. It recalled the French revolution. That was politically problematic at the best of times. In 1933 it was particularly awkward: Hitler's conservative allies were viscerally opposed to it, both at an intellectual and purely emotional level; and in the early years of the Third Reich the Nazis greatly depended on their old-fashioned conservative partners. It is therefore no accident that the article on Cromwell should have sought to contrast the French and English revolutions. The former, it asserted, was based on the 'democratic-mechanistic principle of the greater mass', the latter rooted in 'the most fundamental relationships between citizen and state, individual and God'.[55] The reference to God is further evidence of the attempt to reach out to a non-Nazi audience.

Whether the article achieved its intention is debatable. But such articles did have another, more palpable effect. They reversed the attempts of Weimar's *Anglisten* to challenge the significance of racial ties between Britain and Germany. Instead of doubt, people like Heinrich Bauer offered certainty: there was unambiguously a common Anglo-German outlook; history itself proved it. This, too, can only have been useful to a regime eager to bring about an Anglo-German alliance. Historical or cultural detail about Britain, of which the Nazi party and its leadership had been ignorant, thus began to suggest an ideological consistency in Nazi foreign policy which was in fact wholly imaginary. That this apparent consistency would have been reassuring to the German public, however, hardly needs saying. It encouraged the view that in its foreign policy, as in all other areas of national life, the new government advanced with clear principles, firmness of purpose and conspicuous intellectual integrity.

It may not only have been the public which fell victim to this agreeable illusion. There are some indications that the leadership itself might have been affected. The leadership's views about Britain underwent repeated modifications in the twelve years of Nazi rule, which makes generalisations difficult. Moreover, Hitler's *Table Talk* – the only substantial evidence we have of his day-to-day thoughts – dates from much later; but the *Table Talk* does suggest that Hitler was, temperamentally, receptive to parallels pointed out to him, and happy to trace a grand design where none existed. If this was the case in the early forties, it is likely to have been true also of the preceding decade. Other senior officials, we know, were content to echo their master. But, they too, it seems, occasionally felt the glow of a supposedly common Anglo-German heritage.

A particularly telling instance is recorded in the Goebbels *Diaries*. It concerns an evening at the theatre in 1935. Goebbels had attended a performance of a new 'revolutionary drama' by the regime's favourite living playwright, Hans Johst. The play, *Thomas Paine* was − like similar efforts about Cromwell or Clive − eloquent testimony of the Third Reich's readiness to detect links with Britain[56] (and, as with Bauer's article on Cromwell, it was probably intended to weaken the French associations of the term 'revolution'). What effect *Thomas Paine* had on its general audience is now hard to say. But in the specific case of Goebbels, we know. He committed his feelings to paper. He was 'profoundly moved' by what he saw on stage: 'so much of it reminded me of my own life'.[57] 'Well done, Johst', Goebbels recorded.

That praise seems apt: the flattery was indeed well done; so well done that, as with Goebbels' own propaganda, the intended victim did not notice he was being manipulated. What is at issue here, however, is not the manipulation but its result: Goebbels detected parallels between Tom Paine and himself, and thus between Britain and the Third Reich. The fact that Paine had been unsuccessful in his own country did not matter. The memories of the Nazis' own *Kampfzeit* − the period in the political wilderness − were still fresh. If the immediate effect of this evening is unmistakable, its ramifications are inevitably less certain. It is difficult to quantify the cumulative effect on the leadership of such dubious glimpses of Britain on stage, on screen, in print, or wherever. We lack the day-by-day account of Hitler's evolving thought across the years that might permit more certain judgement. And where such accounts exist, as in the case of Goebbels, the interest in Britain was not sustained enough to provide clear evidence one way or another. But both men, we know, were easily swayed by information they wished to believe in; both had a habit of inflating the importance of welcome news. Both accumulated a considerable store of bizarre detail about Britain in the course of the Twelve-Year Reich. And both, of course, consistently misinterpreted British actions and failed to anticipate likely British responses. To suggest that Ribbentrop's incompetence alone accounted for all this seems scarcely credible.

Disseminating so much misinformation would have taxed even his powers. One will be wise to allow therefore that the leadership's predilection for eccentric sources of information can only have compounded the problem.

It does not require vast powers of imagination to see how this might have operated in practice. Goebbels would presumably have judged the prospects of Anglo-German *entente* more favourably after that 'moving' performance of *Thomas Paine*. Feelings of kinship with Britain had clearly welled up in him. Hitler, too, appears to have experienced moments of profound empathy with Britain. The Führer, we know, was greatly impressed by *The Bengal Lancers*, a vision of the British Empire perhaps not wholly representative of Whitehall policy in the 1930s.[58] The fact that Hitler's views of the Raj, expressed in the *Table Talk*, were decidedly idiosyncratic should therefore surprise no one.

The image of Hitler at the Berghof enjoying repeated showings of *The Bengal Lancers* is one that rightly lodges in the mind. It equals, and perhaps exceeds, in incongruity anything the unhappy Ludwig of Bavaria ever did in *his* mountain fastness. The French ambassador Antoine Poncet was famously struck by the pervasive air of unreality on the Obersalzberg. Poncet was reminded of Wagnerian myth. Yet, though Hitler was certainly receptive to Wagner, at the Berghof it seems images of the Raj brought him even greater delight.

This is not irrelevant to a discussion of Nazi perceptions of Britain. The French ambassador had been favoured with an audience in Hitler's *Teehaus*; German visitors were accorded even greater privileges. They were sometimes invited to watch films with the Führer, and *The Bengal Lancers* was a standard part of the repertoire. Whether or not these guests shared their host's enjoyment is immaterial. His enthusiasm will have communicated itself clearly to them. And in the manner of all courtiers they will have taken due note of it. It is safe to assume that they will have echoed his sentiments assiduously, as they descended from the Berghof back into everyday Germany. One such returnee must have mentioned Hitler's enthusiasm to someone working for the SS newspaper, *Das Schwarze Korps*. The precise route, and the identity of the people involved, is unimportant. It is the consequence alone that matters.

The paper promptly produced a long and glowing article, more of a homily on the topic of *The Bengal Lancers* than a review of the film. *Das Schwarze Korps* did not normally comment on the cinema, which would have made the article stand out. (Even the less observant readers must have grasped the importance of this particular film, after a further reference to it, some six months later.)[59] The title of the first article – 'A Handful of Soldiers Controlling a Nation of 300 Million' – echoes familiar Hitlerean themes. It is worth quoting at length, however, since few things go more to the heart of Nazi perceptions of Britain at the time:

> One must admit the British were fine merchants, but they were even better judges of men, better handlers of men, and better soldiers . . . This film displays throughout the spirit and conduct which is shared, in our new Germany, by the entire *Volk*: loyalty and attention to duty to the last, comradeship and concern for the other, and possibly weaker man. They abuse our new Germany abroad, making it out to be one large garrison where drill and – to use their own idiotic term – 'mindless obedience' suppress and extinguish all humanity; and then from that same world beyond our borders a film reaches us: a scene from the life of a great and powerful nation. A film glorifying precisely that which those vile tongues . . . seek to criticise in us.[60]

This passage is a perfect summary of Nazi reactions to Britain in the mid-thirties. There is, for one thing, the characteristic truculent tone; the sense of being the victim of wilful misunderstanding and outright calumny; there is the imputation of hypocrisy among the Third Reich's foreign critics, which became an abiding theme; there is the unmistakable ignorance about, and incomprehension of, Britain; above all, there is the readiness to see in Britain the Third Reich's alter ego. The characters in *The Bengal Lancers* could easily be mistaken for Prussians, as the SS newspaper opined.[61]

Such coverage, in turn, had consequences. It encouraged those with knowledge about Britain to trace other parallels between the two great Germanic nations. It also meant that the British Empire could be safely celebrated, since it clearly epitomised Germanic – or even Prussian – virtues. In Nazi eyes, praising such virtues was all the more urgent, as they had become eclipsed in Germany by a decade of Weimar pacifism. Eulogies of British imperialism were thus perfectly compatible with German patriotism after 1933. They could in fact provide the platform for oblique, or overt, comparisons with Germany's 'rebirth' – or, to use the Nazi term, its *nationale Erhebung*.

It is this that explains the impressive array of publications about British topics in the early years of the Third Reich. There were historical novels, celebrating among others Raleigh, Nelson, Wellington and the Duke of Marlborough.[62] Cecil Rhodes was the subject of several books, whose titles clearly reveal the nature of the attraction he held for Nazi readers: *The Conqueror, For a Greater Fatherland*, or *The Dream of World Domination*.[63] A volume on Captain Cook was recommended to the Hitler Youth 'because he led an heroic life'.[64] There were books and articles about Dr Livingstone[65] or Lawrence of Arabia whose death, the German public learnt, was all the more poignant for having prevented a much desired meeting with Adolf Hitler.[66] There were English-language publications for use in the Reich's schools (written by politically reliable German schoolmasters). These included such titles as *Heralds of British Imperialism*[67] or a three-volume compendium, simply called *Eminent Englishmen* – Volume 1: *Great Sailors*. Volume 2: *Great Soldiers*. Volume 3: *Great Explorers*.[68] (The tone and topics of these volumes foreshadow very accurately later ministerial guidelines on suitable reading material for schools.)[69] Many of these English-language publications specifically advertised their political usefulness by appearing in a series entitled 'Readings in the Service of National Political Education'.

That there was indeed an ideological agenda underlying all this soon became apparent. It was in the schools of the Reich – or rather it was in the educational debate – that this first surfaced. In 1934, for instance, one influential educationalist suggested as the aim of German schools 'the complete re-moulding of a human being towards an ideological preparedness, towards embracing a future for the *Volk* that will require sacrifices'.[70] This might seem little more than standard Nazi rhetoric.[71] Yet these sentiments were expressed in an article entitled 'English Literature and German Education'. One year on, in 1935, another schoolmaster (and Nazi party activist) thought that teaching about English literature and Britishness (*Volkstum*) offered a wealth of 'topics conducive to character building'; these, he added, were all the more relevant since they were the expression of a 'racial soul closely related to ours'.[72] Another two years on, in 1937, such convictions had reached a semi-official status: they were now voiced in a book edited by a high-ranking civil servant in the Reich Ministry of Education.

This volume, which in turn influenced ministerial guidelines issued a year later, states quite explicitly the political uses of *Englandkunde* – British studies. One passage, in particular, is worth quoting at length. Starting from the premise that any foreign nationality (*Volkstum*) was rooted in race and was the expression 'of the ingredients of its blood', it suggests the peculiar usefulness to political instruction of the British example: 'Studying the English nation, which is related to us [*artverwandt*], and its culture and history will again and again exemplify this.' It was particularly the chief exponents of imperial masculinity that could provide inspiration to German boys: British history demonstrated 'especially in the great leaders [*Führergestalten*] the instinctive rejection of inhibitions alien to the race'.[73]

What these rejected inhibitions were had already been hinted to a wider public in newspaper articles glorifying British conduct at Fashoda or in the India of Clive and Warren Hastings. But Nazi enthusiasm for masculine Britishness and its supposed disdain of moral constraints gets more pointed still. In political coverage a degree of circumspection continued to be observed through much of the thirties. In other fields, it was possible to be more outspoken. Discussions of literature – as much as politics a product of race and of the 'constituent elements in a nation's blood' – are a case in point. Nazi attitudes to Shakespeare, for instance, provide some of the most pointed lessons in 'rejecting inhibitions alien to the race'.

Shakespeare, the Third Reich had decreed, was a Germanic author. The same Heinrich Bauer, who had drawn parallels between Hitler and Cromwell, produced an article to that effect.[74] Amid much purple prose the article contains one striking passage. It comes in a discussion of *Macbeth* (significantly one of the Third Reich's favourite plays). Here is Bauer's final verdict on the play's supposed ethos: 'Great even in committing a crime and unyielding in its loyalty and defiance unto death – that is true Germanic nature.' It is hard not to see in this, published in 1933, and in related remarks by *Rassen*-Günther, a sign of what was to follow in Germany.[75]

Those among the experts who lacked the taste for such full-blooded celebrations of Germanic masculinity found other thoughts to occupy them. They were happy to celebrate less troubling parallels with the new Germany than Macbeth, British gunboat diplomacy, or the record of the East India Company. Education itself was one. And, as in practically all areas of German perceptions of Britain, this too involved a degree of change and of adapting to the Third Reich's known preferences.

Though Weimar educationalists had admired the way the British public school system provided the Empire with suitable administrators,

their admiration had not been total. They were impressed by the importance accorded to leadership, and the early acquaintance with, and
preparation for, political life. They praised also the attention to healthy
bodies, and not just healthy minds, as was the way in some German
schools. Yet it was precisely the ethos of *mens sana in corpore sano* that ultimately troubled many *Anglisten* in the 1920s. During their visits the evidence of *corpora sana* had been abundant, but what of the minds? Dibelius
had diagnosed pervasive intellectual shallowness.[76] There was, moreover,
the suspicion that the long hours on the playing fields were intended, at
least in part, to discourage thought. The emphasis on games seemed part
of a wider tendency to suppress individuality and induce conformity
across a school, and thus ultimately throughout society.[77]

The notion of German authors decrying conformity is less
incongruous than it might seem. It is precisely because Germans had for
prolonged periods lacked political freedom that they cherished their *per-
sönliche Freiraum* – their 'personal bit of freedom'. The life of the mind,[78] as
much as the choice of clothes or the individual design of their houses:
these were treasured freedoms.[79] In Britain, by contrast, they saw a society
of stifling formality and convention, where people knew what to wear for
any given occasion, or what constituted appropriate topics for conversation, etc. Above all, during formative years at school, there was a readiness in Britain to submerge individuality in the team or the house,
whereas in Germany the individual remained essential, as much in ath-
letics, country hikes or mountaineering as at the writing desk.

Even in the first year of the Third Reich, a German commentator
felt able to say that the average German boy would find the regimented
life in an English public school hard to accept.[80] (The increasing problems the regime encountered with rebellious youth once the novelty of
the Third Reich's institutions had worn off, almost seem to prove him
right.) Weimar *Anglisten* thus felt perfectly entitled to accuse the British of
confusing parliamentary democracy with personal freedom.[81] The Third
Reich would, of course, test to destruction the concept of freedom surviving under dictatorial rule, yet that does not totally devalue earlier
German unease about convention or institutional lives.

All this is relevant because German education after 1933 changed
profoundly. There was a vast expansion of hours devoted to cultivating
the healthy body and a concomitant curtailment, in breadth and depth,
of intellectual pursuits. Hitler, a passionate and life-long enemy of learning, had decreed in *Mein Kampf* that the intellect should come last in the list

of educational priorities: *after* physical education and character building.[82] The new institutions created to provide future leaders for the Reich – the *Napolas*: the National Political Academies – emphasised these changed priorities very clearly. (In the most extreme form, the Adolf Hitler Schools, the ability to vault over a horse constituted the height of educational achievement.)

It would be both mischievous and absurd to pretend that these institutions, housed in pseudo-medieval buildings, were in any way copies of British public schools. But they were also wholly alien to native tradition. (Indeed Victor Klemperer, in his study of the Nazi argot, maintains that the adjective *charakterlich* – to go with 'character building' – was a Nazi neologism and did not exist in general usage before the Third Reich.)[83] The ideal of muscular heartiness that had developed during the twenties and the regime's obvious anti-intellectual instincts were new phenomena in German education. The *Anglisten* might therefore perhaps be forgiven for drawing parallels with *non-German* institutions.[84] And Britain's public schools were the only other establishments known to them where a sporting trophy was considered more important than a Latin prize.

After 1933 therefore, official German praise for the public schools became unconditional, and was particularly fervent among those closest to the Nazi party.[85] It was now noted, for instance, that among both the masters and the boys of major public schools, there was a healthy preponderance of the Nordic type, a thought which does not appear to have struck any observer before 1933.[86] There was above all enthusiastic comment about the games field. Indeed, it was only after 1933 that the term 'team spirit' was used with obvious approbation.[87] In all of this Nazi commentators rarely lost sight of the ultimate *raison d'être* of Britain's public schools: the Empire. The pride in the Third Reich's own new schools designed to produce 'future leaders' (*Führernachwuchs*) is therefore probably significant.[88] By 1937, when this observation was made, the Third Reich's perceptible ambitions were no longer constrained by the existing borders.

The debate about Anglo-German similarities in education was, inevitably, of greatest interest to those within the teaching profession itself. It seems doubtful that it would have attracted very widespread attention among the general public, though the schoolmasters' captive audience in the classrooms of the Reich were doubtless treated to full and detailed accounts. But these favourable views of the mid-thirties matter, if only because they were in marked contrast to what was to follow. The shortcomings and supposed iniquities of the public school system would become an important aspect of anti-British propaganda in the war years. As in almost any area of Britain's official image after 1939, this therefore required turning on its head earlier Nazi reasoning.

Another area where the outbreak of war would necessitate a complete re-interpretation was that of British youth movements, and in particular scouting. During the first half of the Third Reich, descriptions of the various British youth movements resonated with obvious Nazi approval. What is more, it was the party itself, through its youth wings, that claimed kinship with Britain. Again, there was the emphasis on 'character building'.[89] But it was not just their ethos that seemed to link British and Nazi youth organisations. Their aims too appeared related. This becomes clear in a series of articles on this topic in the monthly magazine of the Hitler Youth. These articles emphasise the link in Britain between youth movements and the armed forces. The Boy Scouts, the Boys' Brigade, the Cadets, the OTC and the Regular Army are all mentioned as part of the same argument. Though such a military connection is only explored in the case of Britain, the implication about the Hitler Youth itself is clear enough. And the articles' authors were happy to give credit where they felt it was due: 'Of all the European powers, Britain has the oldest institutions for pre-military training.'[90] Nor was the purpose of Britain's youth movements forgotten: it was of course 'the preservation of the British Empire'.[91]

Young Germans in the Hitler Youth were thus in effect told that they were copying the British example. Some were even given the opportunity to judge for themselves. In February 1936 the Hitler Youth magazine *Morgen* described the impressions of Britain recorded by a group of German boys. They had stayed in a boy scout camp on the Isle of Wight and had enjoyed traditional scouting pursuits. But the highlight of their stay – and this is surely significant – was a visit to the Portsmouth naval base. That this article, like the visit, carries a deliberate political message is made clear on the boys' return to Germany. For the organisers had arranged for a final attraction to complement the tour of Portsmouth: a trip to the Kiel naval base to inspect the Reich's new submarines.[92] In other words, parallels between Britain and the Third Reich had been implied to these young Germans (and the magazine's readers) at every stage and in every sphere.

The sight of Germany's new submarines also points to a new factor in Nazi perceptions of Britain in the later thirties: that of German power. With every passing year, the Reich's strength increased. What is more, it did so visibly. The country was no longer defenceless or – it seemed – economically weak. Foreign powers and their emissaries were treating Germany with a degree of respect that provided an eloquent contrast to the superciliousness which democratic Weimar had so often encountered. Inevitably, that began to influence attitudes towards Britain.

It did not at first lead to any perceptible hostility. That needs to be stressed. The group of Hitler Youth in the article above were clearly not shown around Kiel to prepare them psychologically for a future war against Britain. The visit was simply to counterbalance the earlier demonstration of British power. There may even have been some mention of the Anglo-German naval agreement of the preceding year. Britain and Germany were thus portrayed as potential partners and, increasingly, as equals. That was the new element. From the early twenties onwards, Britain had been in the eyes of many in Germany an exemplar or aspiration; 'the way the English do things' seemed a possible way forward, a road to national recovery and perhaps even to renewed greatness. By the mid-thirties, much of that seemed accomplished. Visions of Britain after that time were thus coloured by growing self-confidence. And celebrations of Britishness were increasingly also celebrations of Nazi achievements. It was thus inevitable that the gaze shifted ever more firmly to those areas of national life to which the Nazi party attached the greatest importance. And nothing was more important to the regime than the issue of race.

In the Weimar era the *Anglisten* had consistently questioned the contemporary relevance of the Anglo-Saxon connection. After 1933 the subject was initially avoided. But once the foreign policy intentions of the regime had become clear, and people like Heinrich Bauer had claimed Cromwell as a precursor to National Socialism, there was a renewed emphasis on the ancient ties across the North Sea. This could often be done without intellectual dishonesty. Archaeologists, historians and historical linguists could merely restate familiar facts – though, admittedly, in the certain knowledge that a political message would be read into this. Titles such as *Cultural and Economic Links between England and Frisia* or 'Neolithic links between Lower Saxony and England' thus returned to the fore.[93] Related topics remained a staple throughout the Third Reich. (In the war years they may have seemed especially apposite: *The Germanic Conquest of Britain: The Findings of*

Pre-history and Historical Linguistics[94] or The Sword that Cut Across the Channel: The Victorious Invasion of England according to the Bayeux Tapestry must have quickened patriotic pulses when they appeared in the early years of the war.)[95]

In ideological terms, however, the early centuries of English history had yielded little of concrete relevance. This becomes especially apparent where political relevance was actually being sought. A doctoral thesis published in 1939 with a grant by the Ahnenerbe (Ancestral Heritage) Foundation of the SS proves the point: '"Leading" and "Following", "Ruling" and "Being Ruled" in Anglo-Saxon Vocabulary' claimed to be 'A Contribution to the Research into Leadership [Führertum] and Loyalty in the Germanic World'.[96] It was, in fact, a conventional linguistic study: a patient enumeration of words and of their etymological bases. Old English evidently did not lend itself readily to Nazi purposes.[97] The author therefore had to resort to some anti-Christian flourishes to merit the desired SS funding.

The study is, however, also revealing in another respect. It demonstrates that the Third Reich was not fundamentally interested in 'proving' the ethnic connection between Britain – or England – and Germany. The Anglisten were mistaken in thinking the regime was.[98] It would not have been difficult to illustrate in a study the link between Old English and Old High German vocabulary. Such studies were regularly carried out; yet they did not attract funding from the SS. It was ideological relevance that was sought. Genuine historical links were immaterial.

Confirmation that this was indeed the case comes from an unexpected direction. After 1933, Germany's Romanisten – the academics specialising in the languages and literatures of France, Italy, Spain, etc. – were understandably anxious about their future in the Third Reich. Their response, tinged with desperation, was to emphasise that the Romance languages also revealed historic links with the Germanic world. In linguistic and historical terms those claims were perfectly sound. They were particularly strong in the case of France, a country that owed its very name to a Germanic people. These arguments did not, however, impress the regime. For the Third Reich a sense of kinship depended on ideology (or, at least, on political expediency), not on historical fact. There was nothing about France with which the regime wished to identify. In the case of Britain, however, there was the supposed Anglo-Saxon urge to rule over other nations. It was only this allegedly central aspect of the British character that genuinely caught the leadership's imagination. Other evidence of a common Germanic nature was welcome – not least for propaganda purposes – but was considered largely incidental. The funding priorities of the SS mirror perfectly the regime's wider interests.

The focus of racial analysis was therefore to explain the precise origins of Britain's aptitude for imperial rule – or rather, to confirm that race was at the root of it. There was little room for doubt. As early as 1920 Hitler had conclusively identified the sources of Britain's success: a clear sense of national consciousness, 'which is so signally lacking among our own people'; and, secondly, the scrupulous maintenance of 'racial purity in the colonies'.[99] Both factors were, of course, connected and suggested also a high degree of racial purity at home.

Throughout the twenties and early thirties, when Germany was politically impotent, a contrast between British racial purity and the regrettable lack of it in Germany itself was both permissible and desirable in Nazi circles. *Rassen*-Günther had provided the overall framework for such interpretations. The Anglo-Saxons, he suggested, had been able to maintain greater racial purity than the Germans because of Britain's island nature. (A degree of interbreeding with the Celts had been acknowledged, but was deemed marginal in its effect.)[100]

Yet Britain's geography was only one factor influencing the bloodline of its people. History was the other. The original Anglo-Saxon landings were followed by substantial incursions by people of Scandinavian origin. The Danish presence in eastern England, and the Norse landings in many of the islands and coastal areas of Scotland, Wales and even Ireland had strengthened Britain's Nordic bloodline. This process of *Aufnordung* – 'additional nordification' – had culminated in the Norman Conquests. The Normans, as their name (the North Men) suggested, were of Scandinavian origin: descendants of warriors who had spread fear through much of western Europe during the early Middle Ages. The fact that these Vikings spoke French by the time they landed in England was without consequence. Their blood alone mattered. And here historical linguistics, once again, offered reassurance. Many of the place names in Normandy – Cherbourg, Houlgate, Ouistreham, etc. – still betrayed a one-time Germanic presence. It is this mixture of established fact and wild genetic surmise that characterises Nazi interpretations of history.

If history provided clues to Britain's racial composition, then, with classic Nazi circular reasoning, race explained a nation's history and its foreign policy. It is worth remembering that Rosenberg had invoked that principle in his foreign-policy speech at Nuremberg in 1933. And it was the specific example of Britain that had prompted his thoughts.

Diplomatic reticence – or, if one prefers, low cunning – had prevented him, and others in the leadership, from spelling out the implications. But these were clear enough. The Anglo-Saxons had conquered and enslaved the Celts, before suffering the same fate at the hands of the Norman Vikings. The resulting nation – the English – had conquered and, again, enslaved the neighbouring Celtic nations. The nation resulting from English expansion was Great Britain, which, predictably enough, had continued on foreign shores, and on a scale unparalleled in history, what was in its blood. The result was the British Empire. And, inevitably, there appears before the mind's eye the image of Hitler at the Berghof thrilling to a cinema vision of the British Raj.

It is, of course, possible to doubt a connection between Hitler's cinematic preferences and his later policies or his views about Britain. The frequent mention of the British Raj in the *Table Talk* would suggest otherwise, as would the comments in *Das Schwarze Korps*. But an argument could be made that a fondness for *The Bengal Lancers* is evidence only of well-known personal eccentricity; and that in the scale of Hitler's eccentricities this was one of the more harmless. Yet there remains Rosenberg's Nuremberg speech about race, history and politics. And there remains also the Third Reich's habit of blurring the distinction between Life and Art. If the arts were politicised, politics became overtly visual or theatrical. It is perhaps not wholly irrelevant that the Führer was a failed artist and his *Propagandaminister* a failed *littérateur*. That they did not approach international affairs in the manner of more conventional politicians is scarcely surprising. This might lead one to consider in this context the official commingling of ideology and theatre. A particularly striking example occurred in 1938. The event, recorded in colour print, has become known as the 'Weekend in Munich'.[101]

The leadership had gathered in the *Hauptstadt der Bewegung* – the Capital City of the Nazi Party – for a pageant of *tableaux vivants* representing German art and history. The purpose was to point out, with theatrical *éclat*, real or supposed connections across the centuries. The scenes ranged from the days of the Cheruscii defeating the Roman legions, via the Teutonic Knights, to the Nazi present. It is not just the choice of *tableaux* that is interesting, the concept itself is revealing. Taken as a whole, the procession effectively denied any historical development and suggested a fundamental constancy of national characteristics across the millennia. That spectacle is not unconnected to this discussion, for it provides a key to understanding how the leadership conceived of history generally. It is then not too difficult to sketch in the mind a parallel Nazi pageant of British history: the books recommended to German schoolboys give one a reasonable idea of the likely topics.

The historical perspective might begin, for instance, with the Normans stepping ashore in Sussex. It would shift back to the Vikings in their long boats terrorising the coasts of Europe. It might then sweep across the centuries to the Nazis' own, to the spectacle of the Royal Navy and the *Hungerblockade* of Germany during the Great War. It might return to the Vikings to see them plundering foreign ships and foreign shores, only to dart forward again to Drake and Raleigh, their ships laden with stolen riches. Onwards it might sweep to the other Indies, to disclose Warren Hastings in his treasury. Continuing eastwards, the gaze would fall on ships disgorging opium or firing at those who tried to stop the deadly trade. And back again from eastern seas to western, the eye would light on a fleet of ships with dark-skinned human cargo, on its way to lands cleared of the men who roamed it before the British stepped ashore. And this time it is not Hitler contemplating these scenes but an official in the Reich Ministry of Education; he is preparing a book about the aims of Germany's schools. In it he will recommend the study of British history, because it might teach young Germans 'in exemplary fashion . . . the instinctive rejection of inhibitions alien to the race'.[102]

It will have become obvious why such a Nazi celebration of Britishness would have been impossible to stage before 1939. In a sense, something rather like it – an exhibition entitled *Raubstaat England* (Britain – Empire of Rapine) – was staged in Munich in 1941 as part of the wartime propaganda effort. But that of course reveals the nature of the problem. The exhibition was mounted in the hope that Britain's imperial record would create moral revulsion among the German public. Yet that same moral revulsion would also have greeted *before* 1939 an explicit Nazi embrace of past British methods. Hitler himself, after all, had sought to make political capital out of the victims of British imperialism in the early twenties. This posed clear limits as to what could be said in public after the Seizure of Power.

It is interesting to note therefore that even the most ideologically committed sources observed a degree of circumspection. *Das Schwarze Korps* – often the most uncompromising publication in the Third Reich – is a case in point. In January 1939, its regular column 'Der politische Soldat' – 'The Political Soldier' – specifically considered Britain's racial profile. It duly observed that knowledge of Britain's racial history would be 'useful to us'. But it refrained from spelling out how this might be of use to the Reich.[103]

Part of the problem – indeed the central problem for the Third Reich in the eyes of the leadership – was a lack of time. Britain, as the SS paper pointed out, had enjoyed 'nine centuries of carefree development' during which her 'Nordic ruling caste could perfect itself'.[104] Germany could not wait another nine centuries. The leadership rated the country's chances of survival very low unless immediate action was taken. Such action, in every field, would have to be more radical than anything Britain ever undertook, since the desired outcome would have to be achieved in a fraction of the time. It had taken Britain two and half centuries to subjugate India. Russia would have to be conquered in as many months. The methods to achieve this would, of necessity, differ from those employed by Britain. But success would depend above all on Germany's racial profile. This would have to improve significantly before a Russian campaign – Hitler's principal aim since the mid-twenties – could be undertaken.

The details of Nazi racial policy need not be rehearsed here. They are relevant to this discussion only where the British example itself was considered 'useful' by exponents of the regime. The Third Reich acknowledged obvious differences between Britain and Germany. These related both to the present racial conditions in the two countries and the responses to these differences. The Reich would not, for instance, be able to achieve *Aufnordung* through infusions of Nordic blood from Scandinavia. In that regard, as the SS paper put it, 'our English neighbours have had a happier past than we'.[105] Differences in the two countries' history, Nazi commentators thought, also perhaps explained differing views about the 'Jewish question'. There was a recognition that Britain did not fully share the Reich's anti-semitic agenda (though Hitler seems to have maintained an unshakeable conviction that this was bound to change). Rosenberg mentioned in that first programmatic speech in Nuremberg that 'British insouciance' in this regard was perhaps due to a greater sense of security than a Germany 'threatened from all sides' could ever feel.[106]

Anti-semitism was thus largely absent from Nazi celebrations of Anglo-German kinship in the 1930s. There were references to the British Union of Fascists, whose importance the regime at first greatly overestimated. Yet, in general the evidence was too contradictory to be of propaganda value. Historically, England had been the first country in Europe to expel all its Jews: a fact that would doubtless have featured in the Reich's newspapers, except of course that the Jews were later allowed to return – a decision taken by Cromwell, of all people.[107] To a regime that promised its supporters a permanent solution to the 'Jewish problem' this was scarcely a suitable precedent. (Limited knowledge of Britain was also a factor: events like the Tredegar Riots in South Wales were apparently unknown in Germany.)

Other aspects of racial policy provided more promising evidence. In November 1937 the *Berliner Illustrierte Zeitung* acquainted its readership with the life and work of Sir Francis Galton, the inventor of eugenics.[108] The article was part of the regime's wider attempts to ensure at least tacit acceptance of its eugenic measures. But, even so, the mere existence of the article is remarkable. Here was an attempt to popularise a key Nazi policy by invoking its British roots. Perhaps just as striking is the fact that the experience of other nations went unmentioned. For in terms of more recent eugenic expertise, the record of other countries was more substantial than that of the United Kingdom. This was particularly true of the United States, which has the dubious distinction of leading the field here in the twenties and early thirties. Nazi racial scientists acknowledged their debt to America freely before 1933.[109] Yet it was Britain and Francis Galton that featured in the weekend paper of the German middle classes and not the United States. Invoking *American* precedent might have been counter-productive (nor would it have been popular with the leadership in the later thirties). Yet, once again, this is surely revealing about German attitudes to Britain – both within the party and outside it.

Hans Günther, the father of Nazi *Rassenkunde*, also concentrated on Britain in his attempt to popularise eugenics. He sought, for instance, to exploit British literature for his purposes. In particular, he attempted to demonstrate that Shakespeare had possessed an instinctive grasp of the issues involved, and pointed eagerly to the first Sonnets ('From fairest creatures we desire increase . . .'). Only the Elizabethan poet Sir Thomas Overbury had put it more succinctly, he thought: 'Myself I cannot chose, my wife I may,/ in that choice of her it much doth lye/ to mend myself in my posterity'.[110] That was the best explanation, Günther suggested, of the Third Reich's own aims. And the fact that there was nothing like this in German literature, with its familiar refrain about the universal brotherhood of men, added to the glow of the British example. The SS newspaper had reached similar conclusions: 'This happy breed of men', which Shakespeare had extolled, was the result not of nature but 'of deliberate breeding'.[111]

The British example was also invoked in another area of Nazi racial policy: the regime's attempt to eradicate homosexuality in the Reich. In May 1935 the SS newspaper advocated the killing of homosexuals.[112] This probably makes homosexuals the first category of Nazi victims where mass murder was publicly acknowledged as a policy aim. (Jews, not yet targeted by the Nuremberg Laws, were at the time officially encouraged to emigrate, and eugenics was as yet confined to sterilisation.) Advocacy of murder, in other words, was still sufficiently novel in Germany to warrant explanations. The SS newspaper thus sought to put the matter in a wider European perspective. There was, of course, no precedent – at least no legal precedent – for murder. Even so, an ideological imperative could be discerned: it was instructive to compare the differing attitudes among the nations of Europe to homosexuality. The Mediterranean nations tolerated it. In the days before the Rome–Berlin Axis, this caused no surprise in SS circles. The 'Nordic–Germanic' nations, on the other hand, all sought to remove homosexuals from society. And it was, of course, Britain that had led the way: it had instituted the harshest penal sanctions anywhere in Europe. If the author of the article, an SS-Untersturmbannführer, felt any surprise about this, he did not betray it. On the contrary, he considered Britain's record 'highly instructive'.[113]

There is a double, or perhaps even triple irony to all this. After 1940, cartoons and photographs selected for propaganda purposes would often hint at effeminacy in British men. This presumably owed something to the string of military reverses suffered by the British Army in the first two years of the war and the belief that homosexuals make poor soldiers. It was clearly part of the regime's self-image at that time to contrast an aggressively masculine (and heterosexual) Reich heading for victory with a supposedly less virile Britain which was staring defeat in the face. This was yet again a complete reversal of earlier German – and indeed Nazi – perceptions of Britain. The irony in all this is clear enough. But there is an added twist. Unbeknownst to almost everyone in the early 1940s, a British homosexual, Alan Turing, was doing more than perhaps any other individual during the entire war in ensuring the Third Reich's ultimate defeat. He achieved this, of course, with the very intellect which National Socialism so despised, and which it thought was despised almost as much in Britain. What the reaction to this news might have been among the Nazi leadership is a matter of conjecture; the fact that Britain repaid its debt to Turing after the war by chemically castrating him and driving him to suicide, on the other hand, would no doubt have been considered 'highly instructive'.

The main Nazi objection to homosexuality was that it weakened the national community. It did this supposedly by lowering the birth rate and by compromising the self-consciously masculine image which the regime cultivated. If the Nazi ideal of womanhood was one of complete submission to her mate, that implied an instinctive dominance in the Aryan male. Nazi imagery of square-jawed Teutonic heroes proves that point as surely as do wartime insinuations about British men. The regime may have been scornful of Freudian psychoanalysis, but in their obsession with everything relating to sexuality the Nazis easily surpassed Viennese practice.

The connection between sexuality and power may have become something of a cliché in recent years but it is none the less appropriate in discussing the Third Reich. Hitler himself had suggested such a connection; and significantly he did so in a discussion of British practice. From the earliest days of his political career, Hitler had been fascinated by the concept of the colour bar that operated in the British Empire. This was, of course, to maintain the purity of the race. But it was not simply a matter of sexual reticence, Hitler thought. Politics instinctively came into it too. The British, it seemed to him, had always preferred to be 'masters' rather than 'brothers' in their colonies.[114] That approach precluded inter-racial unions. Maintaining the difference between master race and subject races seemed to him to be at the heart of the British imperial ethos and the secret of its success.

Hitler's views here echo to some extent wider German perceptions. The famous pre-war *Simplicissimus* cartoon about colonial methods that had regimented giraffes parading in German East Africa and an Englishman extracting another piece of gold from a 'native' on the rack, also portrayed a semi-recumbent Frenchman delighting in female African company. Such cartoons depend for their effectiveness on instant recognition. The stereotypes of *Simplicissimus* were not random choices: a cartoon of an Englishman finding contentment in a dark-skinned embrace would have been as improbable as that of a Frenchman reviewing a march-past of African wildlife. There were of course, as everyone knew, French colonial regiments, and some British colonisers no doubt found sexual partners among the colonised. But such exceptions, however widespread, only proved the rule. The wider evidence was of Latin colonialism with its creole legacy, and an unmistakable British penchant for being addressed as sahib or bwana.

Such cartoons disappeared after Versailles, together with Germany's colonial empire. Yet Hitler appears to have struck out on a separate path in the twenties. While most of Germany was concentrating on the fate of Upper Silesia in the looming referendum of 1921, Hitler was apparently preoccupied with the British Empire. And while other Germans might have been impressed by its vastness, Hitler focused on racial purity and Britain's tendency to see in the 'native' not the fellow man – or more particularly the fellow woman – but the subject. The difference between Hitler's perceptions and those betrayed by Wilhelmine cartoons is no less apparent: where imperial Germany saw characteristic French lasciviousness and an equally typical ram-rod stiff, buttoned-up Englishman, Hitler saw the prelude to bastardisation on the one hand and, on the other, British racial disdain. Here, surely, is the nexus between race and empire which came to dominate Hitler's thinking throughout the rest of his life. Here too is perhaps to be found the explanation for another recurring thought: his striking insistence that the Third Reich should copy in Russia British rule in India.

This has always seemed something of a puzzle. Even the harshest critics of British imperialism would hesitate to compare the Raj with German conduct in the occupied Soviet lands. What is more, that much must have been apparent even to the Nazis themselves. Hitler, in the *Table Talk*, repeatedly speaks of the benefits which British rule had brought to India (and, at one stage, took Rosenberg to task for doubting them).[115] Yet Hitler never suggested that German rule would benefit Russia. How, then, could such contradictions be reconciled in his own mind? The answer – in as much as there can be an answer – probably lies in Britain's aloofness towards its non-white subjects.

Whether the aloofness was real or imagined is not the issue. (Hitler had clearly never heard of the so-called Anglo-Indians: *Bhowani Junction* was a post-war film and there was nothing to counterbalance *The Bengal Lancers*.)[116] But racial aloofness was for Hitler the mental link: that was the ideal he advocated in the East. And it was an ideal which he feared did not come naturally to the Germans. The Third Reich, he thought, had to contend here with serious flaws in the German national character. Were the Germans to find themselves in possession of India, Hitler suggested to his inner circle, they should quickly prove incapable of ruling it. They would be inclined to be moved by the poverty of the Indians; what is more, they were certain to be overawed by the antiquity of Indian civilisation. The British, on the other hand, were impressed by neither. They habitually exhibited 'total contempt for all things foreign'. That approach would have to be copied in Russia. 'Whoever betrays the least humanity [in colonialism] is lost', Hitler concluded.[117]

Those sentiments were expressed in 1942. They may be have been influenced, in part, by the difficulties the Third Reich was encountering with its new colonial subjects in the East (they certainly paint a starker picture of British rule in India than those expressed a year earlier).[118] Yet the belief that the divide between the races must be maintained was, as we have seen, much older. And there was always the counter-example of France as a racial *memento mori*. Even before 1933 the Nazi party had concluded that France had become 'an African bridgehead in Europe'.[119] (That made all the more likely a racially defensive alliance between Britain and Germany – what the author of *Brito-Germania: Europe's Salvation* in the 1920s had called 'the two white nations'.)[120]

That Nazi ideas about race and empire drew substantially on what might be called the literature of Western racial panic is obvious enough. The various sources – German, French, American and British – have long been familiar. The roots of National Socialism go deep and they spread wide. But they do not fully explain Hitler's sinister fascination with the British Empire. Here Hitler's own particular background may be of importance. If his colonial obsessions did not seem to be shared by his Munich audiences in 1920, for he made little headway politically, it may be because those audiences were German, and Hitler, originally, was not.

Invoking Hitler's Austrian origin might seem a strange argument in a debate about colonialism: the Austrian Empire, after all, was one of only a handful of European states with almost no colonial experience. But the point is that Hitler was no ordinary Austrian. He had consciously rejected his national background: he moved to Germany; he went to great lengths not to serve in the Imperial Army of Austria (only to volunteer for service in the German Army in 1914); above all, he describes Austria in *Mein Kampf* in tones of almost uniform contempt. What he detested particularly was the multinational ethos of the old Habsburg Empire: the fact that people from different ethnic backgrounds lived next to each other, and did so more or less as equals before the law. This provoked in him a mixture of scorn and retrospective rage. The disintegration of the Habsburg Empire seemed to him directly linked to that multinational ethos of its rulers. An empire that was prepared to blur the distinctions between Slavs and Germans was doomed to fail.

That failure contrasted with a British Empire, larger in 1920, and apparently more powerful than ever: an empire which, as everyone knew, greatly emphasised the difference between rulers and ruled.[121] When, therefore, by the mid-twenties, Hitler's ambitions began to focus on colonising Russia, the British example provided the obvious inspiration. That this was not the case with most Germans in the 1920s, who shared neither his colonial ambitions nor his trauma about the Austrian Nationality Conflict, goes without saying. It was only through his dominance of the Nazi party that he was gradually able to inject his views about a racial empire into wider sections of German society. These views did, however, coalesce with the existing ambitions among right-wing Germans for territorial expansion in the East. They coalesced also with strong and long-standing Prussian prejudice about Poles or Lithuanians. Yet they are not quite the same thing. Prussia had traditionally believed in assimilating minorities, either freely or by state pressure. A glance at the telephone directory of any major Prussian city of the twenties with its endless entries of Slav or Baltic names would have proved the point.

That tradition Hitler rejected. Instead, he advocated what he took to be the British approach: contempt for the foreign and scrupulous adherence to racial purity. The SS newspaper *Das Schwarze Korps* had concluded its 1939 article about Britain's racial origin with John of Gaunt's 'This England' speech. Few other nations, it thought, had ever achieved a comparable tone of self-regard. But, the paper concluded, in the case of Britain it was warranted, for its racial purity was unparalleled. Six years earlier, at the first party rally after the *Machtergreifung*, Alfred Rosenberg had also drawn German attention to the example of Britain. The Third Reich's new anti-semitic policies had not been well received in Britain. But this, Rosenberg insisted, was only a temporary problem. A Germany organised along racial lines was a country for which the British were bound to feel sympathy in the end. For 'it seems to us', Rosenberg explained, 'that the British Empire too is based on a racially defined claim of dominance'.[122]

This may not quite have been the Third Reich's first word about Britain but it remained, in a sense, its last. Throughout the permutations of Nazi policy towards Britain, the regime always regarded the British Empire as the Third Reich's elder brother, linked to it by common assumptions about racial dominance. British politicians who criticised the Third Reich were, in Nazi eyes, denying their country's own history, its true nature and ultimately its future. According to Rosenberg, the British Empire would only survive for as long as the British continued to defend the 'white man's claim of dominance'.[123] It is not difficult to see a connection between those words uttered at Nuremberg and Hitler's repeated offers to help defend the British Empire. It is not difficult either to see a connection with Hitler's favourite film. *The Bengal Lancers*, after all, is precisely about the defence of the white man's claim to dominance. What must have thrilled Hitler especially about its images is not so very difficult to guess: it will have been the sight of dark-skinned multitudes collapsing in a hail of bullets, as the few, the happy Nordic few triumphed once more. That film will have provided a telling contrast to British government pronouncements in the later thirties; and it must have convinced Hitler that the average Briton at least thought as he did. The enjoyment of British cinema audiences of that film spoke for itself. To quote the words of *Das Schwarze Korps*, the film glorified 'precisely what those vile tongues seek to criticise in us'.[124]

The aim, then, as Hitler saw it, was to follow the supposed example of the Raj. The merest glimpse at the *Table Talk* demonstrates this abundantly. Perhaps the most striking instance occurs during the early stages of the Russian campaign. Hitler's thoughts were turning to the post-war world and the tasks that lay ahead. The war was all but won; now it was time to win the peace. It would be essential to find the right men to administer the new lands. Many Germans, alas, would lack the necessary ruthlessness. The solution seemed obvious: one would need to recruit men from Lower Saxony. For that, Hitler explained to his confidants, was 'undoubtedly the home of the ability to rule', since 'the English ruling class originates there'.[125]

If confirmation were still required that Hitler was not a rational leader, this line of thought might serve as conclusive evidence. But it is evidence also of something else: it demonstrates the belief, no less apparent in the *tableaux vivants* of Munich four years earlier, that 'blood' does not change, that the centuries dissolve into nothingness as the same racial encounters are endlessly repeated. It demonstrates also that Hitler had indeed been influenced over the years by Germany's *Anglisten* and Hans Günther's travesty of historical linguistics. A comparison of the *Table Talk* with Hitler's Munich speeches two decades earlier is instructive. In 1920 he had decried the absence of the imperial instinct in Germany: there was no suggestion that the people of Lower Saxony were an exception. When, some years later, he extolled in the *Second Book* the unique British aptitude for colonial rule, there was likewise silence about the Lower Saxons and their innate proconsular abilities. But as in the case of Goebbels and Johst's 'moving' play about Tom Paine, Hitler welcomed information about Britain if it pandered to his hopes and prejudices. And he clung to such incongruous knowledge with all his formidable tenacity. The years after 1933 had seen the development by Germany's *Anglisten* of an image of Anglo-German kinship specially designed to appeal to Nazi tastes. Unsurprisingly, it left the leadership and the country unprepared for the full force of British hostility in 1939.

On some of Hitler's subordinates in the party it began to dawn not long after what had happened. In February 1940 *Das Schwarze Korps* dismissed arguments about racial links with Britain as 'the platitudes of comparative linguistics'.[126] And though the paper acknowledged that ideas of kinship had been universally popular, it charged the Reich's academics with blindness about the truth. There is a rich irony in this. It is fitting that the regime's own anti-intellectual agenda should have driven Germany's academics into political conformity and ever more desperate attempts to provide the misleading information which they thought the regime wanted to hear. It is fitting also that Hitler who by-passed the Foreign Office for fear of *la trahaison des clercs* ended up, at least in part, as the victim of a *trahaison des professeurs*.

But Hitler's ruminations about Lower Saxony also prove one final point: his interest in the British Raj and his enthusiasm for *The Bengal Lancers* were not harmless eccentricities. As he planned and attempted to put into practice the colonial exploitation of Russia, Britain was never far from his mind. However uncomfortable that thought may be, and however grotesque some of the supposed parallels, there is no doubt that the Nazi leadership itself saw a clear connection between the Third Reich and the British Empire, and sought to derive from it legitimacy for its own colonial expansion. In a memorable colloquialism, Hitler's war has been described has 'the biggest land grab in history'. Practically everyone in the Third Reich would have retorted that it was merely the *second* biggest. The organisers of the Munich exhibition 'Britain – Empire of Rapine' put on the first page of its catalogue an old Gillray cartoon.[127] It showed the diminutive leader of a European power – Napoleon Bonaparte – slicing a small piece from a globe-shaped pudding; a gargantuan Prime Minister Pitt, meanwhile, was helping himself to the rest. There was no need to spell out the message.

4 'Their aged bones are rattling': Britain and the Nazi concept of modernity

One of the most famous images of the twentieth century is that of Neville Chamberlain emerging from an aeroplane, waving a piece of paper. It is a painful image, and the painfulness is part of its potency. It is the image of a decent man undone by his very decency. It earned him lasting ridicule, which was only partly deserved, and which the image has helped to keep alive. With its glimpse of an ecstatic crowd welcoming the Prime Minister, it is evidence also of a wider desire for peace, made all the more poignant by the knowledge of what came after. It is an image that has overshadowed Anglo-German relations for much of the century. More than a decade would pass before a British government felt able to trust any German interlocutor again. It would take much longer before the British public felt able to do so.

The image is no less painful for German viewers, and for exactly the same reasons. But there are also additional German ones. Before the photograph was taken, Chamberlain had driven in triumph through the streets of Munich. The city had been his as much as it was usually Hitler's. This, famously, led to the Führer's withdrawal for several days in what can only be described as a huff. The adulation Chamberlain received – much to his own surprise – was evidence that ordinary Germans in 1938 wanted peace as much as the people of Britain did. But it was more than that: it was an expression of long-held hopes of a lasting Anglo-German understanding. Munich stands out in the recollections of many Germans who experienced the Third Reich. It is often the only memory they would like to salvage from its rubble. For Munich was the only territorial revision achieved by lawful means. It was the last time that borders in central Europe were adjusted to fit existing populations rather than the other way round. It was the last time also for half a century that the principle of self-determination was invoked in the region. Munich was what most Germans and Austrians had hoped for in 1919 and of which they had been judged unworthy: Munich was the Good Peace.

The picture of Chamberlain and his piece of paper is therefore all the more poignant for German viewers. It reminds them that the peace Hitler won for them, he had never wanted to win, never valued and promptly threw away. Munich is thus evidence also of a gulf in aims and perceptions between ordinary Germans and those of the Nazi leadership. That gulf had existed throughout the first years of the Third Reich; it had, however, been obscured by the regime's ostensible peacefulness and the apparent breadth and warmth of its anglophilia.

By the summer of 1938 two things had changed: the Nazi leadership felt strong enough to reveal its true face; the pretence of peacefulness began to slip away in every sphere. Yet that need not have affected Anglo-German relations; the regime's hostile intentions had always been directed elsewhere. But Hitler had actually changed his views about Britain. How this came about is no secret. Ribbentrop's unfavourable reports acted like a steady drip of acid into the Führer's ear.[1] They were able to do so because of Britain's continuing failure to respond to Hitler's offers of an Anglo-German accord. Hitler after all was only ever open to views he already half embraced himself.[2] To the dismay of many, including leading Nazis like Goebbels, and eventually even Göring, the Führer began to revise his foreign-policy objectives.[3] The story of Ribbentrop's farcical incompetence, of the resulting anti-British animus that grew in him and confirmed in Hitler an already existing disenchantment with Britain has often been told and need not be repeated here. What matters is that both Ribbentrop and Hitler had wooed Britain. Both had been rebuffed, and neither man was temperamentally inclined to accept rebuffs. Since Britain did not apparently desire their friendship, hostility to Britain was the inevitable consequence.[4]

Nazi hostility, however, came in two distinct forms: it was either mingled with fear or suffused with contempt. Towards the end of the war, the Third Reich's public utterances could never quite disguise a growing fear of the future. In 1938, however, Hitler felt invincible. (And here it does seem appropriate to focus on the Führer: for the decision to go to war in 1939 – and to risk war the preceding year – was his alone.) There can be no doubt that Hitler's hostility to Britain was allied with, or perhaps even born of, deepening contempt.

Put simply, by the later thirties he considered the British Empire a spent force.[5] It was not that he had abandoned his earlier views about British 'ruthlessness'; he had merely become convinced that Britain increasingly lacked the strength to act in character. The suppression of the Arab rising in Palestine in 1937 and 1938 had demonstrated that the old imperial instincts were still alive.[6] (Nazi propaganda in the final months of peace pointed to Palestine whenever a British politician uttered the word 'freedom' or decried the use of violence.)[7] Britain, as Hitler suggested to Goebbels a year later, 'still contained a good ruling race'; 'but', he added, 'for how much longer?'[8] The firmness in Palestine, after all, could not disguise the fact that the Empire was sickening. Since its pyrrhic victory of 1918, it had been forced to accept naval parity with the United States – in itself a humiliation for a country that claimed to rule the seas – and had proved powerless to prevent either Italian or Japanese expansion.[9]

There was, moreover, evidence of internal weakness. The new constitution for India – though dismissed in Berlin as a sham – was none the less a sign of the times.[10] Nor did the fact escape Nazi notice that Ireland under de Valera was able to sever with impunity all ties with the crown.[11] Fifteen years earlier, Britain had refused to countenance an Irish republic. In 1937 she was powerless to prevent it. Whitehall's assertions that nothing had changed was, as the Nazis correctly saw, little more than a bluff. The apparent unconcern might have averted a crisis, but that, as Goebbels noted in his diary, 'was no way to go on ruling the world'.[12]

Britain, in other words, seemed to the Nazi leadership in the later 1930s like an ageing bully. The instinct to threaten and command was undiminished, the voice still carried, but the strength to wield the whips and batons of empire was all but gone. This fatal under-estimation of Britain's remaining power and of the very 'will' which the Nazis had previously so admired led directly to the events of September 1939. Over time, as Britain failed to behave as predicted, Hitler and those closest to him would essentially revert to the Third Reich's original views. The perception of an enfeebled Britain thus persisted roughly from 1937 to 1941. The consequences of that misconception – for the regime, for Germany and the world – were more long-lasting.

Hitler did not speak English and had no personal knowledge of Britain. One cannot repeat these simple facts often enough, for they are at the root of the misconceptions that underlay Nazi policy towards Britain in all its phases. Not a man noted for his sense of humour, the Führer can still raise posthumous laughs with the unintentional dryness of his *aperçus*. 'I've never met an Englishman', he declared in 1942, 'who was not opposed to Churchill.'[13] This, one may safely assume, was no less than the truth. But that encapsulates the nature of the problem. Hitler half realised it himself at times. 'It would be important for me to discover for instance how strong the opposition to Churchill actually is in Britain. Who opposes him? The only way I seem to hear about this is via the press.'[14]

The shortcomings of German intelligence may have been part of the problem. Yet the root of it was Hitler himself. The very entry in the *Table Talk* which bemoaned a lack of information had begun with an outburst about the uselessness of the diplomats who had sought to provide it. Having spurned conventional Foreign Office channels, Hitler was forced to improvise. All the evidence suggests that he depended greatly on personal impressions, and those of people he trusted. His evolving perceptions of Britain were therefore inevitably shaped by the individual British visitors he met and the impressions he formed – indirectly – from photographs and articles in the press.

The succession of rogues and misguided fools who sought him out in the thirties – the Mitfords, Lloyd Georges, etc. – were, in the circumstances, not the most ideal informants. Yet they were only part of the problem. Hitler eventually realised that they did not fully represent public opinion in Britain. Their pronouncements had been too consistently contradicted by events. (The failure of the British Union of Fascists to make headway, for instance, ultimately spoke for itself, and did so even to Hitler's mind.)[15] The problem, however, was more deep-seated. It was not the politics of the visitors alone, but their appearance, their manner, their modes of speech even. And here the growing misconceptions were unwittingly compounded by Britain's official emissaries and the image the British government itself projected. It is therefore worthwhile to attempt to look at official Britain through the eyes of Hitler and of those close to him.

After the outbreak of hostilities in September 1939, one of the flood of books in the Third Reich's anti-British propaganda offensive bore the title *The Old Men Wanted War*.[16] This is a good starting point in the attempt to see the world with Nazi eyes. However improbable it may seem, the basis of the Third Reich's self-image after 1939 was one of outraged innocence. The German attack on Poland was immaterial. It was no different from Britain's forays into the Sudan, the rape of Boer South Africa, or her bloody incursion into defenceless Tibet on the eve of the First World War. Such behaviour – however distasteful – was the mark of a Great Power. It need not provoke a world war and had never provoked Germany into declaring war on Britain. The Reich therefore had a right to expect similar British restraint in the face of *German* expansion.

Responsibility for the Anglo-German conflict of 1939 therefore rested solely with Britain. She it was who had declared war, and she, too, had earlier rejected all Nazi overtures. This was a matter of conviction rather than simply of propaganda. Britain's hostility seemed to Nazi eyes irrational: Hitler's Germany had never sought to diminish or weaken the British Empire. 'It was always our belief', noted the SS newspaper in October 1939, 'that we could live perfectly alongside Britain, and could be mighty and happy alongside each other, though it seems we were mistaken.'[17] The gratuitous unleashing of war, as the Nazis saw it, could only therefore be explained in terms of the character and the individual personalities of the British establishment. In the words of *The Old Men Wanted War*, British policy was dictated by 'the desperate hatred of yesterday's men'.[18]

An irrational hatred of the Third Reich, then, was one aspect the Nazi leadership considered characteristic of Britain's ruling elite. This was closely allied to a second perhaps even more important feature: that of senescence. Seen from Berlin or the Berghof, Britain was a gerontocracy: a nation led and administered by 'poisonous old men, for whom life held out no further promise'.[19] The evidence of that view permeates the Third Reich's official pronouncements from 1937 onwards. A researcher analysing the German press of the period might spend weeks recording all the instances of the name Chamberlain being preceded by the adjective 'old' (and that would not even include related items, such as the headline 'Chamberlain laid low by gout').[20]

This was, of course, intentional malice, as were the cartoon images of a rarely less than cadaverous-looking premier. But, once again, it was not solely a matter of propaganda. The *Goebbels Diaries* – the fullest record we have of the leadership's private views during this period – regularly identify members of the British government and its emissaries as old or at least as ineffectual. Sir Robert Vansittart is thus a 'hyper-nervous man' who 'lacks energy';[21] ambassador Henderson is 'lazy and indolent';[22] Chamberlain is condescended to as an 'old man';[23] a day earlier, Goebbels notes, Hitler himself had described Chamberlain as an 'ancient Englishman'.[24] Six weeks after the outbreak of war, Goebbels dismisses the premier as 'an old windbag',[25] and in February 1940, a prime ministerial speech seems to him little but 'senile chatter'.[26] That impression initially extended also to Churchill, who was judged to be 'a vain and senile windbag'.[27] And though the leadership greatly admired Lloyd George, Goebbels observes, 'but he too is old'; before adding, 'That is the dilemma of democracy. We can sleep quietly.'[28] Hitler himself may have warned, in January 1937, not to judge the 'quality of the British people' by its leadership, yet the overall impression was unmistakably one of senescence.[29] The entire Empire seemed 'decidedly ancient'.[30]

The provenance of these views – the *Goebbels Diaries* – makes them all the more significant: Goebbels was less guilty than other leading Nazis of under-estimating Britain. Through much of the final year of peace he regarded war with Britain as a distinct possibility (and, according to Albert Speer, was ridiculed for this by others in the leadership).[31] The consistent equation of Britain with the ravages of age in the pages of Goebbels' own diary should not therefore be dismissed as propaganda; it may at times have included an element of verbal bravado – an attempt to steady his own frayed nerves – but it clearly reflected genuine conviction.

There is no great mystery as to what might have prompted this: Goebbels had become a cabinet minister in his mid-thirties. He had first achieved high party office in his twenties. Many leading Nazis were not much older than he was, some even younger. The faces of the Third Reich have become so familiar that one fails to recognise now their often startling youth. There were exceptions, of course, but for every lugubrious Rosenberg – still only just into his forties – there was a young Heydrich, Speer or Schirach. The comparative youth of so many in the middle and upper echelons of the Third Reich has long been recognised as a factor in the regime's progressive radicalisation. (This may also be said to be true in the case of relations with Britain: the elderly Baron Neurath had counselled caution, while the younger Ribbentrop exuded arrogant self-confidence.)

The wider question as to whether all this formed part of Hitler's conscious plans misses the point. The Nazis constantly emphasised the role of instinct. And instinct seems a very convincing explanation for Hitler's readiness to entrust important tasks to much younger men. That he was conscious, however, of an age difference between himself and most of those who served him is a matter of record. In April 1939 Hitler celebrated his fiftieth birthday. By international standards he was thus hardly an ancient leader. Even at the time of his death, he was younger than most British prime ministers of the twentieth century had been at the time of taking office. Yet Hitler, as is well known, regarded his life by 1939 as almost over, and regularly intimated to his entourage that he would not live to taste the fruits of his great military labours.

This was in part personal idiosyncrasy, but it was also a reflection of the regime's ethos. One should never forget how much the Third Reich had been constructed upon the idea of youth. Its public iconography revolves around it. The 'New Germany', as it liked to be called at first, was summed up in the parades and the gymnastic routines of row upon row of indistinguishable Aryan bodies. As with photographs of the leadership these have become so familiar that one tends now not to notice that these anonymous columns of German flesh were all young. Youth was the public face of National Socialism. This was reflected in its statuary and painting as much as in its photography or in the imagery of its political posters. All endlessly repeated the same wordless message: we are the future, and the future is ours.

This may not be a new insight, but it is relevant here. The Third Reich's self-image should not be divorced from any discussion of its policies, still less from its perceptions of other countries. The background to the leadership's thinking was always the Reich's youthful strength, youthful vigour and, above all, its youthful fertility. The press regularly printed photographs of the leaders surrounded by their young families. Prominent Nazis may have differed from ordinary politicians in any number of ways, not least in the fact that the babies they clutched for the cameras tended to be their own. Göring, Goebbels, Himmler, Schirach – the list of proud young Nazi fathers is long. Only Hitler – the father of the nation – is the exception here, and it may have compounded his sense of approaching death. When Goebbels records in his diary in 1937: 'Alarming decline of the birth rate in Britain. It's a stricken country', he is thus not just echoing Nazi ideology.[32] He is contrasting – consciously or not – his own large and growing family, and those of his party colleagues, with the Britain he actually knows: a country of desiccated ambassadors and elderly ministers of the crown for whom early fatherhood was, at best, a distant memory.

The youthfulness of the regime was not just in contrast to the image it was beginning to form of Britain, however. It contrasted also with Germany's own recent past. This, too, is important. An elderly and ineffectual Kaiser – appropriately enough with a withered arm – had been followed by Presidents Ebert and Hindenburg, who both died in office.

3   'Club life'

Among Weimar's Chancellors, Stresemann died shortly after leaving office, while of the others few had been conspicuously vigorous. In Austria, meanwhile, annexed in 1938 and probably always part of Hitler's own mindset, the century began with an Emperor of seemingly immemorial age; and after a brief interlude of boyish inexperience in the shape of the Emperor Charles, things soon settled into a pattern of middle-aged mediocrity. It is the combination of advancing years and lack of success that is crucial here. The same combination had struck the Nazis as characteristic about the Weimar Republic. As the Reichstag reconvened in the dying days of German democracy, the chamber seemed to Goebbels 'an assembly of geriatrics'.[33]

All this matters because the exponents of the regime would later draw explicit comparisons between their British enemies and their erstwhile domestic opponents. Ernest Bramsted, in his classic study of Nazi propaganda, has called this 'the lure of historical parallels'.[34] Bramsted noted that Goebbels and Hitler were almost as anxious to mislead themselves as they were to mislead others. This might suggest desperation, and indeed the supposed historical parallels abound after 1942. Yet in the leadership's private views this phenomenon occurs much earlier: at a time, in other words, when few people in the Third Reich experienced much despair – except the silent army of the regime's domestic victims.

There is an extremely revealing passage in the *Goebbels Diaries* about a conversation with Hitler in 1940. It took place on the eve of the great German offensive that would end for the Allied armies in rout and annihilation and would finally bring to a close two centuries and more of British preponderance over the continent of Europe. 'It is becoming quite clear', notes Goebbels,

> that the British are completely stupid and short-sighted. They are exactly the kind of people who opposed us in our domestic struggle for power . . . Precisely like the old bourgeois parties . . . The Führer mentions instances from the Party's history. Weren't our opponents then precisely like the British are today? And shall we not prevail against them as we prevailed against the others?[35]

This is not desperation, this is premature triumph.[36] But the important thing is not that Hitler and Goebbels underestimated British determination in 1940 – that would hardly be a new insight. What matters is the underlying consistency of Nazi views. These had, of course, changed on the subject of Britain (and would do so again in 1941). But the view of an enfeebled Britain connected naturally with existing convictions about the nature and calibre of the Nazis' opponents. National Socialism may have been an irrational ideology, but the irrational mind often produces its own apparently compelling logic. The passage above demonstrates this clearly. It provides obvious links between the theme of supposed British political incompetence in 1940, Goebbels' description in 1932 of an impotent and 'geriatric' Reichstag, and his remarks in 1937 that the age of British politicians revealed the dilemma of democracy.

And this connects harmoniously with the regime's wider perception of the world. Germany and her allies were routinely described as the 'young nations'. This was a key theme in Nazi propaganda for much of the war. (The diarist Viktor Klemperer, who was cursed with a long memory and fluency in foreign languages, promptly recalled an early Mussolini speech; this had described Italian culture as already ancient when the Germans were still illiterate forest dwellers. The youthfulness of nations, Klemperer concluded, was evidently a flexible affair.)[37]

But Klemperer merely reveals here his own complete immunity to Nazi thought. Youth, for the Third Reich, was not solely a question of age but of outlook. The Italian Fascists and Germany's own leadership had both reinvented and rejuvenated their respective countries. From this, they felt, derived the legitimacy of their rule. The Baldwins, Chamberlains and Churchills, and the army of their stooped and greying assistants, had failed to embrace the new. That was the important point: that, more than the kingdom's age or the weight of its history, set Britain apart from the self-proclaimed Young Nations of Europe.

In his study of *Englandkunde*, Raddatz points to an essay in 1933 with the title 'Young Germany – Old England'; and he notes this as a rare exception in those years among professional pronouncements about Britain.[38] In fact, he quotes no other academic voice anywhere that even hinted at British senescence in the early thirties. This indirect glimpse of opinions among Germany's *Anglisten* is important. In 1933, at the beginning of the Third Reich, the perspective of a Britain enfeebled by aged and incompetent leaders did not represent either German or specifically Nazi views.[39] It came about only gradually as the thirties wore on, as Germany's position strengthened and Britain's imperial and international problems multiplied.

At the height of Britain's problems in the 1930s, Prime Minister Chamberlain travelled to Germany. On his return, he famously waved his piece of paper. It might be useful to take a second look at that familiar picture, trying this time to concentrate not on the document in Chamberlain's hand but on the rest of the scene. There is the Prime Minister himself, in his dark old-fashioned suit, and the high collar which immediately dates the picture as pre-war. But behind Chamberlain, massive and yet obscured in a sense by the fatal scrap of paper, is an aeroplane. Chamberlain had flown to Germany. Other stills from the same film reel show him gingerly stepping out of the aircraft. His slight hesitancy is less that of age than of a man still a little wary of an unfamiliar form of transport. It was still a new experience.[40] On his earlier visit to Germany, he had become the first British Prime Minister in history to travel by air. The urgency of the European crisis had made this novel form of transport necessary. Or, to put it provocatively, the Third Reich had just propelled the British government into the age of aviation.

The image of Chamberlain's reception at the aerodrome has no real counterpart in Germany. There is no one photograph that marks as clearly the end of the old and the beginning of the new. By 1938 the German public had been used for years to the spectacle of their leaders bounding in and out of aircraft. Hitler had already relied upon planes in the election campaigns of the Weimar era (this was at a time when campaigning in the United States, the homeland of aviation, still centred on railway sidings). The earliest planes Hitler used did not even possess cabins, and film reels exist of Hitler in aviator's outfit, leaping out of precarious-looking craft. The association of the Führer with this new form of transport was so strong that Leni Riefenstahl could exploit it for the famous opening shots of *Triumph of the Will*. The metallic gleam in the skies identified the leadership of the new Germany as much as the *Pickelhaube* on the ancient President Hindenburg had marked the old.

The wider cult of aviation was a defining feature of the thirties, and both Germany and Fascist Italy exploited it consciously. Göring derived much of his prestige from his status as a fighter pilot in the Great War, and the looming bulk of his Reich Aviation Ministry itself became a symbol of the Nazi government and its embrace of the new. South of the Alps, Italo Balbo, or Mussolini's dashing son-in-law, Count Ciano – aviators both – did much to associate Italy in the public mind with technological advance. (Fittingly, it would also be a plane, albeit a German one, that bore Mussolini years later from mountain-top captivity towards Salò and the butcher's hook of his final public appearance.) Hitler's war would make aeroplanes familiar. Their appearance in vast formations in the skies of Europe robbed them of their romance and associated them with death, terror and destruction. In the 1930s, however, the equation of aviation and dashing youthfulness was strong.

Nor was that perception limited to Germany and Italy. In Britain, John Betjeman's fine poem on the death of George V ends with the image of a young man landing his plane on a runway. This reflects as much the spirit of the age as Betjeman's noted ability to capture it in verse. But at the time the image would have contrasted also with the still fresh memories of the late monarch. Only a year earlier, during his Silver Jubilee, George V and his consort had acknowledged the crowds from a horse-drawn carriage. And that image, which reached the German public via the Reich's newspapers, in turn pointed to the contrast with the 'New Germany'. It did so as surely as, in Britain, it had sustained Betjeman's poem.

For if George V was associated with the horse-drawn carriages of an earlier age, Hitler was identified in the public mind with the new century and its innovations. He was linked with aeroplanes, and perhaps even more strongly with the motor car. Again, innumerable photographs created and maintained that link. In the Weimar days, it is Hitler in his super-charged Mercedes, with the protective headgear and goggles of the period: every inch the daredevil and sportsman. Once in power, he is glimpsed all over Germany, as the autobahn network – the Führer's highways – takes shape. Later still, it is Hitler inspecting the Strength-through-

Joy car: the embryonic Volkswagen Beetle. Nazi propaganda sought to associate this car very closely with Hitler: Professor Porsche's design, the German public were told, had been repeatedly altered and improved at the Führer's insistence. The resulting car, it was thus suggested, was in effect a collaboration between Porsche and Hitler, with Porsche cast in the role of the gifted apprentice. It was only Hitler's long-standing identification as a motor enthusiast that made this kind of propaganda possible.

Yet the most enduring association between Hitler and cars was that of the Führer taking the salute of the crowds in his stretched open Mercedes. The images of Hitler in the *Führerwagen* against the backdrop of various German cities, or, later, amidst ecstatic Austrians and Sudeten Germans provide almost a photographic record of the Third Reich's progress. In a regime expert in the theatrical *mise en scène* of power, Hitler's car was an essential prop. To the embarrassment of post-war Germany, the swastika and the star on the Mercedes grill were closely linked images. Mussolini, something of an expert himself in matters of propaganda, was so impressed with the sleek power of Hitler's limousine that he ordered Italian manufacturers to create a worthy equivalent.

There was also motor racing. And as with Hitler's cars or planes, this had iconic stature. The duels fought between German and Italian drivers in particular – and German and Italian racing cars – amounted to a national obsession in the 1930s. Here were displayed all the characteristics of National Socialism: the powerful machine, controlled by an even more powerful man, and both revealing the might of the nation that had produced them. During the early to mid-thirties – the years of the regime's involuntary peacefulness – the Third Reich's battle honours were won at the AVUS course in Berlin, at the Nürburgring, or at Ventimiglia. The drivers were heralds of the new Reich and of its greater coming victories. (When the most prominent of them, Bernd Rosemeier, was killed in action, so to speak, he received the kind of funeral that would later be awarded to Hitler's most prominent generals.)

All of this may be familiar, but it is relevant to this discussion. For the combination of man and machine – or rather of superman and machine – provided the everyday images of the Third Reich in peacetime; more than that, they were part of its self-image. Against such images must be set occasional German glimpses of Britain: the old King and Queen in their carriage; ministers and senior civil servants in Whitehall, walking to work, complete with bowler hats and rolled-up umbrellas; and Prime Minister Chamberlain hesitating for a moment at the aerodrome, as if

4   *The Duke of Windsor inspecting a racing car during his visit to Germany in 1937*

overawed by what he had just seen in Germany. The precise effect of all this on German viewers – on both the public and the leadership itself – can only be guessed. But by the end of the thirties the contrast was sufficiently strong to strike even non-Germans. Charles Lindbergh famously predicted that Nazi Germany would win the war against Britain. Lindbergh did not claim to know anything about international affairs, but he knew about aviation, and had been impressed by the Third Reich's apparently whole-hearted embrace of technological advance.

Throughout the 1930s, then, the Nazis did everything to strengthen in the public mind the equation of the Third Reich with power and youthful vigour. Britain, meanwhile, seemed to have stagnated; more than that, in the years 1936 and 1937 the country had apparently embarked on the opposite course: an elderly premier had been succeeded by a man of similarly advanced years, and a vigorous and determined monarch by his ineffectual, stuttering brother.

One of the pivotal moments in Anglo-Germans relations this century was undoubtedly the short reign of Edward VIII and the abdication crisis that brought it to a sudden and dramatic close. Indeed, the later Duke of Windsor has been associated ever since in Britain with the Nazi regime. The visit in 1937 of the Duke and Duchess to Germany, and the enthusiasm with which the couple were received, have damned them in British eyes as much as the Duke's apparent wartime readiness to champion an understanding with the Third Reich. The whiff of treason hangs about him even decades after these events. And the publication of the *Table Talk* and the *Goebbels Diaries* with their elaborate praise for the man with whom 'an alliance would have been possible' have only deepened suspicions.[41]

In Germany, especially among those who remember the 1930s, the Duke's name retains a luminous glow. And it is not that of a man who put Germany's interests before those of his own country. There was and is no suggestion in German minds that he was a traitor, a collaborator or even a spineless appeaser. That perception is confirmed by the private views of the Nazi leadership. The *Goebbels Diaries* and Hitler's *Table Talk* are wholly unambiguous in that regard. When the Nazis were dealing with a useful fool, they could never quite disguise an element of contempt in their language; when they met a rogue, their words betray a shared contempt for others. There is nothing of this in the descriptions of the Duke's conversations in Berlin or the later wartime recollections of his actions and opinions. Instead, there is something one comes across only very rarely in Nazi utterances: genuine respect; the respect felt for an equal.

The Duke's motivation in all of this, and his perceptions of National Socialist Germany lie outside the scope of this study. How he was perceived in the Third Reich, however, is central to the story of the final years and months of the peace. It might therefore be appropriate to examine in detail the impression his German hosts formed of him in 1937. Here is Goebbels in what can only be described as gushing mode:

> the Duke is wonderful. A charming, likeable chap; open [in manner], clear [in expression], with a healthy common sense approach, an awareness of contemporary life and social issues. What a delight to talk to him! He responds immediately, is interested in every question. There is nothing of the snob about him. We discussed a thousand things: the Parliamentary system, social and labour issues, national and international affairs. What a shame that he is no longer King! With him an alliance would have been possible . . . The Duke was deposed because he had it in him to be a king in the true sense of the word. That much is clear to

me, now more than ever. I have genuinely grown to like him in these three hours. What an enjoyable afternoon! A great man. What a shame! What a terrible shame![42]

It should perhaps be stressed that this is not Goebbels' usual tone. Except in his descriptions of Hitler, he rarely reaches a comparable pitch of enthusiasm anywhere in the twenty volumes or more of the *Diaries*. This only increases the significance of this particular entry. The Duke of Windsor had clearly charmed his host in the Propaganda Ministry. And what had impressed Goebbels was evidently the man rather than merely his real or supposed political views. Goebbels would meet a string of visitors on any given day who agreed with him on all issues. They tended not to impress him greatly. But the Duke he thought was 'eine Persönlichkeit' – a great man.[43]

What, then, was the precise impression that the host formed of his guest? The Duke was youthful: not just in years, but in outlook. He exhibited 'an awareness of contemporary life'. That observation gains a recognisable edge once one contrasts him with the other members of his family. His predecessor on the throne had viewed the world from a horse-drawn carriage. His successor would be depicted in the German press in ceremonial robes, receiving feudal dues.[44] In other words, the Duke's modern manner alone would have recommended him to the Nazis. (The fact that he had never been crowned, and had thus never been photographed in medieval apparel, had preserved intact the image of the royal innovator.) The Third Reich, it should be remembered, was wholly unnostalgic about Germany's own recent monarchical past (and actively hostile to Austria's dynastic traditions). The Duke of Windsor's obvious preference for modern dress and manners had therefore struck an immediate chord in the Third Reich.

Shortly after the Nazi Seizure of Power, Germany's main illustrated weekly, the *Berliner Illustrierte Zeitung*, reported a minor journalistic coup.[45] It had been granted a brief audience by the then Prince of Wales in his private quarters. The paper was as enthusiastic about the man it encountered as Goebbels would be four years later, and for similar reasons. The Prince seemed simple, youthful and unaffected. There was a boy scout on guard duty outside the palace, as the correspondent noted with delighted surprise. The man inside the palace was equally informal. In keeping with the paper's publishing speciality, image took precedent over text. But it did report his 'firm handshake', his 'fluent German' (with

5   The Berlin crowds cheer the Duke of Windsor, 1937

the word 'fluent' italicised), and the fact that he claimed to have listened to a recent Hitler speech on the radio.

There was in this no suggestion that the Prince actually agreed with Hitler (the paper's own allegiance to Hitler was far from absolute at the time).[46] Politics was not the issue. What impressed the interviewer about the Prince of Wales was his general outlook. Here was a man who used modern methods to keep himself informed, and who evidently possessed the necessary skills, knowledge and initiative to bypass slow-witted officialdom. That such impressions would later have contrasted in German eyes with a British government that claimed to regard central Europe as a faraway place, and loudly boasted that it knew little about it, hardly needs pointing out.

During Edward's brief reign that impression was only enhanced. The King's visit to the destitute coalminers of South Wales created an enormous impression in Germany. It moved the country by reminding it of its own recent economic nightmare. Just as importantly, it contrasted with the apparent indifference to the suffering of the unemployed among the *elected* officeholders in both countries. The King's visit to South Wales had once more highlighted the failure of democracy to provide even a minimum standard of living for those it claimed to represent; and it had done so as dramatically as any Hitler speech during the Depression.[47] Hitler had subsequently vanquished unemployment in Germany; now, in Britain, there was also someone who recognised the problem and who was not too caught up in the agreeable life of London clubs or in share dealings at the stock exchange to notice the victims of what the Nazis called 'the system'.

The link between the Third Reich's concepts of modernity and its anti-capitalist leanings will interest us later. That the Duke of Windsor brought alive that connection is of more immediate importance. Edward VIII, it seemed, had – independently – reached similar conclusions about the contemporary world as the National Socialists. When, therefore, in 1937, the Nazi leadership showed the ex-King its model housing estates, or a film about the various schemes of the German Labour Front, it did so not because they saw in him a Nazi sympathiser but a fellow social innovator. Quite simply, they remembered his visit to the Welsh valleys. And the cheers that greeted the Duke among the crowd of German workers in 1937 showed that they evidently remembered it too.

As the final crisis of Edward's brief reign gathered momentum, the German press focused on the simple unaffected man and his reluctance to be constrained by outdated protocol and convention. He answered his own telephone, German readers were told. He preferred to travel incognito: as Prince of Wales, he had apparently once been reprimanded by a loyal subject for a flippant remark about himself; on a visit to Turkey, meanwhile, the Prince had explored Istanbul in a taxi like a 'modern-day Harun-al-Rashed'.[48] Such *Volksnähe* – literally, 'proximity to the people' – had long been a German political ideal. In the absence of participation in government on the part of the *Volk*, it helped legitimise autocratic rule. The Nazis, too, embraced the ideal, though not the practice of it: on the Obersalzberg, or later in the various Führer HQs, the leadership sequestered itself from its subjects as firmly as any monarch of the *ancien régime*.

One of the chief expressions of *Volksnähe* had always been language. And here the concept did reveal a strong connection with modernity and innovation. Luther had first revolutionised Germany by 'observing popular speech'.[49] Some of Germany's most revered monarchs had favoured a similar approach. Those most closely associated with modernising their realms, Frederick the Great in Prussia, or in Austria Maria Theresa and Joseph II, had also simplified and made more effective the language of their administrations. It is therefore perhaps significant that Goebbels should have described the Duke of Windsor in 1937 as being *klar* – a quality that combines clarity in expression with perceptiveness and logical thought. And this may be more than a mere detail, because he adds to this the exclamation, 'What a delight to talk to him!' It is worth entertaining the thought that this delight might have been due as much to the Duke's manner as to what he actually said to his German hosts. This is possibly of wider significance.

There is an intriguing passage in Hitler's *Table Talk* that might be relevant here. In it Hitler holds forth on the relative merits of the various English accents he had heard over the years. Since Hitler did not speak English, he judged what he heard merely in terms of pleasing or less pleasing noise. All this may sound characteristically grotesque, but there may be more to it. The English Hitler claimed he had found most agreeable was that of Lloyd George, the sounds he had disliked most were those of Anthony Eden.[50]

It is tempting, therefore, to conclude that what Hitler is really saying is that he preferred visitors to agree with him. Yet one should not perhaps dismiss his remark quite so easily. Lloyd George's speech was that of a common man who had risen through the ranks, Eden's that of the upper class. Hitler might not have been able to identify their accents sociologically, but he can scarcely have been unaware of their respective backgrounds, and he would doubtless have observed their differing manner. And there is the fact also that Eden's languid aristocratic tones and general deportment did not just provoke Hitler and the Nazis. Decades later, it would compound Britain's international isolation over Suez. A mixture of resentment and contempt for Anthony Eden probably constituted the only thing Hitler and President Eisenhower ever had in common.

Eden might be regarded as a special case. Yet the perception of arrogance dogged most official British emissaries to Germany in the later thirties. That this was in part a simple reflection of the deteriorating relations between the two countries is undeniable. Yet might it not also have been connected with the manner of the visitors? In Britain their accents induced, in the 1930s and beyond, automatic deference. Abroad, the significance of the accent might not always have been recognised, but the tone and the manner that went with it would have been unmistakable. It was not simply a matter of being imperious, but of politeness laced and saturated with instinctive condescension. While Britain was pre-eminent

6   'Eden'

in international affairs, other countries had little choice but to accept this. As British power eroded, they would have been less inclined to do so. This hypothesis would explain Nazi reactions in the later thirties (and would fit also with anecdotal evidence after 1945 of patrician or would-be patrician ministers increasing Britain's diplomatic isolation in the councils of Europe and elsewhere).

Deportment, and the use of language, are factors in Anglo-German relations that are readily accepted when the gaze falls on the Nazi leadership. However, might this not have worked both ways? The nation-alist writer Hans Grimm, who lived in Britain for several years and spoke English fluently, provides possible evidence in support of this view. In 1937 he published his thoughts on a speech by the retiring Prime Minister Baldwin. The piece, entitled 'Baldwin – or the Difficulties of Compre-hension', is worth quoting at length. 'Whoever . . . might have heard or read Baldwin's speech in the original English', begins Grimm,

> would have found it neither strange nor peculiar; it would have seemed to him, as it did to me, a sincere and not unimportant pronouncement. It was only when I started translating the speech into German and began to listen to it with German ears, so to speak, that it started to grow strange and almost irritating . . . And yet there I was, a well-qualified listener with more goodwill than most . . . It might . . . be that the British and the Germans have grown apart through the different ways in which they have tended to interpret each other's language.[51]

Reinhard Spitzy, Ribbentrop's assistant in London, reached strikingly similar conclusions. In his post-war memoirs, he writes, 'As absurd as it may sound, this war was caused at least in part by the fact that neither side understood the language of the other . . . The representatives of each side were separated by worlds of culture and education.'[52]

Spitzy's remarkably unapologetic memoirs – full of regret but without a scintilla of remorse – practically invite the riposte that British politicians understood Hitler's language perfectly; that the war, moreover, was caused by the Third Reich's actions and not simply by its rhetoric. But the wider point is not so easily dismissed. That holds true of Anglo-German relations in the decades before 1933, and it is true also, in a sense, of the Nazi years.

Spitzy is surely right to suggest that British understatement, and the phrases of purely mechanical English politeness – 'I am afraid', 'I am not sure about that', 'I rather doubt', 'I tend to disagree', etc. – can be acutely misleading in translation. To those unfamiliar with British conven-tions, they can sound hesitant, uncertain or wavering. That can give a speaker the appearance of being what a later Prime Minister liked to call 'wet'. This effect is all the more pronounced if observed against a back-ground of real military or economic weakness, a position in which British ministers found themselves with increasing frequency as the twentieth century wore on. If the reality of British difficulties, further amplified by the appearance of hesitancy, is then combined with a manner betraying the old conviction of effortless superiority towards the foreigner, the consequences can be explosive.

'The British', Goebbels noted in his diary in 1937, 'are currently engaged on a spectacularly idiotic foreign policy. They are all mouth, picking quarrels with everyone, but lack the gumption or the strength to act.'[53] This is a perfect summary of Nazi views about Britain in the later 1930s. But all politics has human features. So too it is with Goebbels. His diary entry ends with the observation, 'Eden is a blockhead of rare proportions.'

This in turn points to an important thought. It was not simply that the Nazi leadership chafed at the real or supposed arrogance of the British government. They were struck by the apparent mismatch between British rhetoric and actual power. With internal challenges to Britain's imperial rule in India, the Middle East and elsewhere, and challenges from outside by a newly assertive Japan in the East and an expansionist Italy in the Mediterranean and East Africa, Britain simply could not afford to 'pick a quarrel' with Germany, as Goebbels put it. To do so was to imperil the very survival of the British Empire.

In the light of this, the mixture of patrician *bonhomie* and rhetorical defiance that characterised British policy towards Germany in the later 1930s seemed to the Nazi leaders grotesquely inappropriate.[54] One does not alienate gratuitously people on whose goodwill one is dependent. Germany held the key to the continued survival – or the disintegration – of the British Empire. The apparent inability of the political class in Britain to grasp that point suggested its fundamental incompetence. It was this thought, more perhaps than any other, that set the Third Reich on a course of deliberate confrontation with Britain from 1937 onwards. Bottomless contempt for Britain's political class led more or less directly to the events of 1938 and 1939. And it is this thought also that leads back once again to the only British visitor in those years who impressed the Nazis.

The Duke of Windsor had favoured an understanding with the Third Reich. This was in a sense what Hitler had been predicting since the mid-twenties. Britain, as he had suggested in his *Second Book*, would enter an alliance with Germany only if it was in her own interest to so.[55] Edward's overtures – both before and after his abdication – thus revealed him not primarily as a friend of Germany but as a hard-headed defender of the British Empire. And just as manner, policies and manifest incompetence went together in Eden or Chamberlain, so acumen and conduct were of a piece in the Duke of Windsor.

It is no accident that Goebbels noted the absence of all snobbery in the Duke. This is more than simply a reminder of Nazi class resentment. It has clear political implications (and it connects Goebbels' observations about his royal visitor with Ernest Bramsted's 'historical parallels'). Snobbery, quite simply, seemed to the Third Reich the last refuge of the incompetent.[56] In the Weimar years the Nazis had been treated *de haut en bas* by Germany's old-style conservatives. This had only deepened their contempt for the country's aristocracy. For in the end, Hitler and his followers had outmanoeuvred their supposed elders and betters. Abroad, too, snobbery invariably masked incompetence. (The leadership formed a very low opinion of the House of Savoy – technically their allies – and of various haughty Italian officials they encountered during their state visits; events swiftly confirmed these impressions.)

The Duke of Windsor's unaffected manner is therefore highly significant. And so, of course, was the fact that Britain had forced this man to abdicate. 'The Duke was deposed because he had it in him to be a king in the true sense of the word. That much is clear to me, now more than ever', as Goebbels had put it. The abdication, in other words, had been brought about by politically third-rate minds who feared for their future careers in a country led by a competent ruler. (The fact that both in Germany and in Austria the crown retained until 1918 the right to over-rule Parliament and dismiss governments probably misled the Nazis about the constitutional realities in Britain.)[57]

There was, of course, a recognition that Edward's choice of consort had brought matters to a head. Hitler detected – perhaps with reason – more than a hint of xenophobia in the hostility to Mrs Simpson, and though he sympathised with the smitten monarch, he regarded such xenophobia as perfectly natural. It was most unwise for a leader, he thought, to marry a foreigner.[58] The suggestion that ecclesiastical opposition had been decisive, on the other hand, did not strike anyone in the Third Reich as remotely credible. An institution expressly founded for the furtherance of royal bigamy, which had remained silent even when its founder added murder to his other misdemeanours, was unlikely to develop moral scruples unless encouraged to do so. The great thing about the Church of England, Hitler suggested a few years later, was that one could 'depend on it'[59] (a melancholy thought for the Führer, faced as he was with a hostile Catholic hierarchy in the Reich).

Whatever the precise explanation of the supposed political plot in the autumn of 1936,[60] the fact that Edward had given up his throne for a woman emerged clearly and only added to his attraction.[61] Several leading Nazis were either divorced themselves or married to divorcees, and thus likely to sympathise. But there was more than that: not a few found time for additional extra-marital encounters – though none quite equalled Goebbels' own formidable energies in this field. Surrounding oneself with attractive women was part of the Nazi style of government. This could induce an automatic sense of kinship with visitors who seemed to share the leadership's tastes. One does not have to read too far between the lines of Goebbels' diary, for instance, to find that Mrs Simpson's charms, and her husband's evident awareness of them, increased the Duke's stature in Goebbels' eyes.[62]

The issue of how the sexual lives of statesmen are perceived by their colleagues, and the extent to which these perceptions might influence their judgement, is rarely examined. A natural and laudable reticence by the parties concerned makes the matter difficult to assess. But it might be worth remembering in this context that President Kennedy – another self-consciously youthful leader of a young nation – reduced Prime Minister Macmillan to embarrassed silence with a casual remark about his sexual appetites. This may be the only crassness the Nazi leadership hesitated to inflict on visiting dignitaries, but the imagination, we may be certain, ranged freely. In a regime obsessed with the birth rate it could hardly have been otherwise. And the contrast between a happy Duke of Windsor beside his attractive young wife and the apparently asexual political class that ousted him must have seemed suggestive to the Third Reich.[63]

With Edward VIII removed from the political scene, the perception among the leadership of a Britain in terminal decline quickly took root. There was occasional intelligence that challenged this view – the restructuring in December 1937, for instance, of Britain's military command – but, for the most part things seemed reassuringly decrepit.[64] 'Speech from the throne by George VI', Goebbels' diary entry reads in October 1937, 'it's enough to make anyone stutter.'[65] The brazenness with which the King's disability is linked to the supposed incompetence of his Prime Minister may seem astonishing, since Goebbels himself walked through life with a noticeable limp. Yet it is entirely characteristic of the Third Reich and its beliefs.

Perhaps just as important in its symbolism as the King's stutter was the anachronistic ritual that surrounded the Gracious Speech. From 1937 onwards the Third Reich sought to present Britain in the German media as a Ruritanian nation. In this it was greatly helped by Britain's obvious fondness for ceremony and tradition. Many of the Third Reich's own ceremonies and its excessive love of uniforms struck outside observers – one merely has to think of Chaplin's *Great Dictator* – as farcical. Inside Germany, however, they represented real power and the effect was different. Much the same goes for British ceremonies and the elaborate outfits associated with them. To outsiders, the combination of stiff-necked dignity and music-hall splendour often seems distinctly comical. Hostile eyes are easily tempted to dismiss the officials in such scenes as mere stage buffoons. The simple fact that Britain retained the use of wigs, for instance, was an enormous boon to Nazi propaganda.

Wigs had become obsolete in Germany at the end of the eighteenth century. In some regions of the country this was due to the direct influence of revolutionary France; in others, it was part of the successful attempt of German monarchies to survive the upheaval through bold modernisation. The actual word for wig – *Zopf* – and its related adjectives soon reflected the changed perceptions: they acquired a secondary meaning of 'old-fashioned' or 'fuddy-duddy', which they retain in twentieth-century usage. A simple photograph of a wig or a bewigged British official therefore carried all the linguistic and cultural associations the Nazis might have wished for. The weekly newspaper *Das Reich*, which regularly featured editorials from Goebbels' own pen, thus printed a photo in 1940 of a row of wigs in a London shop window. It contrasted this with the famous sculpture of Queen Nefertiti, and invited its readers to marvel how fresh and youthful Pharaonic Egypt seemed in comparison to contemporary Britain.[66]

A few months earlier, the *Berliner Illustrierte Zeitung* had featured a bewigged British official outside the Mansion House in London. He was reading a royal proclamation about the defence of the realm. Britain was fighting for her survival at the time. This stirring document, German readers were informed, began with the word 'whereas' (and the German translation – *sintemalen* – suggested even more strongly the language of bygone centuries). As for the robed and bewigged official reading out the proclamation, he did so, the paper reported, 'with dust cascading from his wig'. It all seemed symbolic of the way Britain had 'sought to hold out against the modern age'.[67]

Some three years earlier – at a time, in other words, when the German press still retained the very last vestiges of editorial independence – the same paper had carried a notably sympathetic article about the English sense of humour.[68] The piece was illustrated with several of the celebrated cartoons from Pont of Punch's *The English Character*. Among those reproduced were two, entitled respectively 'A Weakness for Everything Old' and 'A Reluctance to Admit Defeat'. It is tempting to speculate whether the paper's readers would still have recalled these in the late summer of 1940.

This might serve as a useful reminder, however, not to confuse Nazi propaganda with the actual perceptions of ordinary Germans. The two might overlap, or share similar assumptions, but they were not necessarily always the same thing. The view of British senescence was not originally part of the German image of Britain. There was no suggestion of it in the Weimar years. The fact that Germany's *Anglisten* had not been struck by a supposedly enfeebled nation even after 1933 has already been noted. It might be worth remembering, therefore, the wartime observations of Ernst Kris and Hans Speyer about Nazi radio propaganda. Their contention, it will be recalled, was that the frequency of a particular theme in Nazi broadcasts, and the stridency with which it was asserted, might indicate a gulf in perceptions between the leadership and the led – and the leaders' desire to narrow it.[69] The theme of the 'Young Nations of Europe' versus a British Empire displaying 'all the signs of age-related weakness and decay' might be a case in point.[70]

After Dunkirk and Britain's astonishing refusal to withdraw from the conflict, it may well have seemed judicious to forestall anxious questions among the public with confident predictions of Britain's *inevitable* defeat. Certainly, the supposed contrast between Britain and Germany (and Germany's allies) becomes omnipresent in the Reich's press in the summer of 1940. The fact that the theme of an ageing British Empire had been sounded intermittently for several years, and more loudly since the spring of 1939, gave this line of propaganda a helpful hint of consistency. Yet there is something new in 1940: it is the glance at the Reich's allies. This, too, is significant.

During the final stages of the war, Viktor Klemperer noted in his diary that reports of Japanese victories were a reliable indication that 'things were in a bad way' nearer to home.[71] Given the Nazis' self-regard, praise for Germany's allies was fundamentally out of character. When it occurred, it was a sure sign that the regime was somehow in trouble. In the summer of 1940, only weeks after the Wehrmacht's entry into Paris, this might have seemed unlikely. Britain was admittedly behaving in a manner not foreseen by Hitler, but the German public were as yet not aware of the leadership's failure to plan for such a course of events. There was, however, a much more immediate problem: the Italians.

The Rome–Berlin Axis had never been popular in Germany. Italy's double dealing in 1914 had been neither forgiven nor forgotten. The failure of the Italian allies to enter the war in 1939 therefore carried uncomfortable historical echoes. Nor did the timing of Italy's eventual offensive – when the British and French armies were in full retreat – improve matters. Again, this recalled in the most unfortunate manner the previous war: in 1915 it had been the apparent weakness of the Central Powers that had suddenly fired Italy's warrior spirit. 'Kicking a man when down' was evidently something of an Italian habit. The Nazi leadership therefore perceived an urgent need to improve the image of Germany's southern ally.[72] This was easier said than done. Italian actions tended to speak for themselves (and would continue to do so for the rest of the war).

The theme of the Young Nations of Europe therefore helped the regime out of an uncomfortable propaganda impasse. Italy could at last be presented in a positive light. As an added bonus, this connected harmoniously with existing anti-British themes. Photographs of the Italian War Minister Muti in aviator's outfit were thus contrasted with Anthony Eden peering out wearily from under his fedora; bronzed and athletic Italian youths on a beach, meanwhile, were juxtaposed with diminutive Etonians balancing on tiny heads grotesquely outsize top hats.[73]

The retention of Victorian dress by Britain's major public schools was, like the use of wigs by officials, of considerable propaganda value to the Third Reich. Photographs of a boy all but disappearing under his top hat demonstrated wordlessly the cliché of 'putting old heads on young shoulders'. It thus allowed even British youth to be associated with the general theme of senescence.[74] But it also encouraged other, no less useful associations. School dress – particularly tails – could make older boys appear distinctly *louche*. This made for a welcome contrast with the clean-living members of the Hitler Youth, or of the various youth movements of Germany's allies.[75] Above all, it hinted usefully at degeneracy: the theme that in the prudish Third Reich dared not speak its name, but was never far from the surface.

Here, too, the Propaganda Ministry was greatly helped by British custom. The flamboyant leisure wear of the upper-class British male – extravagant blazers and dandyish boaters – could look most suggestive to continental eyes. Pictures of the Henley Regatta or other fixtures of the social calendar were prized by the Nazis not just as reminders of a class divide. The same went for the Empire's more exotic uniforms. Turbaned Englishmen, for instance, tended to look anything but martial. The richly illustrated publications which characterised the early stages of the propaganda war, such as *Die verlorene Insel* (*The Doomed Isle*), could therefore limit themselves to the driest of commentaries and allow the pictures to speak for themselves.[76]

What was hinted at was not necessarily any particular sexual proclivity as such: it was an air of being generally ineffectual. And here the various Nazi preoccupations (and prejudices) did coalesce: Britain's low birth rate, the country's senescence, the inability – or unwillingness – to move with the times, and the resulting technological backwardness. These were no longer the empire builders, explorers or naval heroes who had made Britain powerful. They were merely the characters familiar from the works of Aldous Huxley, Bernard Shaw, Evelyn Waugh and P. G. Wodehouse: capable only of dissipating their inheritance.[77]

In an extraordinarily revealing editorial in late October 1939 the SS newspaper provided a comprehensive digest of the inter-linking Nazi perceptions of Britain. It started by reminding its readers of the patriotic prayer of 1914: 'Gott strafe England'. There was no need, in 1939, to call on divine help, the paper suggested. Britain herself had been working ceaselessly towards her own downfall: 'the British people are punishing themselves with the leadership they have chosen, and will be destroyed because of their failure to recognise their [racial] mission. That we are hastening their fate, that, too, was Britain's wish.' The editorial reiterated the Third Reich's earlier hopes of coexistence with the British Empire. But it went further than that: it suggested that many committed Nazis regarded Britain's decline as 'a severe blow to Nordic leadership of mankind'. The war was thus a double tragedy. But such views, the paper explained, ignored the evidence of racial decline in Britain itself. The country's natural leaders had for several generations now settled in the colonies, preferring frontier life to the debilitating luxury that would have surrounded them at home. What was left in Britain was a leadership by default, made up of 'insider dealers at the stock exchange', estate owners and 'politicking lawyers'. Their lot, and that of the country, was sterility:

7   *Henley*

'fresh blossoms', after all, did not grow 'on a dung heap'. And switching nimbly from horticultural metaphor to palaeontology, the paper continued, 'Just as the dinosaur, bloated by an abundance of food, did not survive the ice age, so too the . . . British Empire will fail to make it into the new era.' Its end would not even be Germany's doing. 'The dinosaurs did not die out because other creatures sought to kill them but because they had outlived their age. The changed environment was not kind to inert gluttons.'[78]

8   Officers at a reception

The social themes in Nazi propaganda will interest us later. More urgent is the question of how persuasive all this sounded to the paper's readers. *Das Schwarze Korps* was perhaps the most uncompromising of the Reich's newspapers. Its core readership – members of the SS – were the regime's ideological vanguard. Unease among their number about the effect of the conflict on the British Empire is therefore significant. (Those cherishing the film image of Nazis ceaselessly plotting Britain's downfall might perhaps find this as troubling as the Nazi leadership itself did in 1939.) For a continued belief in the basic viability of the British Empire was hard to reconcile with the official party view of relentless British decline. The tone, length and intensity of the SS editorial is perhaps a tacit admission of a failure to persuade even the most fervently National Socialist stratum of German society. Britain's positive image during the Weimar era and the elaborate praise for all things British in the early years of the regime seem to have counteracted to a large extent the propaganda efforts of the later thirties.

A nation's opinions on various issues might be likened to a fleet of vessels on an open sea. Where the public is not substantially engaged – merely gliding, in the way of small craft, on the surface – a sudden blast from its government and media can suffice to blow it in the desired direction. Germany's positive image of Britain, however, was in its weight and solidity more like a giant liner. Winds and waves barely affected it; and when the ship's captain suddenly decided in 1937 to throw around the rudder, then – to his well-documented annoyance – the vessel stubbornly continued for some time on its old course.

This leads to a wider point. The theme of British senescence has at its heart a racial component. The idea that an entire nation might be affected by senility is credible only to those who find racial theories persuasive. And racial theory was the weak point in the Third Reich's ideological armour. This may sound astonishing. After all, everything about the Third Reich – its laws, its policies and the unimaginable horror of its crimes – was racially based and racially explained. That racial theory fired the Nazi elite is beyond question; whether it was equally effective with ordinary Germans is much less certain.

Large numbers of the German public, we know, believed in Hitler; they believed – to a lesser extent – in the Nazi party. They believed very strongly in the technological and social innovations of the Third Reich, and therefore in its superiority over other systems of government. They believed, after 1939, in German valour and German armour, and thus in German victory, often against all the evidence. They believed also in the absolute evil of Bolshevism, and the right and indeed the duty to fight it; and many of them clearly believed in the shadowy and satanic power of 'world Jewry'. But the strength of anti-semitism among ordinary Germans does not disprove the weakness of racial theory. For anti-semitism existed before Nazi racial 'science' was born, and in many cases flourished quite independently of it.

Support for the regime, therefore, was not conditional on a belief in *Rassenkunde*. But without such a belief the notion of Britain undergoing the effects of de-nordification was less than persuasive. And that belief, it seems, was not even fully shared among the SS. It can hardly be an accident that, in one way or another, *Das Schwarze Korps* should have kept returning to the thorny topic of *Rassenkunde*. In October 1940, the paper finally sought to confront the issue overtly.[79] It claimed to be responding to the specific questions of its readers. Soldiers at the front had written in, wondering how the anti-German stance of the British, the Dutch and the Norwegians could be reconciled with the notion of a common Nordic identity. A schoolmaster, on the other hand, related his classroom difficulties. Teaching Mendel's law of heredity and the various colours of peas was easy enough. But how should he respond to the puzzled question from his young audience as to how and why this should form the basis of National Socialist policies? He confessed he was unable to give a scientific reply to that question.

Nor was this all: the paper had sought to reassure its readers about *Rassenkunde* before. With the shameless honesty to which the Nazis sometimes resorted in *extremis*, it had declared that the basis for Nazi racial views was not science as such but instinct.[80] This had brought a furious response from scandalised readers. If that were indeed the case – which they absolutely refused to believe – then, surely, Nazi racial policy would amount to 'a catastrophic and decisive error'.[81]

Whether these various correspondents were genuine or merely a journalistic device is in a sense immaterial: for the questions they raised were evidently real enough. And they make it seem unlikely that Germans less committed to the Nazi cause than the readers of the SS newspaper would have believed the more colourful theories of a Nordic – or, alternatively, a de-nordified – Britain. This still leaves the question of what they did believe. And the answer is not straightforward. In a dictatorship the private views of the public leave few traces: some letters, a diary here and there, and occasional files by the Gestapo or the SD. The rich stream of publications of the Weimar era, which had flowed in slightly reduced breadth even into the Third Reich dries up after September 1939. Or, rather, it is replaced by official Nazi propaganda. One must therefore approach the issue obliquely.

What had charmed right-wing Germans about Britain in the 1920s, it will be recalled, was the country's apparent conservatism: the rural life, the glorious feudalism of the British constitution, the resolute rejection of modern art, the apparent disapproval of modern manners, and the rigid conformity which held together this antique social structure. From a view of a country defined by its traditions, it is but a small step to that of an old-fashioned nation. This need not be an indication of hostility. A present-day parallel may be instructive here. Contemporary Americans are, in the general consensus, broadly sympathetic to Britain. Their liking, however, is not entirely free from condescension. It is informed by a belief in their own country's modernity and the perception of an essentially Ruritanian Britain.

That also describes rather well the way German attitudes towards Britain were developing in the later 1930s. As in the case of the Americans, there was both an underlying sense of kinship and a hardening perception of a fundamental contrast. German power, success and influence, growing more pronounced as the thirties wore on, contrasted with Britain's deepening imperial problems. The contrast, however, was not merely perceived to have political roots; it was, almost inevitably, seen in terms of German modernity and Britain's noted love of tradition.

This was not simply the effect of Nazi propaganda. An intense pride in Germany's scientific and engineering prowess had been one of the few obvious sources of shared patriotism across the political divide after 1918. The embrace of modern technology extended even to the most unbending of old German conservatives, and could coexist with their preference for large estates and country pursuits, and their dislike of modern manners. (George V may have toured London in a horse-drawn carriage; the ancient President Hindenburg – fully a generation older – preferred to acknowledge the crowds from an open Mercedes, and did so long before Hitler acquired one.) The Third Reich merely appropriated, and highlighted further, Germany's existing identification with technological advance.

A gradual change in perceptions of Britain was therefore inevitable as Germany recovered after the Depression. Nazi propaganda will doubtless have nudged it a little further, but was able to do so only where it did not fundamentally contradict existing views. The argument of an old-fashioned nation was persuasive because it tallied with the evidence of British culture that had reached Germany in the twenties, and the photographs that did so after 1933: debutantes driving to the Palace to be presented, ermined dignitaries at the opening of Parliament, and the public face of the reigns of both George V and George VI. The theme of racial degeneracy, on the other hand, was far less credible. It contradicted too obviously earlier German admiration for Britain's power and the Nazis' own initial fascination with British imperialism.

Nazi propaganda about Britain was most successful where it was least strident and its ideological motivation not too apparent. Reports about open fires failing to heat up British houses, for instance, seemed entirely credible, and so was the explanation that 'installing central heating would be to compromise tradition'.[82] In much the same way, photographs of signs urging Londoners to conserve water revealed not merely the perils of an English summer but endearing features of Britishness: the thought that more reservoirs and pipelines might help alleviate the recurring droughts was, *Das Schwarze Korps* suggested, uncomfortably radical for British minds.[83] Such articles presumably appealed because they were seen as evidence of British eccentricity rather than of incompetence, as the Nazi ideologues were hoping to suggest.

Overtly anti-British propaganda, both before and during the war, was rather less effective. Himmler's intelligence services frequently reported on the limited impact of propaganda where the German public had recognised the underlying intention. The SD report for 8 August 1940 goes to the heart of the matter: 'intelligence from all regions [of the Reich] indicates that the public are getting tired of polemical articles about Britain. They seem *interested only in facts*.'[84]

Perhaps the clearest indication of why such anti-British propaganda was comparatively ineffective is furnished by a popular film. *Die englische Heirat* – 'The English Marriage' (1934) – has little artistic merit to commend it. Its plot and images are, however, highly revealing. The film is ostensibly a love story between an English aristocrat and a young German woman. But the young man is a mere cipher. The real focus is the determination of his German bride to overcome the obvious hostility of her prospective parents-in-law. The film depends for its lighter moments on the contrast between an ancient Britain, set in its ways, and a modern girl, arriving in a high-powered German sports car. As such, it is not unlike the treatment of Anglo-American romances in Hollywood films, and points once again to unmistakable parallels in German and American perceptions in that regard. The difference, however, is the degree of hostility that the young woman encounters. It is clearly more than simply snobbery or mild prejudice. This she eventually overcomes; the crucial moment occurs when her fiancé's grandmother — a lady in the Edith Evans mode of booming bass voice and masculine aspect — encounters her by chance and recognises that the girl, though German, might be the right woman to take in hand her somewhat ineffectual grandson.

The familiar themes of later Nazi propaganda are thus all anticipated: the obsession with tradition, the comparative technological backwardness, the contrast between an unequivocally youthful Germany and a generally older Britain, between German initiative and British passivity (the supposedly counter-intuitive casting of the couple's respective genders is particularly revealing). Yet, for all that, the film's ultimate theme — Anglo-German understanding — clearly remains intensely desirable. And the old lady who has so long opposed it is described as a figure of consequence. Here the otherwise trivial film connects with the real world of Anglo-German relations in those years. It is difficult not to be reminded of the crowds that cheered Chamberlain in Munich. They saw the Prime Minister's age and old-fashioned appearance, but evidently did not react in the way the regime would have wanted them to. Chamberlain — and by extension the country he represented — were no objects of ridicule to ordinary Germans. The aim remained, as before, Anglo-German partnership.

This was not to be. Yet there was no enthusiasm among ordinary Germans for war in 1939. The scenes that had characterised the summer of 1914 were not repeated. Nor were there, this time, cries of 'Gott strafe England'. Inevitably, though, hostility grew once it became clear that Poland's surrender would not be the end of the war. In a sense, this is hardly surprising. In wartime nations close ranks; doubts are suppressed; and the favourable opinions once held about an enemy are, at least temporarily, in abeyance. Only the absence of hostility in such circumstances would be genuinely surprising. Hostility to Britain from the autumn of 1939 onwards is therefore no more proof of an underlying anti-British animus than Chamberlain's firmness over Poland is evidence of earlier hawkishness. It suited both combatants, however, to pretend otherwise.

If the German public had not been swayed quite as much by Nazi propaganda as the regime would have wished, events soon altered that.

The astonishing German victories of the first twelve months of the war – for once Goebbels' hyperbole of an 'unprecedented age' seemed justified – left an inevitable impression. 'I no longer need to produce any propaganda', noted Goebbels in July 1940, 'our enemies are doing the job for me.'[85] For a few dizzy months the war seemed won. An ecstatic German public was now ready to believe almost anything its leadership might have wished to tell it. That also went for Britain. It was, after all, a *fact* that the British Army had been humiliated and chased from the continent, first in Norway and then in France. The theme of British senescence suddenly seemed credible.

And yet, even in 1940, the evidence of a nation united in its contempt for, or hatred of, Britain is not wholly persuasive. In May 1940 the Princess Vassiltchikov, an objective and often shrewd observer, noted in her diary: 'Many Germans have still a lurking admiration for the English.'[86] Some six months later, she was astonished to come across a vast building site where the Third Reich was constructing a new British embassy for use after the war.[87] The fact that such a building was envisaged at all in Hitler's gigantic new capital is surely revealing.

But perhaps the most striking, and the most moving, evidence comes from the pages of Goebbels' own diary: his entry for 11 October 1939 records a widespread rumour throughout the Reich that day that George VI had abdicated, and the Duke of Windsor, once more in possession of his crown, was calling for an end to the war. Work in shops, factories and offices (including some ministries) was suspended amid spontaneous celebration. Complete strangers embraced in the streets as they told each other the news.[88] There would later be an exact repetition of this in July 1940, after the fall of France. This time the rumour ran that the Duke of Windsor had not merely been restored to his throne but had flown to Berlin to negotiate an end to hostilities.[89] It is worth noting that there was no suggestion in this of Britain having surrendered. The restored monarch was not suing for peace: he was seeking to bring about an end to an unnecessary war. Like Chamberlain's rapturous reception by the people of Munich in 1938, and indeed the welcome everywhere in Germany for the Duke himself in 1937, these rumours provided telling evidence. They are among the rare moments when the stage-managed façade of the Reich parts before the viewer to permit a glimpse of how ordinary Germans at the time actually felt about Britain.

5 'The class struggle of the nations': Britain and Nazi anti-capitalism

'Why do we argue about "social" or "socialist?"', a young Joseph Goebbels asked in the twenties. 'I don't want to be called a National Socialist for nothing.'[1] The controversy has never entirely abated. It has merely moved from the realm of politics to that of historical analysis. The question of how socialist National Socialism was, or indeed whether it was so at all, lies beyond the scope of this study. But the fact that some Nazis – at all levels of the party – did not simply consider themselves nationalists is of relevance. For in the second half of the Twelve-Year Reich, Nazi anti-capitalist leanings influenced substantially the official German image of Britain. The theme of a socially retrograde and ruthlessly exploitative British ruling class was at the heart of the Third Reich's domestic propaganda in the war years, and remained so to the end. Since it was never the sole theme of anti-British propaganda, however, it is useful to approach it in context.

By the later thirties, as we have seen, a gulf had become apparent between the leadership's views of Britain and those of ordinary Germans. The regime responded with a major initiative that grew in scope and intensity as war approached. This went beyond what might be called mere news management: the leadership now sought actively to mould the German image of Britain. Previously it had relied on (selected) voices from below to provide it and others with information; now it indicated what the tone of such information should be. There was no need even for formal guidelines. Daily newspaper coverage itself gave the authors of articles or books sufficient indication of what was expected of them. And both journalists and academics duly became more cautious in their praise of Britain. Yet even in the final year of peace, admiration and the old longing for an understanding with Britain often shone through. In 1939 an *Anglist* still felt able to observe in print that the 'kinship of spirit' between Germans and Britons ultimately 'transcended all [political] disputes of the day'.[2]

After the outbreak of war, however, all remnants of individuality vanished from the printed page. From September 1939 onwards, German perceptions of Britain essentially take three forms: official propaganda, to which everything published now conformed; the private opinions of the leadership; and the equally private opinions of the public, which reach the modern observer only in the rare cases where they were somehow committed to paper. The range of sources narrows, in other words, even as overall coverage of Britain is stepped up by the political centre.

Given the Third Reich's fragmented power structure, however, there were in fact several centres from which propaganda emanated. Apart from Hitler himself, who was always able to intervene when he chose to, this left three principal players: Goebbels, Ribbentrop, and Rosenberg. Of these, Rosenberg was perhaps the least influential in the war years. He retained control over publications directed in the main at party members, but his impact on the wider public was limited. Ribbentrop was *politically* important, at least in the early stages of the war, but his ability to reach a mass audience at home was similarly circumscribed. Lastly, there was Goebbels himself. He, of course, controlled all the major sources of propaganda inside the Reich; what is more, his actual power increased, as the military setbacks made his skills indispensable to the regime.

The output of these rival bureaucracies reflected the preoccupations of their respective masters. Rosenberg's main platform – the *Nationalsozialistische Monatshefte* – concerned itself principally with ideology and philosophy, along with the supposed machinations of Freemasons and 'world Jewry'.[3] Ribbentrop relied on the expertise of the academics working in his *Deutsches Institut für außenpolitische Forschung*. The books and articles they produced were therefore devoted to foreign policy, and aspects of international law or of Britain's history.[4] Goebbels' propaganda, by contrast, was more wide-ranging in scope, theme and target audience. But as with his rivals, the topics were connected with his personal interests, opinions, and, above all, prejudices.

Goebbels' crusade against what he called 'plutocracy' was central to the Third Reich's wartime propaganda. The theme of social injustice, which provided the emotive core of Nazi anti-capitalism, might seem directly connected with Goebbels' own beliefs. Yet, in reality, the Propaganda Ministry had stumbled across it almost by accident. There is little indication of concern in the early thirties about the fate of the British working class. National socialism, after all, was not interested in diluting by appeals to class consciousness the allegiance of any section of society towards the Volk. In that regard labour activists were as suspect as the aristocrats whose family ties cut across national borders, or Catholics, who owed obedience to a rival authority beyond Nazi control. Internationalism amounted to a lack of völkisch consciousness, and was not something the regime wished to encourage, even indirectly.

There was also, once again, simple ignorance about conditions in Britain. Nazi pronouncements in the early thirties were not merely guided by hopes of Anglo-German partnership; they were defined almost as much by the circumscribed factual knowledge of the leadership. One gets a clear indication of this from their response to Edward VIII's famous visit to South Wales. In a testy memorandum, an official in the Propaganda Ministry complained about the failure of German foreign correspondents to provide Berlin with adequate information: 'After all, the representatives of the German press might have been expected to become interested in British slums, even before the thing became topical because of the King's visit.'[5]

This is doubly revealing because there is in this no hint of sympathy for the plight of the British working class. If wartime propaganda later sought to suggest otherwise, it was merely another act of Nazi deception. Further proof that the regime had not suddenly embraced the workers' cause comes from another memorandum circulating in the Propaganda Ministry some six months later. It relates to a report about a failed strike in Britain. This elicited the comment that it was always useful to provide German workers with evidence of the futility of strikes.[6] Photographs and moving commentaries in wartime publications about the effect of lockouts in Britain are thus evidence only of the utter shamelessness of Goebbels' ministry.

Yet the two memoranda also reveal something else: they demonstrate a Nazi readiness to use events in Britain for essentially domestic purposes. The objective was at first not simply to blacken Britain's reputation – though, increasingly, that was a welcome side effect – but to point a political lesson for German audiences. The intended message might be the iniquity of strikes, or the equation of democracy and mass unemployment on the one hand, and, on the other, of National Socialism and

'Freedom and Bread', as the Nazi slogan put it.[7] Edward VIII's tour of South Wales and his subsequent visit to Germany must therefore have alerted several leading Nazis – Hitler and Goebbels included – to the topic of social conditions in Britain; and it must have suggested to them that this constituted a rich seam to be mined by Nazi propaganda.

Its usefulness was twofold: it would remind Germans of the achievements of National Socialist rule, notably the economic revival after 1933; and domestically it might counteract foreign criticism of the Third Reich. The former point is obvious, the latter may need explaining. As the thirties wore on, there was progressively more outspoken British criticism of what in modern parlance might be called the Third Reich's human-rights record: persecuted members of the clergy, for instance, or well-known pacifists incarcerated in concentration camps, to say nothing of the ever more overt harassment of Germany's Jews. There was no obvious answer to such criticism simply because it stated the truth. And it was difficult to ignore because of the high regard many Germans had for Britain. (British criticism was much more serious for the regime than French, Soviet or American criticism, which most Germans tended to reject out of hand.) The only possible response, therefore, short of alter-ing domestic practice, was to retaliate by undermining the moral cre-dentials of British critics. Sarcastic references to 'British humanitarianism' became a constant in Nazi propaganda.[8] It is therefore no accident that even such apolitical publications as the *Berliner Illustrierte Zeitung* started in the later thirties to print pictures of South Wales, Tyneside or the East End of London to demonstrate to German readers what British humanitarian-ism entailed at home.[9]

It is worth noting that this tactic effectively anticipated a similar response decades later by another totalitarian power: the Soviet Union. The Kremlin would habitually counter Western criticism about human rights by reminding the world of the unemployment rates of the major democracies; the right to work, the Soviets would point out, was enshrined in the United Nations Declaration of Human Rights.[10] Western politicians, it was thus suggested, invoked human rights only when they found it politically convenient; such blatant hypocrisy should therefore be treated with the contempt it deserved. Of course, Soviet defiance did not in any way invalidate Western criticism. But, equally, Western politi-cians were noticeably unable to respond to the Soviet argument directly, and their silence no doubt spoke for itself.

The concept of human rights had not been invented in the 1930s.

9   *A lockout*

Political pronouncements were thus couched in slightly different terms; but otherwise the parallels between the tactics of Soviet Communists in the final decades of the Iron Curtain and of the Nazis after about 1937 are striking. It may not necessarily prove that National Socialism merited its name, but it is a useful reminder that Nazi rhetoric at least was often undeniably socialist in tone. This was recognised by observers even at the time. What is more, the recognition was prompted specifically by the Third Reich's anti-British propaganda. In one of its regular reports about conditions in the Reich, the German Social Democrat party-in-exile noted the extraordinary similarity between Nazi and Marxist rhetoric: 'It is almost the old slogans of the Communists that are [now] being used against the "Western capitalist imperialists and plutocrats".'[11] It might thus be said – a little provocatively perhaps – that in 1939 the Nazi party rediscovered its left-wing heritage.

For the talk of 'plutocracy' was not just a matter of propaganda. It had obvious ideological resonance. It connected in particular with the aims and beliefs of the old radical wing of the Nazi party, which had been in abeyance since the expulsion of the Strasser brothers and the violent suppression of the faction around Ernst Röhm in 1934. It may be an exaggeration to suggest that this was a calculated appeal to a neglected Nazi constituency; but that anti-capitalist rhetoric would have appealed to

10   'I say, how about focusing on Britain for a change?' (The board in the background
reads, '2 million unemployed in Britain')

11   *A homeless woman*

that particular group, providing it with once again with apparent legitimacy and a renewed ideological focus, is surely undeniable. And to believe that Goebbels and Hitler himself – the chief exponents of the new line – were wholly unaware of this is surely to under-estimate the intelligence of the former and the very considerable political instincts of the latter. In the on-going debate about the internal dynamics of National Socialism and the Third Reich's social agenda the theme of 'British plutocracy' may thus represent significant, and neglected, evidence.

The explicit linkage between Britain and capitalism connected, moreover, with a strong political undertow inside the party, perceptible even after the Röhm affair. The influential SS newspaper, for instance, regularly excoriated the supposedly selfish practices of German business. There was also Robert Ley with his followers in the DAF – the German Labour Front. In an article in *Das Reich*, Ley was explicitly associated with 'what was socialist about National Socialism'.[12] This is directly relevant to German perceptions of Britain: Ley it was who had organised the Duke of Windsor's famous visit to Germany, which had confirmed in German minds the association of the Duke with social innovation (and by implication had identified as reactionaries those who had brought about his abdication). And there was Goebbels, who had enjoyed talking to the Duke about social issues, and who in the twenties had insisted that he was national *and* socialist. There was also Schirach who declared, neatly linking generational and class themes, 'Youth is Socialism, as the Hitler Youth . . . proves.'[13] Lastly, there was the Führer himself. In the *Table Talk*, Hitler remarks in late 1941 – significantly on the question of why Britain entered the war – that private enterprise 'everywhere was run by the same crooks'; the only time it ever invoked idealism was when the workers requested a pay rise. 'What . . . have you no sense of idealism?', would come the scandalised question.[14] This is not propaganda, this is conviction. And it leads to the curious thought that Hitler and Stalin – allies between 1939 and 1941 – might have shared the view that events at the time constituted a capitalist war.

This thought in turn reveals the true importance of the plutocratic theme to the Third Reich: it was used to explain why Germany was fighting Britain. As such, it holds the key to understanding how the war was 'sold' to a German public which had been noticeably unenthusiastic in 1938 about the prospect of going to war.

The unmistakable longing for peace among ordinary Germans during and after the Sudeten crisis had demonstrated to the Nazi leadership that there could be no simple repetition of 1914: appeals to patriotic sentiment would not necessarily motivate the country to the extent desired by the regime. It was therefore imperative to portray the Third Reich as the victim rather than the aggressor, hence the grisly charade in Upper Silesia of the supposed Polish incursion at Gleiwitz, where German political prisoners, dressed in Polish uniforms, were shot to provide suitable photographic evidence. In a sense, the very first victims of Hitler's war were German; and his first words to the German people on the morning of war were a lie written in blood. The regime was – and remained – determined to disguise at home what was obvious abroad. The desire to expand and acquire *Lebensraum* may have been the worst-kept of Nazi secrets, yet officially all the Third Reich was seeking was the return of German-speaking Danzig. The demands for Polish territory were not acknowledged. (As late as 1943 the SS newspaper exclaimed, 'And all this – it needs to be repeated again and again – solely to prevent Danzig from staying German'.)[15]

Given such apparently modest German aims, Britain's unexpected declaration of war provided a problem for the propagandists. It needed to be explained to the German public without revealing the true extent of earlier Nazi demands. References to the malice of specific British politicians were part of the strategy.[16] So were hints about the mental inflexibility of age. The Nazis' true stroke of genius, however, was to suggest that Danzig, or even Poland, were merely excuses for underlying British aggressiveness. The roots of the conflict were ideological. What was at issue supposedly was the future of capitalism itself. The Anglo-German war was, in a sense, a class war between capital and labour: 'the decisive struggle of Europe's revolution'.[17] It was fought by the 'moneybags' which featured so prominently in anti-British cartoons and targeted the toiling Aryan masses who, under the leadership of Adolf Hitler, had escaped the Tyranny of Gold.[18] The war was a conflict between a British plutocracy defending its right to exploit others at home and abroad, and a Reich whose guiding principle was the dignity of labour. 'It is not the German people as such they wish to destroy', declared the SS paper, 'but the socialist German people.'[19]

It is worth reflecting on how ingenious this line of argument was. It did much more than merely divert attention from Germany's attack on Poland. For one thing, it put the blame for the war, against all the evidence, on Britain, and did so by supposedly enabling ordinary Germans to see through enemy propaganda. The titles of anti-British books and

12   *'In the supposedly free democracies the police act in the interest of the ruling class'*

pamphlets of the early years of the war reveal that strategy clearly. The recurring imagery is that of 'slipping masks', of Britain's 'true face' exposed or of 'the truth revealed'.[20]

Explaining the war in economic and social terms, moreover, referred directly to the self-image of the Third Reich. In the Nazi view of the 1930s, Germany had overcome class conflict by rejecting the capitalist system. Instead, the leadership provided an overall framework in which employers and employees were co-operating for the good of the nation. Actual ownership of a company, suggested the SS newspaper, was now 'completely irrelevant'.[21] The new economic order had, in the Nazi phrase, put 'the common interest before individual interest'. National Socialism had 'turned the unemployed into workers and workers into genuine citizens'.[22] Freeing Germany 'from the clutches of capitalism' had changed the lives of millions: workers now enjoyed guaranteed holidays and the means 'to travel through their fatherland like lords in chequered trousers'; cars were being designed for them, and even foreign travel on cruise ships had become possible.[23] In a remarkable anticipation of post-war stereotypes, the SS paper suggested that here lay one of the roots of hostility to the Reich: British tourists resented having suddenly to share beaches with Germans. After all, as the French said, *Egoïste comme un anglais.*[24]

Germany's revolution was thus profoundly unwelcome to the moneyed classes in Britain. It represented a double threat: at home, the working class might start to wonder why their country was unable to provide them with the standard of living Germany offered her nationals.[25] The British Empire owned a quarter of the globe but supposedly lacked the means to offer its workers a minimum level of comfort. Germany's example was therefore acutely dangerous and had to be destroyed at all costs.[26] 'They [i.e. the British government] hate us for our social convictions', Hitler said in 1940 at the beginning of Winter Relief, 'and our plans and actions [in the social field] seem dangerous to them.'[27] Abroad, other nations might follow the Third Reich's example of autarky, which would ultimately affect the banks in the City of London, and thus 'the Lords of the interest rates'.[28] Britain's future standard of living would depend on what she was able to produce by the sweat of her brow rather than by demanding lucrative commissions.[29] Neither thought was welcome to Britain's political class with its banking and landowning background.

Lord Halifax's reported claim that the war was in defence of everything 'that made life worth living' was therefore in propaganda terms the wrong thing for a peer of the realm to say. The German press conceded gleefully that it had an undeniable ring of honesty about it.[30] It seemed to prove the Nazis' point: war had been unleashed by a small and utterly irresponsible group in Britain, eager to protect their sectional interests. (Here, propaganda blended with conviction: Britain's decision

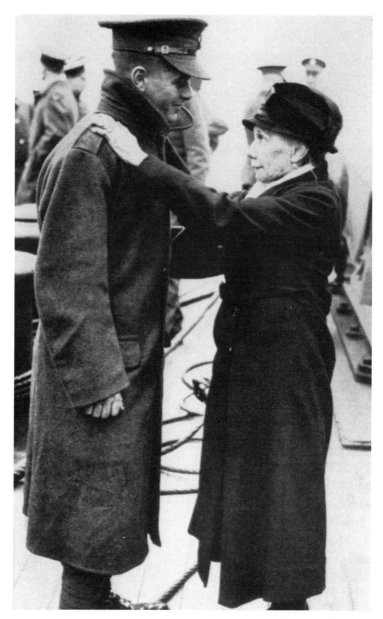

13   'Called to service to defend the interests of the ruling class'

to go to war, Hitler confided to his inner circle in 1942, had been reached 'in a couple of country houses before 1939';[31] Nazi social measures had been 'much resented' there, and judged 'unfair' practice, because they threatened the 'carefree' existence of Britain's ruling class.)[32]

This account of plutocratic self-interest had a further advantage: it allowed the regime to distinguish between the British people and their rulers. This left a door open to future reconciliation. The Nazi leadership believed for a long time that Britain would withdraw from the conflict eventually. In the meantime it was best to be circumspect. 'Nothing must be said to offend the people of Britain', noted Goebbels in his diary in 1940; our quarrel is only with 'Churchill and his clique'.[33] Even if a reconciliation were not to occur, such self-restraint would have been worthwhile in propaganda terms. It would have demonstrated at home and abroad the goodwill of the regime, and would thus have conciliated those Germans who still harboured friendly feelings towards Britain. Lastly, it would have denied the British authorities the opportunity to exploit German hostility to shore up domestic support. (Hitler always maintained that Churchill's failure to distinguish, in threatening retribution, between ordinary Germans and the Nazi leadership was a colossal error, which had greatly strengthened the Nazis' position at home.)[34]

Distinguishing between an exploited British nation and its morally bankrupt rulers also tied in conveniently with previous observations about an effete, pleasure-seeking and ineffectual leadership, whose only perceptible qualification was that in their youth they had worn 'top hats at Eton'.[35] This gave official pronouncements a welcome logical coherence. Indeed, it is striking how seamlessly the strands of Nazi propaganda connect at this stage of the war. The subject of capitalism, of banks, shares and the stock exchange offered a natural opportunity to introduce familiar racial leitmotivs. Photographs of British financiers were carefully chosen to illustrate the point.[36] The supposed political ramifications were explained by the SS newspaper in characteristically distasteful style: once 'a certain bank balance had been reached', Jewish businessmen found it easy 'to glide' into the House of Lords, guided 'as if on rails' by 'the gentle . . . curvature of their noses'.[37]

In the words of a study published in 1940, the Jewish penetration of Britain's aristocracy by elevation or intermarriage had been 'pointed out too many times in recent years' to require further elaboration; it would suffice to note that 'Half-Jews were closing in on the throne itself.'[38] (There was even a hint that the Jews had advanced further than

14   *'Characteristic features at the British stock exchange'*

the throne room. A photograph of Edward VII – traditionally associated in Germany with the *entente cordiale* and the 'encircling' of imperial Germany – was accompanied by the observation that the King looked remarkably semitic; his mother, Queen Victoria, the study added, had admitted Jews freely to her court.)[39] Such observations, in turn, helped explain why a Nordic nation should be fighting the Third Reich. (Nazi *Rassenkunde*, which had earlier attested to Britain's Nordic status, now pointed portentously to Manchester or the East End of London, and spoke of progressive de-nordification in all strata of British society.)[40]

Above all, the plutocratic theme allowed the regime to revive memories of the Depression. The first ever issue in May 1940 of Goebbels' publishing showpiece *Das Reich* – a Nazi equivalent of a British Sunday broadsheet – demonstrates that strategy clearly.[41] Germany, the paper explained, was now waging war against those 'who had regarded the permanent impoverishment of the German people as the surest guarantee for their own affluence and bloated luxury'. Their 'brutal financial policies' had resulted in the unemployment of millions of German workers. (The article uses the emotive word *brotlos* – literally 'breadless' – to described the fate of the unemployed.) 'Such was the order, such the freedom which the Financial Powers of the West had introduced to Europe'. Now, with Germany throwing off her chains, and able once again to feed and clothe herself, the cry was going out to save '"the freedom of the world and the highest values of mankind"'. Germany had tasted that freedom and knew exactly 'what the British have in mind when they speak of the highest values'.[42] The British war aim, the article concluded, was to preserve Britain's 'financial dictatorship' over Europe.

This piece probably speaks for itself. Two observations, however, should perhaps be made. *Das Reich* had as its target audience the educated middle classes — the so-called *Bildungsbürgertum*. It is worth noting that an article about the plight of unemployed workers was apparently considered likely to motivate such an audience politically. The explanation for this lies in the scale of the Depression which Germany had experienced at the beginning of the 1930s: almost everyone had been touched by it in some way. Companies were bankrupted, businesses were forced to close, banks and insurance companies collapsed, and those who escaped unemployment were cheated of their savings and had their earnings sharply decreased. For the second time in a decade millions had been reduced to destitution.

The Depression remained a national trauma long afterwards, scarcely lessened by the subsequent recovery. Its effect was still perceptible in West German financial policy decades later. Before and during the war, it was one of the most potent weapons in the armoury of Nazi domestic propaganda. It is no accident that it should have been deployed in 1939–40 to help reconcile the German public to the war. It is no accident either that it was used again in the Third Reich's dying days: a desperate attempt to rally support not just for the war this time, but for the regime itself. In one of its final issues in 1945 — appearing by an unhappy coincidence on April Fools' Day — *Das Reich* proclaimed, 'We are fighting for freedom, we are fighting for socialism, which alone permits dignity and freedom.'[43]

It will have become clear that Britain was effectively used as a foil by Nazi propaganda. The country represented not merely the forces ranged against the Third Reich, it also served to remind the German people of the values for which they were supposedly fighting. It is therefore useful to examine more closely one of the numerous anti-British books produced in the early years of the war. *Die verlorene Insel* ('The Doomed Isle') is a particularly striking example. It might be described as a coffee-table book: it is lavishly illustrated and offers only brief comments on each page. It relies, in other words, on the effect the images would produce on German readers.

15   *Hungry and unemployed*

Analysing the selection of photographs therefore provides useful clues about the ideological intention that had shaped the volume.

The book starts with geography: images of dramatic coastline, dry stone walls in bleakest Yorkshire, and sheep grazing on barren Highland landscapes. It then switches to the Home Counties with its country houses set in extensive grounds. Already important points have been made subliminally: the richest soil is held by the richest landowners, while the rural poor eke out an existence on marginal lands. The rich, moreover, and this the accompanying text states explicitly, do not use the land for agricultural purposes but have turned it into parks 'ideal for fox hunting'.[44] (The house chosen to illustrate the political fecklessness of the aristocracy is, amusingly enough, Cliveden: clearly no one in Berlin recognised it.)

The same page also contains a reference to the Highland Clearances, which, readers were informed, had created perfect conditions for shooting. Photos and text combined, therefore, made a solid political point. For this was an island, as the Hitler speech in the book's introduction had emphasised, which did not produce enough food to feed its people, and not enough work to allow them to purchase food. The fate of the rural poor in the past two centuries was thus directly related to that of the miners of South Wales in the 1930s or of the Jarrow Marchers – of

16   *Jarrow Marchers*

whom the book also contained photographs. None of these phenomena had been accidents; they were the consequence of Britain's style of government. They were proof of the callous indifference of Britain's rulers to the suffering of those they nominally represented in Parliament.

The supposed readiness of Britain's ruling class to ignore the needs of others was a recurring motif – not least because it was intended to point to the superiority of Germany's *Volksgemeinschaft*. Sometimes this took the form of malicious misinterpretation: images of huntsmen riding past a bombed house, for instance, or Duff Cooper finishing his breakfast during a German air raid on France were not treated as examples of sangfroid in Goebbels' press.[45] (The image of the huntsmen enjoying a day's sport amid the devastation was allowed to speak for itself; the undisturbed breakfast occasioned the observation that raids on *France* evidently had not diminished British joie de vivre.)[46]

But there was also more substantial evidence. The wartime evacuation of British children to Canada was as suggestive as the differing diets in the West and East Ends of London. Photos of working-class children being told to seek cover under their desks during an air raid drill at an East End school were contrasted with well-groomed boys disembarking at Montreal in the safety of distant Canada: 'third from the left is Lord March' explained the *Berliner Illustrierte*, the boy to his 'right is Lord

Edward Cavendish'.[47] A week later the paper showed society ladies arriving in North America.[48] Tales of gold, jewellery and race horses heading across the Atlantic were likewise common in 1940, and all the more effective for using the tones of old-style society reporting. 'War', gloated the SS paper, 'reliably demonstrates people's true worth'; the same, it added, went for forms of government.[49]

The German public, however, never got to hear about aspects of the Blitz that might have borne out the regime's anti-plutocratic propaganda. The catastrophic shortage of air raid shelters in the East End, highlighted by the appalling loss of life in Bethnal Green tube station, and the often uneasy reaction in the West End to temporary refugees from the eastern parts of town were deliberately not covered in the German press. The Propaganda Ministry was fearful that this might incite adverse comments about shortcomings in the Reich's own provision of shelters.[50] Stories of British aristocrats paying their way to safety, or rewarding themselves with lobster and champagne if they could not, therefore were evidence above all of the Nazis' own cynicism.

The effectiveness of such tales is hard to gauge. In the specific case of shellfish extravagance it seems doubtful. Much of Germany is continental rather than maritime in outlook, and beyond the coastal regions seafood traditionally held little allure to German palates. Most seafood remained unrationed. In an unmistakable dig at Goebbels' propaganda, the Princess Vassiltchikov thus records in her diary on 27 November 1940: 'Dined with [Prince] Paul Metternich . . . Ate lobster and other unrationed plutocratic delicacies.'

Evidence that Nazi propaganda did not always have the intended effect also comes from the files of the SD. Lurid accounts of plutocratic excess in Mayfair and of destitution further east had acquainted some Germans with the rudiments of London geography. This had unwelcome consequences. Himmler's agents overheard people wondering why the Luftwaffe kept bombing the East End; did that not mean that the poor rather than the rich were being hit?[51] Reports about the plutocratic lifestyle had also led to 'the wish being expressed to hear more about life in English clubs'.[52] Evidently, as the Communists were also to discover in Eastern Europe, tales of capitalist extravagance could captivate as much as repel.

This thought brings us back to the photographs of *Die verlorene Insel*. It is by no means certain that the images of the plutocratic lifestyle which take up about a third of the book would have induced outrage in German

17   'Growing old in the East End'

readers. The more effective ones may well have been those whose intention was apparently satirical: images of debutantes practising their curt-
sies before an empty throne, or effete young men in extravagant outfits at
Henley. But Nazi propaganda aimed at a cumulative effect. This is also true
of *Die verlorene Insel*. Individual photographs all carried an overt or sometimes merely a coded message; but only taken as a whole did they achieve

their full impact. All the familiar themes of anti-British propaganda – senility, degeneracy, Jewish infiltration, the links between government and business, etc. – are sounded but the effect lies in their synthesis: what emerges is the notion of a misgoverned land.

Housing conditions in Britain exemplified this. The insistence on building individual houses rather than flats was characteristic. In a small island with limited space, it was evidence of inefficient land use. This was nothing to do with individuality: a visit to any British suburb would quickly dispel the notion that the British valued architectural variety: 'the monotony is unimaginable to Continental minds', as one newspaper put it.[53] The true reason, it seemed to the Nazis, was that the interests of the developers always took precedence. Mass-produced suburban houses were cheaper to build. Construction on cheaper land at some distance from the town centres increased profit margins.

The result was a brick tide advancing in all directions from town centres, eating up Britain's glorious countryside.[54] The absence of planning in all this was striking. London was the only major city in Europe that had no overall authority to take strategic decisions. The property speculators would not have welcomed one. Freedom in a plutocracy, as countless Nazi books and articles pointed out, was the freedom of the rich to become richer still, even if that meant compromising the national interest. The spread of suburbia, for instance, created further problems: people had to commute to work, where in a continental city they might be only a short tram ride away. It was not uncommon, German readers were told, for people in London to spend an hour and more each day in dirty and overcrowded trains.[55] As for the railways, the state of the trains and of many stations was lamentable. There was in this, one of the world's most affluent countries, a startling lack of investment. But then, as the SS newspaper pointed out, Britain's railways were not state-owned. And private enterprise put the interests of shareholders above those of passengers.[56] Wherever Nazi observers looked, the evidence seemed to point in the same direction: Britain was a country organised for the benefit of the richest section of society. The plutocrats misgoverned with apparent impunity.

This notion leads to one of the most lavish and ingenious examples of Nazi anti-capitalist propaganda: the German film about the sinking of the *Titanic*. The plot of the film provided ample scope for displays of plutocratic callousness.[57] The lack of lifeboats, the company's reckless pursuit of profit, and the instinct of the British authorities to put free

18   First-class passengers abandoning ship

enterprise before passenger safety, were all grist to Nazi propaganda. The ship itself, and its fate, seemed symbolic of Britain. The different classes of passengers were strictly segregated, just as the social classes were in Britain. (It was possible, noted an article in *Das Reich*, 'to spend a lifetime in Britain' and hardly ever come into contact 'with the centres of poverty';[58] suburbs were popular not only with developers but with a middle class which tried to emulate its betters in their contempt for the poor.)[59] The *Titanic* with its different decks allowed such points to emerge clearly.

On board the *Titanic*, your income decided not merely what food you ate, but whether you were allowed to see the sun and breathe fresh air – for the sleeping quarters of the poor were hidden away in subaquatic gloom – and ultimately whether or not you stayed alive: places in the life-boats were given by preference to the more affluent passengers. The poor were left to drown. This, the Nazis thought, reflected life in Britain most accurately. Everything from cradle to grave, from schooling to health care, depended on whether or not you had the funds to pay for adequate services.

19   *Water flooding the lower decks of the* Titanic

Intriguingly, the film was not actually shown in Germany, though it was released in occupied France. The reasons for this are not entirely clear. The film's director had been denounced by an informer for defeatism and committed suicide. This may have affected his film, but it is also possible that the scenes of mass panic were judged inappropriate against a background of intensifying RAF bombing.[60] Whatever, the precise circumstances, Titanic thus achieved the rare distinction of being banned both by the Nazis and by Allied censors after 1945.

Titanic may have been the most spectacular example of Goebbels' ministerial campaign against the plutocratic enemy, but it was by no means its only vehicle. At the height of anti-British propaganda, between the fall of France and the Russian campaign, a vast number of articles, books and pamphlets were produced. These often provided quite detailed information about social conditions in Britain and the history of British capitalism. Foreign sources were given great prominence, in the hope no doubt of heightening the impact of their damning descriptions of Britain. From Ledru-Rollin's *De la Décadence de l'Angleterre* to the writings of Shaw, H. G. Wells or George Orwell (who thus featured in propaganda on both sides), or

Lloyd George's parliamentary speeches, the range of sources was impressive.[61]

Such wealth of material was largely due to the quiet dedication of German students. In November 1939 the Nazi Student League had offered the Propaganda Ministry its services in collecting material to discredit Britain. In February 1940 Goebbels and Rust, the Minister of Education, formally asked for student help.[62] The so-called *Studentischer Kriegspropagandaeinsatz* seems to have involved at its height in 1940 about 6,000 volunteers.[63] It is not quite clear, however, how voluntary such services really were. Students were a privileged minority in wartime society, and conscious of their privilege; and conscious, too, one imagines, of how easily their sojourn at university might end. Even so, enthusiasm seems gradually to have flagged. This was in part because the Third Reich had, true to its instincts, instituted a division of labour: female students had been allotted the gruelling task of collecting material; men then wrote up what their intellectual handmaidens had amassed. 'The girls are not really enjoying the constant trailing through books . . . since they never have the chance to use the material', noted a report from Berlin's universities.[64] This adds a certain piquancy to a publication in the *England ohne Maske* series, which excoriated the exploitation of women in Britain.[65]

The purpose of this vast amount of material was twofold: to discredit Britain and her rulers in German eyes, and to emphasise the superiority of National Socialism. No opportunity was missed to portray Britain's governing class as hypocrites, concerned about the welfare of humanity in every country but their own. The study on exploited women, for instance, referred to a Victorian parliamentary debate in 1842 to make that point: as the peers turned their attention to social issues, 'the Archbishop of Canterbury and the Bishop of London left the House'.[66] Already in December 1938, the German press had reported about a debate on the plight of the South Wales valleys: out of 615 MPs, a total of nineteen had attended the debate.[67] Goebbels' own *Das Reich* painted an atmospheric picture of supposedly archetypal British gentlemen agreeing over the port about the iniquity of wasting taxpayers' money on the indigent; for the poor, God willing, would always be with one.[68] A study about British slums invited its readers to reflect on the fact that there was no German word for 'slums'.[69] (It then proceeded to explain what a 'back-to-back' was.)

There were references to the startling discrepancies in the life expectancy of the inhabitants of the West and East Ends of London. Health

20   'Growing up in the East End'

statistics were also given for industrial areas further afield: in Newcastle
17 per cent of schoolchildren had been judged in 1938 to be suffering
from malnutrition. The figure for Gateshead was 22 per cent, that for
Durham 21 per cent; 'and this in a nation which controls the riches of half
the globe'.[70] It was pointed out that rickets, a classic illness associated
with deprivation, had traditionally been known in Germany as *die englische
Krankheit* – the English disease. Mention was also made of the fact that
London had only acquired proper sanitation once the ruling class itself

began to die of cholera. Then, suddenly, taxpayers' money had become available. The picture that emerged of Britain's rulers was at best one of callousness, at worst of criminal irresponsibility. 'Do not even try to understand the British ruling class', Goebbels suggested in one of his articles for *Das Reich*, because they defied comprehension; theirs was 'a different, an alien, an evil world'.[71]

It is no accident either that the Third Reich enthusiastically embraced the novels of A. J. Cronin. Now largely forgotten, they were once popular in Britain too. They centre on Cronin's own experience as a doctor and inspector of mines in South Wales. The picture they paint of workers and their families all but abandoned to their fate and unable to afford the treatment that might cure them is as powerful as it is disturbing. Without being overtly political, they are undeniably an indictment of Britain in the 1930s, and were recognised as such in Berlin. Cronin's work was printed in large numbers and remained available after other British authors had been banned. Germans might have been prevented from reading about British detectives, or British drawing-rooms, but novels set in British slums were readily available. As late as April 1944, when paper shortages had all but destroyed the Reich's publishing, Viktor Klemperer noted Cronin's literary presence in the windows of practically every bookshop in his hometown of Dresden.[72]

What will have become clear is that anti-capitalist propaganda relied on a perception of a contrast between Germany and Britain: a contrast that did not have to be elaborated but was immediately, implicitly felt. It was enough to show photographs of a street in Stepney or Whitechapel.[73] It was enough to show people sleeping rough on the Embankment. It was enough to show the unemployed queuing up outside the labour exchange. The people in such photographs, the Nazi press conceded, were technically free. It was just that 'they lacked the freedom to work, the freedom to earn their living, the freedom to care for their families'.[74] There was no democracy in Germany, the press admitted, but objectively Germans had greater freedom: for without freedom from want there could be no freedom worthy of the name. Democracy, in the title of a book published in 1940, was simply a *Komödie der Freiheit* ('A Freedom Farce').[75]

This was not simply socialist thought, it also appealed in a sense to a German tradition going back to Bismarck, or even further to Germany's enlightened rulers in the eighteenth century. The notion of a special responsibility for the weakest of their subjects had been taken

21   'In a British slum'

seriously by some of the most celebrated monarchs of German absolut-
ism, both of the Habsburg and the Hohenzollern dynasties. But with that
concern came a re-affirmation of their own unlimited authority. The
notion of the state (or of the crown) as a benevolent factor in society thus
predated socialism in Germany by a century and more. It was here that
Bismarck famously detected a way of neutralising socialism, hence the
development in Germany, under an autocratic regime hostile to democracy, of the world's first welfare state.

National Socialism therefore could portray itself as being the
rightful inheritor of a German tradition in social welfare. And the economic catastrophes of hyperinflation and mass unemployment, which
had destroyed the Weimar Republic, could be credibly associated with
parliamentary government. The evidence both from Germany itself, or
from Britain, seemed to prove that point. To put it in the crude terms of
modern political advertising, the Nazi message was: 'democracy is not
working'. And however uncomfortable the thought may seem to us now,
that notion was entirely persuasive in the 1930s. Part of the success of the
Nazis was their ability to allow ordinary people, buffeted by twentieth-
century history, to make sense of their experience. The faceless and anonymous forces that had deprived them of their income, their savings, their
property were explained in apparently convincing terms. More than that,

22   'Homeless men on the Embankment'

the Nazis gave ordinary Germans the illusion of recovering control over their own lives. The international forces ranged against the individual had been challenged by the Third Reich, and dignity had been restored to their erstwhile victims. The economic revival, moreover, seemed to demonstrate the validity of Nazi arguments. The observation that it is difficult to argue with success may be trite but it certainly described the Third Reich in 1939. Economic historians may point out that the Nazi economy was unstable and heading for crisis; the great mass of the German public, at the time, saw only the success.

This meant that the Nazis, too, were able to suggest in 1939 (and beyond) that the war was about the defence of ideals and moral values. The combatants on the Allied side, we know, were motivated not just by patriotism; images of invading Nazi armies, of Jews assaulted in the streets as their shops and synagogues burnt, were potent factors. Less familiar may be the notion that the Germans, too, were not merely following patriotic instincts. They were driven by memories of the Depression: of 'the British peace', 'or the blessings of democracy', as the Nazi media called them in retrospect.[76] And they were driven also by the thought that beyond the Third Reich's borders these conditions of unemployment and destitution persisted, and were ready to return should Britain win the war. Commenting on Britain's initially mild plans for Germany, the SS paper explained: 'They [i.e. the British government] are being generous: they do not intend to treat us any worse than they have treated their own countrymen.' Germany would have to give up National Socialism and be given as its reward 'what the Welsh miners had been granted'.[77] It is a sobering thought that the domestic record of British governments between the wars – rather than talk of *Lebensraum* – was considered the supreme argument to persuade ordinary Germans to fight for a Nazi victory.

News of Britain's plans for a post-war welfare state therefore acutely threatened the effectiveness of Nazi propaganda. Goebbels countered by claiming on behalf of the Third Reich intellectual parenthood for those reforms. The British plutocrats had agreed to Beveridge's proposals because they saw no other way of winning future elections.[78] The example of the Third Reich had changed British politics. The suggestion that this was an indigenous British initiative was brushed aside. Why, after all, had such native British idealism not flowered before the Third Reich came into being? The current British government was made up of individuals who had held various offices in the inter-war years. Goebbels suggested a simple question: 'You were in power [then]; why did you not act?'[79] Any British cabinet minister would experience the 'most severe embarrassment were he to be called upon to explain what British democracy had achieved since Versailles . . . in the way of enabling the masses to lead lives more commensurate with human dignity'.[80]

Already in 1940 *Das Reich* had commented on British plans for social reform by claiming direct Nazi influence: 'Strange though it may sound, it is an undeniable fact that the British discovered that there is something wrong with their [political] system only after they got to know National Socialism.' The Third Reich had 'become the tutor' to 'British democracy'.[81] (After the war, British officials in Germany – many of them left-leaning – congratulated themselves on having taught Germans how to construct a successful parliamentary democracy. Their students were in no position to argue. Yet it seems likely that some of them secretly congratulated themselves on having taught the British about the need for a welfare state. Anglo-German relations abound in ironies.)

The effectiveness of the Third Reich's anti-plutocratic propaganda is, inevitably, difficult to determine accurately. The regime certainly believed in the picture it painted of Britain. Hitler judged a revolution 'of gruesome proportions' a distinct possibility, and thought it likely that Britain's rulers had at least tried to prepare for it: 'I fancy there are certain regiments that they [the British government] would be reluctant to send overseas.'[82] Ordinary Germans, too, evidently came to believe in large numbers that a revolution was probable. The SD monitored widespread rumours in December 1940 of imminent upheaval in Britain.[83] (Rumours about the return to the throne of the Duke of Windsor should also be borne in mind: the Duke, after all, was strongly associated with social reform.)

The limitations are no less obvious. As Britain held out, confounding both the regime's private and public prognoses, the German people began to revise their judgement. Only seven weeks after the rumours of revolution, the SD reported doubts about the reliability of the German media: 'Reports about social conditions in Britain continue to meet with a critical reaction: the people of Britain surely did not feel they were languishing under a plutocratic regime.'[84] Even less welcome to the Nazi leadership must have been the second part of that report. It records that popular reaction to descriptions of social inequality in Britain and preferential treatment for those who could pay frequently led to the observation, 'Well, it's no different here.'

To this should be added anecdotal evidence of an even more fundamental kind. Viktor Klemperer records an incident in June 1940, at the height of the anti-plutocratic campaign. An acquaintance turned to him and enquired, 'what does plutocracy mean?' Klemperer duly noted in his diary 'I wonder how many of the *Volksgenossen* [the National Comrades] actually know.'[85] Even if this were a relatively isolated incident, it is a useful reminder that there were limitations to Nazi propaganda: not everyone was interested, not everyone even understood it, and not everyone, of course, was ready to believe it. It follows that limitations of propaganda grew apace with the worsening situation at the front.

Yet there can be little doubt either that the theme of social reformers in Germany versus Britain — *the Reactionary, Britain's Social Backwardness*, or 'The Land without Socialism', as wartime titles put it, was one of the strongest cards the Nazis held.[86] It is surely no accident that politically minded university lecturers had identified social issues, in a submission to the leadership, as the most promising avenue of anti-British propaganda.[87] Among the enemies of National Socialism there was much the same impression. In their report of 6 July 1939, the agents for the German Social Democrat party-in-exile had noted with despair the effectiveness of the Nazi argument about full employment.[88] All political arguments of covert Social Democrats were powerless against the simple mantra that there was no one without a job now.

But it is again an entry from the Klemperer diaries that puts it most succinctly. In 1944, when he began to doubt that as a Jew he would live to see the Nazi defeat, the renewed anti-plutocratic theme – this time with an added American angle – led to this mournful observation: 'the Nazis may have miscalculated strategically but assuredly never in propaganda terms'.[89]

6 'The chorus of hypocrites': history and propaganda

'I have never left the slightest doubt', said Hitler in a speech in April 1939, 'that the existence of this Empire [i.e. the British] . . . represents an inestimable value for the culture and economy of mankind.' He admitted that it had been founded 'through violence' – 'often the most brutal violence' – but history was interested only in 'success' and 'less in the method' employed to achieve it.[1] Paradoxically, the fact that Hitler had indeed been unstinting in his praise presented a problem for Nazi propaganda as war approached. It was difficult suddenly to attack what one had habitually extolled.

This put the Third Reich in an unprecedented position. Britain's historic rivals – the United States, France and Imperial Germany – had always been able to point to the record of the British Empire to achieve a contrast between the iniquities of Albion and their own conspicuous virtue. The founders of the American constitution – slave owners almost to a man – decried the lack of liberty in Britain's Empire. The France of Napoleon was shocked at Britain's bellicosity; Imperial Germany was appalled by the brutality of British colonialism. A large measure of hypocrisy, in other words, had traditionally oiled the wheels of history and helped sustain the image of unique righteousness which each of the Great Powers claimed for itself.

Having publicly identified with the British Empire, the Third Reich was initially reluctant to use imperial history as a weapon against Britain. There thus existed on the level of propaganda much the same problem the Nazis faced more generally: how to react to British hostility, which had simply not been anticipated to such a degree. The solution came to the Nazi leadership almost by accident. As Britain (and America) raised their voices in protest against German entry into Prague, Hitler and his collaborators were genuinely angered by that response. It seemed to them unwarranted. Each of the Great Powers had its sphere of influence. Britain possessed an Empire: in the late thirties British forces were in action, suppressing 'native' rebellion in India and the Middle East. The United States in its sphere of influence preferred to maintain the fiction of Latin American independence, but deposed governments, and invaded countries in the region at will, and largely controlled their economies. Germany was now expanding into Eastern Europe. It was surely unreasonable to deny the Germans what one demanded as of right for oneself. To do so was an act of hypocrisy. This represented Nazi convictions, not simply propaganda. Yet out of such conviction arose the Third Reich's public response to Anglo-Saxon criticism.

The defining moment perhaps came after an intervention by President Roosevelt in April 1939. In a well-intentioned but thoroughly ill-advised move, the President had demanded guarantees that the freedom of a long list of named countries would be respected. Hitler glanced at the list, saw his chance and seized it. In a bravura performance before a specially convened Reichstag, he declared himself happy to give the requested assurances in the majority of cases.[2] There were some countries on the list, however, where he declared himself unable to do so: Syria's freedom, for instance, he would not guarantee, on the grounds that one could not uphold what did not exist; Syria was not free, but a French mandate. Roosevelt had in effect given Hitler the opportunity to remind the world of Allied colonialism, and, more particularly, of the secret Anglo-French agreement on the eve of the Paris peace conferences. Britain and France had decided to divide the Arab world between themselves, in flagrant violation not just of Wilsonian principle but of solemn wartime undertakings to the Arabs.

There was more. Roosevelt had also mentioned Ireland. Hitler promptly reminded him that Prime Minister de Valera had only recently spoken of threats to Ireland's independence. 'Oddly enough', said Hitler, de Valera did not appear to have in mind a *German* threat.[3] (Churchill periodically thought aloud about the need to seize Irish ports.) Lastly, there was Palestine. Like Syria, it was the result of broken promises. It had, moreover, featured regularly in the news during the later thirties: its native population had been engaged in prolonged protest against British rule and Jewish immigration. Britain suppressed this by force, thus providing the Third Reich with useful propaganda targets. (In December

23   'Christmas 1938: in Germany and in the British Empire'

1938, for instance, there were cartoons of mangers being blown skyward, or of German Christmas trees and British machine guns; the captions read, 'Christmas in Germany' and 'Christmas in the British Empire'.) The Third Reich's public response to British criticism in the final months of peace is probably best summed up by the editorial headline, 'People in glass houses'.[4]

After September 1939, the Nazi leadership mounted a comprehensive attack on Britain's reputation in Germany. Public speeches were accompanied by the publication of a wide range of books and pamphlets about British history. These started to appear rapidly after the outbreak of hostilities. Much of the material had already been used in shorter form. The intense press campaign following the annexation of the rump Czech state in the spring of 1939 had served as a dress rehearsal[5] (some of the material was also simply recycled from the more improvised efforts during the First World War).[6] These publications were designed to appeal to different sections of the public, though together they aimed to reach the entire nation.

Anti-British material ranged from pseudo-academic studies to lurid accounts of British iniquity. A book like *England ohne Maske* ('Britain Unmasked'), which became the source of much derivative material, supposedly aimed at objectivity. Its dust jacket insisted that it sought only to offer facts and would leave it to the reader to decide whether the absence of such facts in German history was a matter of regret or something to be profoundly 'thankful' for.[7] *Das ist England:Weltherrschaft durch Blut und Gold* ('This is Britain: World Domination by Blood and Gold'), evidently did not wish to burden its readers with such decisions.[8] (The title, incidentally, echoed almost verbatim Hitler's own sentiments in his earliest Munich days).[9] There was also *Bibel, Scheckbuch und Kanonen* ('Bible, Chequebook and Cannons').[10] Such books were supplemented by more detailed studies. Most of these were published by Ribbentrop's *Deutsches Institut für außenpolitische Forschung*. Its series *Das britische Reich in der Weltpolitik* ('The British Empire in World Politics') ran to some two dozen volumes, covering with thoroughness every doubtful aspect of British rule from Aden to Zanzibar. If the anti-plutocratic campaign was Goebbels' hour, then the examination of Britain's imperial record was Ribbentrop's moment. This did not mean, however, that the Propaganda Ministry had no input. There was in effect a division of labour: Ribbentrop's academics catered for the educated middle classes, Goebbels for the masses. (The books' titles are usually a reliable guide to their respective provenance: *Britain's Political Morality in Her Own Words*, for instance, versus *Britain's Trail of Blood*.)[11]

Initially, there were often explicit attempts to relate British history to contemporary events. The most obvious one was Britain's declaration of war itself. As in 1914, it had been Britain that had declared war on Germany, not the other way round. It was thus useful to examine Britain's wider record. The book *England ohne Maske* did so in a chapter entitled 'British militarism'. Quoting no less an authority than J. R. Seeley, it noted that in the period between the Glorious Revolution and the Battle of Waterloo, Britain had been involved in seven major wars; during those 126 years, she had been at war for sixty-four years: in other words, for more than half the time.[12] In the ensuing period from Waterloo to the Great War, it was noted that Britain was again more often engaged in conflict than not; during the same ninety-nine years, Germany was at peace for all but ten. Another source calculated that in the last 500 years Britain had fought some 250 wars.[13] A Berlin newspaper published 'A Balance Sheet of British Peacefulness for 1854–1914': from the wars against the Ashanti, to those against the Zulu it counted forty-two in eighty years.[14] The figures surely spoke for themselves.

The Royal Navy's blockade was likewise analysed. In the early stages of the war it not only affected Germany but inconvenienced the neutral vessels of Scandinavia and the Low Countries. This, too, was not without historical resonance. Did not the roots of the British Empire lie in the piracy of Drake? Britain, in other words, was merely reverting to type. (Nazi *Rassenkunde*, after all, considered national characteristics to be fixed for all time in a nation's 'blood'.) It was significant, therefore, that Britain, alone among the nations of Europe, regarded pirates as national heroes and gloried in their bloody attacks on foreign ships and shores. *Seeräuberstaat England* ('Britain – Nation of Pirates') – a book written by a retired rear-admiral of the Kaiser's fleet – sought to provide the historical detail. The rear-admiral nimbly spanned the centuries. Had not Nelson seized the fleet of neutral Denmark, bombarding Copenhagen without war even being declared? And did the British not admire him for it still? It was not at all difficult to imagine what Britain's reaction would have been if Germany had carried out such an unprovoked attack. One merely had to look at the example of Belgium in the First World War. The bombardment of neutral Copenhagen (by Britain) was a glorious deed, the bombardment of neutral Louvain (by Germany) was an act of singular infamy. The explanation for this was provided by the title of another book, *Cant: British Hypocrisy*.[15]

Cant – it was invariably pointed out that there was no German word for it – had long featured in the German debate about Britain. During the First World War it had been one of the central topics of anti-British propaganda. Even in the Weimar years, when attitudes towards Britain softened, turning gradually from hostility to admiration and frequently even affection, cant remained a preoccupation among the *Anglisten*. The more thoughtful experts sought to avoid simple condemnation. People like Dibelius suggested that this was a cultural issue rather than simply a character defect: British Protestant culture demanded constant public reaffirmation of the highest moral standards.[16] In reality these were of course quite impossible to achieve, let alone to maintain. The resulting gap between a collective moral ambition and actual practice (which inevitably fell short of it) was the origin of cant. But even Dibelius admitted that Britain's habitual readiness to gloss over the disreputable aspects of British history – or current policy – was an unappealing feature in an otherwise admirable country.[17]

This points to a real difference between Anglo-Saxon political culture and that of many continental countries. Continental statesmen have traditionally judged it unwise to occupy the loftier summits of the moral high ground because they know that *Realpolitik* would quickly expire there for want of oxygen. Anglo-Saxon politicians – both British and, more recently, American – enjoy the higher reaches. They breathe in moral purity and then descend, refreshed, to the plains of everyday affairs. The resulting gap between rhetoric and politics is apt to strike the continental observer forcefully.

When European politicians have their moral shortcomings pointed out to them by their British or American counterparts they therefore often feel a degree of irritation. In cynical continental ears, talk of ethical policies merely serves to amplify the ethical limitations in the policies of their Anglo-Saxon interlocutors. Before the Second World War, Britain was what is now called a superpower. Superpower status is neither achieved nor maintained by observing a strict moral code. There was thus an unmistakable gulf between British rhetoric and British practice. Abroad, that gave rise easily to a perception of pervasive and ingrained hypocrisy. This was an important factor in Anglo-German relations because it produced much resentment. From Bismarck to Hitler, the list is long of German leaders who bridled at British criticism. It was often not the criticism as such, it was its source that irritated most. High moral principle from the spokesmen of Denmark or Luxembourg was perhaps not surprising. In a country with Britain's record, it seemed more than a little incongruous. 'Any European with a knowledge of history', observed the SS newspaper in July 1939, 'is bound to respond with the observation: "They of all people".'[18]

There is yet another factor: language itself. Anglo-Saxon political culture depends on the unrivalled subtleties of the English language. It allows politicians proficient in it to bend and twist the truth to a degree that would fracture it in continental mouths. If 'he wanted our advice' can refer both to a wish, and, just conceivably, to a need: this offers possibilities for subsequent denial undreamt of in other cultures. Germans, conditioned by their own language, have traditionally cherished a national image of forthrightness. *Der deutsche Michel*, the German equivalent of John Bull or France's Marianne, was thus before the war always the *honest* Michel. To others, such honesty can look like boorishness. By the same process, subtlety can seem to others merely a variant of dishonesty. The cliché of perfidious Albion may owe much to the English language

24   'Lord Halifax's hearthside dreams: "The principle of British policy has always been respect for other nations and their right of self-determination"'

and the way it has been used by successive generations of British statesmen, diplomats and journalists. Goethe, in *Faust*, alludes to this by exploiting a double meaning in his own language: *englisch* in the eighteenth century could mean both 'angelic' and 'English'. Goethe thus observes of the fiends from the underworld, 'Sie lispeln englisch, wenn sie lügen': the forces of evil counterfeit the sound of angels for their lies; or, alternatively, for such purposes they resort by preference to the English language.

All of this is relevant because the better informed (and more dispassionate) observers noted its effect at the time. Reference has already been made to the comments of the writer Hans Grimm on Baldwin's use of language. The valedictory speech of that Prime Minister had moved Grimm when he read it in English, but had irritated him once he started translating it into German. The problem was less one of ambiguity or euphemism as such. It lay in the second characteristic feature of Anglo-Saxon political rhetoric: its often highly coloured style and moralising inflections. (Some of its effect on continental ears can be captured by trying out the process in reverse: for instance by translating literally everyday expressions of French politeness into English: the result is an astonishing pomposity that is largely in the translation.) Phrases used by Baldwin such as the 'triumph of light over darkness' – many of them rooted in scripture – do not translate well. They sound either absurdly overblown or vaguely blasphemous. Seen against a record of Britain's past political practice, they can also suggest, once again, dishonesty or, in a word, cant.

In an article written on the very eve of war, an *Anglist* – not unsympathetic to Britain – analysed the tropes of speech of Britain's leadership.[19] He noted Halifax's view of Britain's imperial role as 'service to mankind' and as a bastion of 'freedom and toleration', before arriving at Baldwin's description of the Empire as 'an instrument of Divine Providence'. One can see why anglophile Germans were made uncomfortable by such phrases. They recognised Baldwin's sincerity, but they realised that some of their countrymen might be less inclined to do so. For Baldwin or Halifax, it seemed, had both successfully exorcised from their memories all the problematic aspects of Britain's imperial history. And the Third Reich was keen to remind the world of these after 1938.

There were references in books and newspapers to Tasmania, where in a conscious campaign of genocide the entire Tasmanian people had been exterminated. There were references also to what would now be called bacteriological warfare; in North America blankets infected with the smallpox virus, to which, it was known, Indians had no immunity, were left for them to find. (This killed at a stroke men, women and children, thus opening up new lands for settlement.) There were, inevitably, references to slavery, to the selling of opium, and Britain declaring war on those who tried to stop the trade in narcotics. There were references to Ireland: to Cromwell, the Famine and the Black and Tans. There were references to India, from the days of the nabobs to such recent events as the

25   'What would the British say if we were to do this even to a single Jew?'

Amritsar massacre in 1919, or the ordinance which followed it: that Indians were to cross a square in the town centre only on their hands and knees.[20]

This raises several points. For one thing, one is bound to recall Hitler's remarks about India or North America as exemplars for future German rule in Russia, and his general admiration for the British Empire and Britain's essential 'ruthlessness'. One recalls also the suggestions from the Reich Ministry of Education in 1937 that young Germans should study Anglo-Saxon history to learn how to overcome their moral scruples. What is clear, then, is that the Nazi leadership were not in any way discountenanced by Britain's imperial record. They were hoping to equal it.

Why, then, highlight it in domestic propaganda? There was no perceptible need to do so. The regime might have concentrated on the highly effective theme of Nazi anti-capitalism, and the real or supposed injustice of the Danzig Corridor. Why risk the appearance of inconsistency by attacking what had previously been praised, at least by implication? Part of the answer is no doubt the wish to blacken Britain's reputation in Germany. Britain was still highly regarded by many Germans. What is more, some of them at least appear to have remained receptive to the

British point of view even in the final months of peace. British broadcasts were widely listened to, and as the affair of the King-Hall letters demonstrates, the regime considered the possible echo in the Reich of British arguments a serious threat.[21] It was precisely because ordinary Germans were evidently not at first united against Britain that Nazi propaganda had to 'unmask' the British.

There was also the fact that the Third Reich, by its own actions, had been forced on the defensive domestically. It is surely no accident that German newspapers suddenly reported about British colonial atrocities after *Kristallnacht*. The suggested contrast was between premeditated murder by Anglo-Saxons hands (America, Tasmania, etc.) versus popular anger boiling over in Germany. The SS paper, with its ugly mendacity, declared that such anger had been spontaneous and yet not 'excessive': but the note of defensiveness is unmistakable.[22] Substantial numbers of ordinary Germans evidently did not share their leaders' cynicism, and Nazi propaganda is indirect evidence of that. The fact that Himmler's SD still reported popular discussions in January 1940 about whether the *Protektorat* constituted a breach of the Munich agreement reveals likewise the genuine, and on-going difficulties which Nazi propaganda encountered domestically.[23]

For a regime whose image was thus tarnished even at home, it was useful to highlight British practice. Most of the histories of the British Empire published in 1939 and afterwards contained detailed lists of where and when Britain had reneged on past promises or actual treaty obligations. The favourite example, inevitably, was Palestine, because it was both recent and particularly colourful.[24] There had been three British promises in all: one to the Arabs in general to create an Arab national state out of the ashes of the Ottoman Empire. This promise had been broken after the First World War. Second, there had been, almost simultaneously, a promise to create a Jewish homeland in Palestine. Such a homeland had not materialised by 1939, and renewed restrictions on Jewish immigration made it seem an unlikely prospect at the time. Third, there had been formal undertakings to the League of Nations to govern Palestine in the interest of its native population. Widespread Palestinian demonstrations suggested that Britain had fallen short of that obligation. Finally, German observers pointed out, it was worth noting that the second promise was of course plainly incompatible with the other two.

Britain's double dealing in Palestine and the broken promise of Dominion status for India were therefore crucial to Nazi propaganda. The

26   'What exactly is Democracy, Ahmed?' – 'It's wearing the same manacles'

details were useful in themselves. They could moreover be contrasted with the grander flourishes of imperial rhetoric. One account of recent British history, for instance, used as mottoes selected extracts from Stanley Baldwin's speeches: 'the tricks of diplomacy', 'the exclusion of morality' and 'a harvest of cynicism'.[25] Baldwin had directed these observations at the Third Reich. Nazi propaganda relished the opportunity to turn them against the man who had made them. The director of Ribbentrop's research institute used a similar strategy. In a lecture entitled 'The Principles of British Foreign Policy', he suggested that he was aware of course that these words were 'a contradiction in terms'.[26]

The implied lesson of all this was twofold: Germany would have to copy British methods to flourish, something which, as we have seen, the Reich's newspapers had been suggesting for some years. The British

27   'British cavalry charging Gandhi's supporters'

example in India or the Middle East demonstrated that Great Powers were always free to bend, if not to break, undertakings they had given: they were answerable to no one but themselves. This line of argument was of obvious relevance as the Wehrmacht entered Prague, supposedly at the invitation of the Czechs. The fact that the British Empire had in recent years offered more concessions to its captive nations was immaterial to Nazi minds: it merely reflected growing British weakness. Britain's sudden championing of moral causes was utterly transparent. The country was reminiscent of those 'ancient roués' who, having grown too old to go on sinning, start preaching abstinence to others.[27] For the second lesson of imperial history was this: that Britain, because of her own record, had forfeited for all time the right to criticise others.[28]

This leads to what was perhaps the most important factor in this propaganda initiative: Hitler's own growing rage at British politicians and journalists. From the autumn of 1938 onwards, particularly after the notorious outburst at Saarbrücken, where Hitler said in effect that he would not accept lessons in morality from Britain, one senses that Hitler can often barely control his anger.[29] He clearly found the high moral tone of British pronouncements intolerably provocative. Here was a country whose record was common knowledge, yet which did not hesitate to associate that record with Divine Providence. This Hitler was probably happy to accept as a British version of his own political cynicism. But to be criticised by Britain for trying to emulate her example, that seemed an act of extraordinary brazenness. When Hitler's rage subsided, after the Battle of Britain, he concluded that the British were 'of incomparable impertinence'. And he added, 'We still have a lot to learn there.'[30]

There is, therefore, about the Third Reich's campaign against supposed British cynicism a multiple irony. Both *sides* effectively used the record of the British Empire as an important argument for why their respective countries should go to war; and both pointed to that record to suggest that victory for their own arms would make the world a better place. British pronouncements relied on a view of imperial history which suppressed all its problematic aspects; the Third Reich, meanwhile, omitted all the redeeming features. On the German side, there is the added irony of a regime forced to criticise what it actually admired, thus inspiring in the German people revulsion for the very things the regime was planning to bring about. The level of deception involved is astonishing even by Nazi standards.

But there is also something else worth considering here: the role of ordinary Germans as the target audience of Nazi anti-imperialist propaganda. The fact that these themes could be used by Goebbels' ministry is surely significant. The strategy worked because in 1939–40 Germany still retained the very last vestiges of an old innocence and sense of honour, which the Nazis were busy destroying. The regime's outrage about Britain's imperial record was wholly synthetic. The revulsion of ordinary Germans was genuine, and these were perhaps the final moments in their country's history when Germans still felt entitled to voice such revulsion. A few of the more quixotic publications that appeared at the time suggest that their authors were indeed motivated not exclusively by patriotism. A retired professor of classics, for instance, published a book about Cyprus, which burned with indignation at the thought that Hellenes should languish under a foreign yoke.[31] The book appeared in 1940, and had presumably been completed the previous year. It is difficult to imagine that particular book being written a year later, after the Axis had imposed a far heavier yoke on Greece herself. With the onset of Barbarossa, much of the anti-British propaganda simply disappeared from the newspapers and the bookshops. That too is suggestive.

28   *Some topics he will not be preaching about:'The Boer War','The Hunger Blockade of Germany in 1918','India','Palestine'*

Tales of mass slaughter and genocide, of slavery and theft of land had simply become too topical.

A related effect can also be seen in the case of Ireland, which had been given prominence on the eve of war and in its early stages. Apart from books and articles about the country, the profile of Ireland had been raised more generally.[32] Plays by Yeats were performed for the first time; Shaw was now specifically identified as Irish, and the German public with its hazy notions of the British Isles were informed that 'English' and 'Irish' were not necessarily the same thing. That point was made at greater length in two films: *Der Fuchs von Glenarvon* ('The Fox of Glenarvon'), directed by Goebbels' own brother-in-law, and *Mein Leben für Irland* ('My Life for

29   *Miss Britannia, the governess: 'Why do you keep bringing me news about the Empire? I'm trying to register outrage. So obviously I need news from Germany'*

Ireland'). These films demonstrate perfectly the way that anti-British themes were progressively blunted by events. *Der Fuchs von Glenarvon* had been completed on the eve of the Western Offensive in April 1940. It was shown in occupied France later that year. *Mein Leben für Irland* was not.

Doubts had been expressed among the leadership itself about its possible effect.[33] Was a film about a small nation refusing to submit to the despotism and brutality of its powerful neighbour an appropriate message to air in 1940? How would it be received in countries recently conquered by Germany? Viewers in the Reich's border regions seem to have been in no doubt: SD agents overheard cinema audiences in Silesia suggesting that such films were surely unsuitable for occupied Poland or the *Protektorat*.[34] In December 1940 Goebbels recorded in his diary that Ireland was no longer a desirable theme.[35]

That Ireland should have disappeared as a topic in occupied Europe is perhaps not surprising; that the subject was also dropped inside Germany, however, is striking. It might suggest that the regime feared uncomfortable parallels might occur even to the people of Germany (as in some cases they clearly had). This connects with wider evidence of the German public reacting in a way not originally anticipated by the regime. The fall of France was a case in point. There was enormous pride and joy. The war seemed won and Alsace-Lorraine – the abducted daughter of nationalist iconography – had returned home. But the SD reported hearing among the public frequent expressions of sympathy with the people of France: 'Since the armistice attitudes towards France are completely transformed', it noted.[36] At least some Germans, it seems, remembered the taste of defeat and occupation in 1918. And now that Versailles had been symbolically erased, their instinct was to be magnanimous in victory. The regime, of course, had different ideas. Repeatedly, in July 1940, Goebbels noted the urgent need to counteract pro-French sentiment. At one point, he decries the incorrigible 'sentimentality' of the German people.[37]

That 'sentimentality' was, however, precisely what anti-British propaganda had sought to exploit. Had the German people been as ruthless as the Nazi leadership wished them to be, the attacks on Britain's imperial record would simply not have worked. These depended at the very least on a residual sense of right and wrong. Yet, as the Third Reich's own conduct became ever more blatantly criminal, and did so in an ever growing number of fields, such sentimentality – and such innocence – could not survive. It had to give way to complicity with the regime or to harden into opposition. The domestic limitations of the anti-imperialist stance are thus clear. In the short term the propaganda campaign could continue by concentrating on the most glaring examples of Britain's moral shortcomings; in the long term it would cease to be viable.

One of the most lavish anti-British films of the war, *Ohm Krüger*, demonstrates this clearly. As German audiences in large numbers flocked to the cinemas to see it, the blood of innocents which Nazi propaganda was conjuring up on the screen had already become bloody reality outside the cinema: it was turning from a trickle to a torrent and soon

30   Boer victims

began to wash around the feet of the audience itself. *Ohm Krüger*, a film about British concentration camps during the Boer War, is certainly evidence that Nazi propaganda was nothing if not hypocritical. The scale of Nazi crimes, even in 1941, exceeded by far Britain's culpability in South Africa. Yet one can appreciate why the topic was tempting for the Third Reich. The Boer War was not distant history; the film's older viewers and some of Britain's leaders had lived through it. Churchill had actually been in South Africa at the time. Their silence about British conduct then contrasted suggestively with their vocal outrage now about Germany.

Even more important for the regime, however, were German memories of the Boer War. It had left an immense impression on Germany, perhaps directly comparable to that in Britain of Germany's own attack on Belgium a decade later: it was the rape of a small country by a Great Power amid scenes of gruesome inhumanity. Nazi propagandists, in other words, were hoping to rekindle the outrage that had galvanised Imperial Germany, and much of continental Europe, at the beginning of the century. Then the news from South Africa had produced a conviction among many that civilisation would not be safe until the Boers had been avenged and Britain punished for her misdeeds.

„OHM KRUGER"
Der Emil Jannings-Film der Tobis

31   *A camp inmate*

The Boer War, moreover, held an additional attraction for the
Nazis: here the victims of colonialism had been white. This was indeed one
of the most striking aspects of British colonial practice. It alone had
sought to encompass white populations overseas, and had not hesitated
to use against them practices which the other European powers reserved
for non-white nations. The Nazi press had referred, for instance, to the
fate of the French-speaking Acadians of Nova Scotia. These communities
had been robbed of all their belongings and had then been deported by
the British Army to the swamps of Louisiana, where they were left to fend
for themselves. The conditions of this enforced relocation – lack of sanitation and basic care for the deportees' welfare – had been such that mass

32   Feasting in the British camps while the Boers starve (Note the fake pineapple on
      the sideboard — the real thing was unobtainable in the wartime Reich.)

death ensued en route.[38] The methods thus seemed to Nazi observers
remarkably similar to events in South Africa or Ireland. Duff Cooper and
Vansittart were suggesting after 1939 that the Third Reich's actions were
no accident but formed part of a wider historical pattern of German
behaviour. In an almost exact mirror image, the Third Reich's propaganda
turned to British history because the Nazis too thought they could detect
a recurring pattern.

Concentrating on white victims, however, held a further crucial
attraction to the Propaganda Ministry. *Ohm Krüger* demonstrates this clearly:
the Boers looked like ordinary Europeans. This made more immediate the
impact of the starving hands held out accusingly on screen towards their
British tormentors. It thus revived useful memories of the famine conditions of 1918 brought about by the British blockade of Germany. Already
on the eve of war, in July 1939, the underground agents of German Social
Democracy-in-exile reported that in northern Germany local Nazi
branches were warning about British plans to starve the Reich into submission: it might therefore be necessary to strike pre-emptively against
the habitual merchants of famine. And the Social Democrat agents

33   Starving Boer family

reported that even in a country which they described as 'fearful of war'
such propaganda was having a visible effect.[39]

The memories of the Great Hunger of 1918 remained a potent
weapon in the Nazi propaganda arsenal.[40] The regime insisted that famine
had always been a British weapon of choice to subdue both hostile and
captive nations. When, therefore, as if on cue, the Great Bengal Famine of
1943 broke out within a year or so of Gandhi's 'Quit India' campaign, the
German press did not fail to report it; there was no need by 1943 to spell
out the wider message: only German arms and the Führer's foresight stood
between Europe and the fate of Bengal, Ireland, the Acadians, or the Boers.[41]

Such wilful Nazi misconstruction should not be allowed to
obscure an uncomfortable point: Britain's imperial record made the
country genuinely vulnerable in propaganda terms. There was no need,
for the most part, to invent stories of imperial atrocities: history furnished
them readily enough. Responsibility for these could not, of course, fairly
be laid on the British politicians of the 1930s and 1940s. But there were
three things that counted against the country and its political spokesmen.
The first was the rhetorical style noted earlier. For against the full background of British history, official pronouncements about 'Divine Providence' seemed problematic to say the least. If nothing else, it hardened
doubts about the sincerity of British regret even where such regret had

been expressed in the past. The most shameful practices had ended, but was there any remorse? Britain's self-satisfied tone suggested otherwise. Remorse, moreover, needs to be accompanied by an attempt at restitution. Without such an attempt it counts for nothing. Yet there was no evidence anywhere that Britain had attempted restitution. Nazi propaganda accepted that slavery, which had enriched Britain, had ended. But the profits of slavery – translated into country houses, art collections, or even charitable endowments such as colleges, hospitals and alms houses – continued to percolate through British society down the generations. Parliament had felt it appropriate to offer compensation when it abolished slavery: the payments, as the Third Reich noted, had gone to the slave owners not the slaves. The exercise then had allowed Britain to keep the profits from slavery *and* feel virtuous for having abolished it. This was not remorse, this was hypocrisy.[42]

And so it was with land. Hardly an inch had been returned to its original owners. In temperate climes suitable for settlement, the 'natives' had of course been so severely decimated that it was almost impossible to return lands to their original owners. But even on inhospitable shores Britain was not noticeably inclined to withdraw. Apart from minor tactical retreats in the Middle East, where indirect rule had been substituted for the more costly direct authority, only Southern Ireland had been given back. And that withdrawal had been neither entirely voluntary nor particularly graceful.

Our perspective of the Second World War today is informed by our knowledge of what came after. Against Nazi accusations about British imperialism we set the subsequent record of rapid decolonisation. Yet such a course of events seemed most improbable in 1939: there was talk of independence for India but some British Conservatives advocated a transitional period of 600 years. Churchill himself made it abundantly clear what he thought of Gandhi and the Congress. President Roosevelt sought to encourage more flexibility, but the King's first minister, famously, was not inclined to preside over the dissolution of His Majesty's Empire. Hitler, significantly, was on the side of Churchill: 'I share the opinion of the British Tories: what is the point in subjugating a free country if you then intend to give it back its freedom?'[43] And this thought, it may be noted, was prompted by a discussion inside Führer headquarters about the future of Russia.

Britain's past record and the pronouncements and evident convictions of her wartime leaders thus undermined substantially the credibility of Allied intentions. The British Empire as an institution was fundamentally incompatible with the principles of the Atlantic Charter for which Britain claimed to be fighting. Since Britain chose to take her stand on the loftiest moral ground, the Third Reich was happy to highlight, domestically and in occupied Europe, the limitations of that stance. (Nor were the Nazis inclined to accept a contrast between Britain and America: the United States, after all, had no intention of surrendering its own grip on Latin America.) 'What utter frauds Churchill and Roosevelt are!', as Hitler put it.[44]

From a German perspective, then, the determination of Britain and America to hold on to their lands and to make no amends for their past was striking. Together with the persistence of their attitudes to their own 'subject races' amid the talk of Liberty and Justice, Self-evident Truths, Service to Mankind and Divine Providence, this allowed for just two possible interpretations. One was that the great democracies shared as their guiding principle an almost boundless cynicism. This was the view of the Nazi hierarchy. Alternatively, it might suggest that the Anglo-Saxon nations had compartmentalised their past so success- fully that they had become unable to associate cause and effect. Their power and affluence obscured the memory of how that power and affluence had been acquired. In other words, Britain and America could not be accused of hypocrisy because they had become incapable of recognising it in themselves. This was the view propounded in the article on the British political rhetoric referred to earlier.[45] As evidence it quoted a British Member of Parliament: 'as Anglo-Saxons, we find it easy, without conscious dishonesty, to mask our motives even from ourselves'.[46]

Hypocrisy, then, was the overarching theme that connected Nazi percep- tions of Britain during the first two years of the war. It was as relevant to the anti-plutocratic campaign as to references about the Empire. To talk about democracy while people lacked the very basics of life was cant. To promise freedom to other nations while withholding it from one's own captive territories was fundamentally dishonest. Alternatively, to deny Germany and her allies what one demanded for oneself, or had enjoyed in the past, was no less dishonest. That message could emerge in speeches or histories or even in bedtime stories for the youngest generation of Germans. The magazine *Der Pimpf* – written for those still too young for the Hitler Youth proper – published the imaginary adventures of a little

German boy who has infiltrated Britain.[47] He has even managed to bluff his way into a parliamentary debate by 'assuming a haughty air' and 'draping an umbrella over his arm'. But inside the chamber he makes a fatal mistake. As he listens to a debate about Freedom, he is so moved by the fine sentiments expressed that he advocates independence for India, freedom for the people of Palestine, and a return to Argentina of the Falkland Islands. The faces around him turn to stone: his cover is blown.

That story appeared in March 1940. A year later Germany had not merely extinguished freedom in much of central, northern and western Europe but was preparing to subjugate the very Greeks whose fate in Cyprus had so outraged elderly German classicists. A little later still would come the brief but horrific realisation of the Third Reich's colonial ambitions on Baltic, Russian and Ukrainian soil. Inside Führer headquarters the comparisons with the British Empire occurred more frequently than ever. In public, however, the topic became taboo. Already in *Mein Kampf*, two decades earlier, Hitler had complained about the German 'mania for objectivity'.[48] Goebbels reprimanded the German people in 1942 for their habitual *Überobjektivität* – their 'hyper-objectivity'.[49] This, he suggested, clouded German judgement, particularly in the case of Britain. With their 'mania for fairness' the Germans 'made much of [Britain's] few redeeming features' instead of concentrating on 'British cynicism' and the 'repulsiveness' of British conduct.[50] But as Himmler's agents regularly reported, such remonstrations did not succeed in changing the German public. The implications for Nazi propaganda were therefore clear: to anyone less cynical than the Nazi leadership, the suggestion of hypocrisy would now only have damned the Third Reich itself.

7   'The land without music': culture and propaganda

The year 1935 marked the high point of Nazi hopes for a partnership with Britain. It was also, by fortuitous coincidence, the 250th anniversary of the birth of George Frideric Handel. The regime was not slow to recognise the political usefulness of the anniversary. Handel (or Händel, as Germans would insist) was nicely symbolic of past Anglo-German ties, and the festivities of February 1935 in his native city of Halle clearly aimed at a wider resonance. Alfred Rosenberg, the intellectual figurehead of National Socialism, officiated. In his address he conjured not merely the spirit of Händel but of Shakespeare who, he reminded his audience, had become to the Germans what Händel had become to the British.[1] Such sentiments were uncontroversial and well founded. And so, in a sense, were Rosenberg's wider remarks. He contrasted Shakespeare's extraordinary impact in Germany with the more limited echo of Italian and French writers. (This was *before* the days of the Rome–Berlin Axis, and there was thus no need to dissemble about Italy.) Shakespeare, Rosenberg explained, had 'helped free' Germany from alien Latin convention and 'smoothed the path' for German dramatists.[2] Germany had always been conscious of her debt to the Bard and his native land, and had been happy to repay it in such figures as Händel or Holbein.

Rosenberg's speech was thus, by his standards, a relatively graceful affair. Nazi ideology shone through only occasionally. There were references to a 'fundamental kinship' between Britain and Germany (and there was a characteristically inept description of Händel as the 'mighty Viking of music').[3] But the significance of all this lies neither in its tone nor, for once, in ideology. It is Rosenberg's mental link between Händel, Holbein and Shakespeare that is crucial here: cultural influence over the centuries had been a reciprocal affair. Neither Britain nor Germany could claim absolute dominance; neither could deny the other's greatness; and both found that celebrating their own cultural inheritance pointed sooner or later to connections, and the debt they owed one another.

This may not seem a particularly surprising thought. Yet it was one which National Socialists were normally reluctant to entertain. Nazi ideology perceived artistic creativity as an outcrop of race, or of 'blood', as the Third Reich preferred to call it. (Rosenberg's speech about Händel itself was later published in a volume containing the word 'blood' in its title.)[4] Such a view of culture made the very idea of foreign influence problematic to say the least. It suggested bastardy and racial decline. Britain's artistic impact on Germany, however, was ideologically above suspicion. Rosenberg's own speech had demonstrated as much. The perceived racial ties between the two countries allowed the Third Reich to acknowledge publicly Anglo-Saxon influence. English drama and fiction, in particular, were cultivated almost as freely as in Weimar days. Yet the very readiness with which the Nazi state embraced British culture became problematic in 1939, after the outbreak of war.

This first became obvious in the theatre: the initial dilemma was simply how to keep German theatrical life viable without the continued presence of British drama. In a country which valued its theatres as much as Germany had traditionally done this was no trifling issue. The regime itself had consistently proclaimed the supposed rebirth of German culture as a core aim of National Socialism. *Mein Kampf* contained a lengthy section about the theatre and its political significance.[5] Nazi ideology transformed the German stage after 1933: it deprived it of its greatest talents in every artistic field: actors, directors, designers, and, above all, writers. There had been such a severe pruning of the native German repertoire for ideological reasons that there was by the later thirties a clear shortage of politically acceptable plays. The regime's efforts at cleansing the arts had thus, paradoxically, led to a greater reliance than ever on non-German, and particularly British, dramatists. In 1938 Goebbels found it necessary to remonstrate with the Reich's theatre managers about this: there were 'too many foreigners' in the repertoire.[6]

The outbreak of war provided an opportunity to remedy this. Yet this only brought things to a head: a ban on Shakespeare and Shaw – two of the central pillars of the Third Reich's theatre – finally threatened to bring about its collapse. Pragmatism therefore prevailed. Shakespeare was declared an adoptive son of Germany – perhaps not without justification.[7] Shaw, meanwhile, was conveniently discovered to be a native of de Valera's neutral Ireland.[8] Both helped sustain the Third Reich's increasingly precarious cultural ambitions throughout the war. Shakespearean drama was among the last things staged in several theatres in the East, where the sound of the German language was silenced for ever in 1945: in Königsberg or Breslau, Shakespeare's verse effectively accompanied the death of German life. As theatre became increasingly rare throughout the Reich, lectures and readings drew large audiences. At Hamburg University, for instance, there was a series of public lectures in 1944 on Shakespearean themes. A contemporary account speaks of the extraordinary effect achieved by *Lear*'s Blasted Heath, or *Macbeth*'s Birnam Wood at Dunsinane, amid the charred ruins of Hamburg, 'the wailing of the air raid sirens, the sounds of the flak' and the unending casualty lists from the Eastern Front.[9]

The Hamburg lectures had carried an unmistakable political message. The academic who delivered them had exhibited similar coded signals throughout the twelve years of Nazi rule.[10] In his case, dissent was expressed through a choice of English verse. At the other end of the political scale, English literature was employed for more questionable purposes. Numerous *Anglisten* had enlisted George Bernard Shaw for the Third Reich's intellectual war effort. Shaw was, admittedly, an obvious choice: he had long been an acerbic commentator on modern Britain. In particular, he had satirised Britain's habitual self-delusion about her own political motives. The preface to *A Man of Destiny*, for instance, explained with studied seriousness that, alone among the nations of this world, the English had acquired their empire out of sheer altruism. Unsurprisingly, this became a central text in wartime academic analysis of Britishness.[11] Shaw's various utterances acted as a suitably sardonic counterpoint to the bombast of imperial rhetoric. They undercut Halifax's 'service to mankind', Baldwin's 'instrument of Divine Providence' or indeed Kipling's 'White Man's Burden'. (Germany's *Anglisten* liked to point out that whenever another power had offered to help shoulder that burden, Britain had been strangely reluctant to accept assistance.) Shaw thus provided welcome corroboration of Britain's essential hypocrisy.[12] Since this came from a non-German source, it was invaluable to the Third Reich. Without Shaw, Goebbels suggested, Nazi domestic propaganda would have been 'perceptibly' weakened in its impact.[13]

The example of Shaw demonstrates that English literature itself offered material for the Propaganda Ministry. The novels of A. J. Cronin have already been mentioned. Carlyle and Ruskin, Aldous Huxley, George Orwell, H. G. Wells and many more were regularly invoked in books and articles. The relevant information was either furnished by *Anglisten* with Nazi leanings or by their students. The undergraduates involved in the *Kriegspropagandaeinsatz* – the Wartime Propaganda Service – had been given as one of their tasks the collection of suitable quotations from English literature. ('British authors criticising Britain' may well have been one of the less tedious assignments, compared to 'the provision of health insurance in Britain', 'unemployment benefit in Britain' or 'English financial law'.)[14]

Satirical writing was particularly useful, not least because the satirical intent survived translation into German even if individual phrases did not. The most striking case is a now forgotten novel: *The Autobiography of a Cad* by G. A. Macdonnel, which was endlessly quoted in books and articles. Nor did the Nazis hesitate to enlist Swift and his *Modest Proposal* for their propaganda purposes.[15] As in the case of Macdonnel's satire on political and commercial life, this might suggest a Teutonic failure to recognise irony. Yet this is to under-estimate the intelligence of Nazi propagandists. They were perfectly able to identify satire, but they knew also that satire, for all its exaggeration, provided a glimpse of the truth. It depended for its effect on that connection with the real world. Cannibalism in the British Isles clearly belonged to the realm of fiction. But Swift's suggestion that the English would hardly mind if Irish infants perished gained a recognisable edge, if viewed against the background of the Irish Famine a century later. Taken together, they illustrated perfectly the Third Reich's views on what it called 'British humanitarianism'.

The Propaganda Ministry's effort to collect instances of 'British authors criticising Britain' was, in other words, a peculiarly cynical exercise. It exploited the very mechanisms of democracy which the Nazis had suppressed in Germany. More than that, it misrepresented the motives of the authors it quoted. Nazi propaganda throughout sought to suggest that British self-criticism was the result of unguarded moments, rather than of moral principle. This connected with the wider theme in anti-British campaigns of 'slipping masks' and 'the truth revealed'. As a strategy this is perhaps not very surprising: deception was the Nazis' basic currency, and they produced it with inflationary recklessness.

This was not always without risk: instances of British self-criticism might also contain themes and motifs that were hardly consistent with wider Nazi propaganda. Victor Klemperer wondered, for instance, how a novel like Howard Spring's O *Absalom* managed to pass the censors: not only was it 'uncompromisingly pacifist and internationalist', it contained a highly sympathetic portrait of a Jewish theatre director. Klemperer provided his own answer: the book had passed because in it the rebellious Irish chant '*Gott strafe England!*'[16] (Ireland, of course, had been another suggested topic for the *Kriegspropagandaeinsatz*.) Whether German readers, however, were struck most by the rebellious Irish or the Jewish theatre director is impossible to say. But it highlights once again the importance of *belles lettres* not just to Nazi propaganda but to actual German perceptions of Britain.

British literature remained a factor in German national life after 1939. Examples of its official or covert presence could be extended almost indefinitely. Even books deemed undesirable – like the detective stories whose 'glorification' of Scotland Yard had so exercised Goebbels and Himmler – remained available if one knew where to look.[17] Proscribed books had disappeared from shops and lending libraries, but it was not illegal to own them. The millions of copies sold before 1939 therefore continued to be read, and were passed from hand to hand among friends and acquaintances. The Princess Vassiltchikov thus records in 1940 that a Berlin 'anti-aircraft gunner . . . was locked up recently for having been caught reading an English novel instead of scanning the skies for English planes'.[18] Another anti-aircraft battery in Berlin used their off-duty periods in the same year for rehearsals of A *Midsummer Night's Dream*, which they staged with official permission.[19]

There is also, once again, the diary of Viktor Klemperer with its usual inexhaustible detail. Not only did Klemperer read the Third Reich's own earlier paeans to Britishness (a life of Wellington as the Wehrmacht completed the destruction of Poland, for instance),[20] he continued to have access to English novels even after his own books had effectively been confiscated as Jewish property. Few things in his diary are more incongruous and more poignant than his references to Galsworthy amid reports of Theresienstadt and rumours of Auschwitz.[21]

Such glimpses of individual lives do not merely add colour to our understanding of life in the Third Reich. Their function is even more important. By their mere existence, they highlight the limitations of the Third Reich's efforts to control the thoughts and emotions of its subjects. Nazi ideology was not quite as all-embracing as some observers have imagined, and considerably less so than the regime would have wished. It is surely no accident that the SS newspaper should have been concerned about the possible effect of English literature on German readers.[22]

Nazi propaganda, and indeed Nazi ideology, dealt in types: the Aryan, the Jew, the German, *der Engländer*. Literature, on the other hand, is usually interested in the individual. The secret of its effectiveness, it used to be said, lay in its ability to be both personal and universal. A novel, a poem, or a play might be born of one man's preoccupations but it spoke to all its readers of their own lives. That was its function: it reached out to the readers. That this is of relevance in a discussion of German perceptions of Britain will scarcely need to be pointed out. If literature is escapism, as it is sometimes dismissively asserted, then English writing offered ordinary Germans a temporary escape from the Third Reich. More than that, it allowed them access, through fiction, to Britain itself. English literature, as *Das Schwarze Korps* explained to its SS readers, 'gave the Englishman a human face'.[23] Therein lay its danger for the regime.

The point becomes clearer if one recalls the diary entry of the Princess Vassiltchikov mentioned earlier: the young man on the factory roof in Berlin's Siemensstadt was reading an English novel while, intermittently, scanning the skies for English planes. The novel he was reading provided a link with the creatures inside the planes: it gave them faces. And in war that is fatal. It is easier to fire an anti-aircraft gun if one does not think of the men it might kill. (By the same token, it is easier to drop bombs without thinking that 'the target' is actually men, women and children.)

How widespread this effect was is of course very difficult to quantify. Not every German can have been in the habit of reading English novels. Some may rarely have read in their leisure time at all. Social class and educational background will have played a part. It may even be the case that someone who took along an English novel to his anti-aircraft duty was already a confirmed anglophile, and hardly needed reinforcement of his anglophilia. But it should perhaps be remembered how widespread the appeal of English literature had been before 1939, and how much more so than that of any other foreign country. It should be remembered also how vastly popular, in all sections of society, English detective fiction had been. This is not irrelevant to the discussion. In 1938, in the weeks after the *Anschluß*, Viktor Klemperer was reading Dorothy Sayers.[24] The contrast between life in the newly enlarged Third Reich and the world of Lord Peter Wimsey made him wish he were in England. Klemperer had no personal knowledge of Britain: it was apparently the effect of the book alone that caused such thoughts.

Klemperer may, or may not, have been a special case. But it is worth remembering the wider picture of the Weimar years. The fictional working-class man in Alfred Döblin's *Berlin Alexanderplatz* comes to mind. In the 1920s the words 'Conan Doyle's Collected Works', had echoed through his mind. A decade later he might not have been thinking of emigrating, unlike Klemperer; but neither would he have forgotten Conan Doyle. He, and millions like him in real life, may have lacked education and experience of foreign travel, but they too knew at least one Englishman very well: Sherlock Holmes. And again, this is not as trivial as it might seem. As in the case of Klemperer and Dorothy Sayers, Conan Doyle's detective gave Britain a highly appealing face. One merely has to contrast Holmes' intelligence, courage and resourcefulness with the Nazi propaganda image of a senescent and ineffectual nation to understand why Goebbels had banned English detective fiction. In fact, Goebbels must have come to regret giving permission in 1937 for a German film version of the life of Sherlock Holmes. Hans Albers, the Third Reich's greatest matinee idol, had played the detective in *Der Mann der Sherlock Holmes war*, thus ensuring that even those who never read had got to know the celebrated Englishman.

In the first two years of the war, therefore, there existed in effect two German images of *der Engländer* which contradicted each other. To put it in the terms of Nazi films, there were the brutal, arrogant and cowardly Englishmen who terrorised the Irish or the Boers in *Der Fuchs von Glenarvon*, *Mein Leben für Irland* and *Ohm Krüger*, or who showed their contempt for the rest of humanity against the African backdrop of *Germanin* or *Carl Peters*. But there must also have been a memory of *Der Mann der Sherlock Holmes war*. Much the same applied to the printed word. The readers of the *Berliner Illustrierte Zeitung*, for instance, were offered in 1940 a serial about the British Raj. It was from the pen of Thea von Harbou, the right-wing authoress – the word seems appropriate – who had written the script for Fritz Lang's film *Metropolis*. 'Aufblühender Lotus' ('Blossoming Lotus') provided a contrast between a young Indian nationalist and a German nurse versus Sir Charles Trelawney and his wife. Idealism in the 'native town' was thus set against the atmosphere in Government House, where the 'soul, thoughts and feelings dwelt in arrogance as in a fortress'.[25] Yet the same weekly newspaper in which this literary lotus unfolded over successive weeks had published throughout the 1930s short stories by Somerset Maugham – the last of which had appeared exactly a fortnight before the outbreak of war.[26] As in the case of German cinema audiences, some sense of inner

34   *Hans Albers as the Great Detective*

tension must surely have existed in the paper's readers after September 1939.

All of this may not be unconnected with the fact that, through most of the war, the German public thought much more highly of Britain and the British than would have seemed likely in the circumstances. There were, of course, periods when the public do seem to have been swayed by Nazi propaganda, but only if British conduct seemed to bear out what the regime was saying. Thus, in the summer of 1939, after years of appeasement, the notion of British passivity seemed persuasive enough. Likewise, the Allied military disasters of 1940 made Nazi confidence seem credible. Viktor Klemperer's diary is once again instructive here. It records much the same impressions which Himmler's agents provided in their weekly SD reports, but adds to these Klemperer's own anti-Nazi perspective. On 3 September 1939, he recorded a general confidence in continued British passivity. Germany, Klemperer thought, was 'ten thousand times more arrogant than in 1914'. Two weeks later, his tone suggests that he himself was having to battle the effect of Nazi propaganda: 'Peace in a few weeks . . . or are Britain and France going to fight? But how, where, and with what chances of success?'[27] By May 1940, he records, 'I no longer think it impossible that Hitler will have entered London by 1 August', a prospect which he knew might seal his own fate.[28]

As Britain continued to hold out, however, public opinion changed. The regime's propaganda no longer tallied with reality. The Propaganda Ministry found it difficult at first to provide an explanation for continued British defiance. Yet, for the public, there may have been less of an enigma: earlier German views of Britain explained perfectly recent events. To put it in the banal terms of detective fiction: the nation of Sherlock Holmes or Lord Peter Wimsey was unlikely to be deterred by initial setbacks, however severe. As an 'Aryan' friend of Viktor Klemperer remarked, in May 1941, 'I always knew the war would be lost in the end. It is this idiotic underestimation of Britain.'[29]

Doubts about the regime are perhaps not very surprising in Klemperer's circle of friends, but the explanation given for why the war was being lost, and the insistence always to have known, are surely striking. One does not claim 'always to have known' if one has actually shared such knowledge with others. Klemperer's friend, in other words, had succumbed to Nazi propaganda herself in the first year of the war, and the sense of irritation ('idiotic') is clearly directed in part at her own temporary credulity. This is perhaps of wider significance. In the case of Britain, some Germans at least felt that they themselves ought to have known better, even if the regime did not.

It is not difficult to see, then, why the Third Reich should have been uneasy about the continuing effect of British culture on its subjects. Yet the topic could not simply be ignored. And just as British criticism of Nazi brutality before 1939 had been answered with an attack on Britain's good name, the Third Reich now sought to undermine Britain's cultural credentials. In part, this was simply a case of following Nazi instincts. Culture mattered to the Third Reich, since it defined national and individual identities. In wartime, therefore, enemy culture became a target: literally so in the case of Poland and Russia – more often, however, at the metaphorical level of propaganda. Britain was no exception; yet the task was more difficult and more urgent.

Conscious perhaps that it could not win openly the argument about English literature, the Third Reich silenced most discussion of it and concentrated on specific areas. Some authors, as we have seen, were effectively co-opted. Others were identified as exponents of 'cant'. A particularly ingenious line of attack was chosen to solve the unavoidable problem of Shakespeare. Here Germany's indirect claims on Shakespeare were emphasised, those of Britain systematically questioned.

Already before the outbreak of war, the regime had cast a self-satisfied glance at respective theatrical practice in Britain and the Reich. In Germany, Shakespeare had long been omnipresent: there was hardly a theatre that did not schedule at least one Shakespearean play per season. British theatre, on the other hand, which was commercial rather than government-funded, staged Shakespeare much more intermittently. Statistics of productions and performances thus suggested that Britain was neglecting her greatest dramatist. In an average year, new productions of Shakespeare in Britain might scarcely reach double figures. This compared with three hundred and more, which was the Reich's average throughout the 1930s.[30] Hitler, ever discriminating and well informed, was also critical of the quality of British productions: 'in no other country in the world is Shakespeare played as badly as in Britain', he opined in 1941. (One of the most interesting aspects of the *Table Talk* is to see actual Nazi propaganda not merely initiated by the Führer but refracted by him too: the resulting detachment from reality was absolute.)[31]

In propaganda terms, several useful conclusions could be drawn from Britain's comparative neglect of Shakespeare: first, that Germany was the natural repository of all that was great in Western civilisation – the nation to which, in the eighteenth century, the mantle of Ancient Greece and Renaissance Italy had been passed. It was unsurprising therefore that a Shakespeare posthumously ignored in his own country had found a natural home in Germany. This did not merely have cultural implications, however: it connected perfectly with the propaganda theme of the Reich as guardian of continental Europe, shielding it alike from 'Asiatic' and Anglo-Saxon depredations. Second, it suggested that Britain was irredeemably philistine: a nation that had traded its racial soul for plutocratic gain. (Variations on this theme had already been sounded. Wren, it was pointed out, had designed a sublime city to set off St Paul's: it had never been built because commercial interests would not allow it. Nash had constructed noble terraces in the Strand: these had only recently been knocked down to make way for architecturally worthless property development.)[32]

Above all, English theatre after Shakespeare indicated a more general decline. The rapid collapse of the Elizabethan theatrical tradition, and the preference of subsequent generations for lightweight comedy, melodrama and music hall, seemed to bear out the findings of Nazi *Rassenkunde* elsewhere. A history of the English theatre could thus rehearse again all the familiar themes of Nazi propaganda: the Restoration marked the beginning of national decline with French fads replacing Aryan wholesomeness; the undeniable falling-off in the eighteenth century, and the almost total eclipse of the English stage in the nineteenth, could be contrasted all the more effectively with Germany's own golden age. A selective panorama of 'English' culture was thus able to bear out neatly the Nazis' generational theme of a senescent Britain and a youthful Germany.[33]

It is enough to note that such propaganda connected with other themes and created the apparently compelling logic which National Socialism frequently achieved through its selective use of the facts. And the Third Reich was undeniably adroit in reinterpreting Britain's real or supposed cultural record. Hypocrisy, of course, helped. Before 1933, it will be remembered, Britain's limited artistic impact in various fields was judged to be reassuring by many conservative Germans. London might have been a little staid, but it seemed 'healthier' than the fevered creativity of many continental capitals during the twenties. Now the Third Reich was inconsistent enough to castigate London as 'the most provincial place on earth'.[34] And a regime that had prized British character building and suspicion of learning, now decried the dislike in Britain of all things 'highbrow'.[35]

The main target for Nazi cultural propaganda, however, lay elsewhere. It was, inevitably enough, Britain's comparatively meagre contribution to Western music. This was not only because Germany's musical record was particularly strong, but because the Third Reich itself had always accorded music very high status. Nazi ambitions in this realm often outstripped reality: the first Nuremberg rally after the Seizure of Power, for instance, had included a compulsory evening of Wagner for the party faithful. The exercise was not a complete success. Large numbers of party members had unaccountably lost their bearings on the way to the opera; stewards had to be sent out and discovered them on licensed premises in advanced stages of disorientation. By contrast, German soldiers were grateful, after the outbreak of war, to be offered a chance to visit Bayreuth or the Salzburg Festival. Their enjoyment of music was no doubt heightened by the thought of having temporarily escaped the fighting. The film *Stukas* (1941) demonstrated the power of music even more memorably: a concert miraculously restored a wounded Luftwaffe pilot to health and allowed him – for such are the glories of culture – to rejoin his bomber squadron.

Nazi crassness cannot, however, disguise the fact that here the regime was exploiting successfully not merely German preferences but undoubted German strength. The richness of the Austro-German tradition made British music, or the supposed absence of such a thing, a tempting propaganda target. British composers had not achieved much resonance either before or after 1933. Many German music lovers were unfamiliar even with Elgar.[36] The fact that the only name conjured readily by British musical tradition was that of Händel thus spoke for itself in German minds. 'They love music', as Hitler observed of the British, 'but music does not love them.'[37]

Other voices doubted even a British love of music. In September 1939 it was reported that Sir Thomas Beecham had ended his long association with Covent Garden 'because he had grown tired of the constant battle with the indifference of the audience'.[38] Nor did it escape Nazi notice that Covent Garden was subsequently used as a dance hall. In Berlin, meanwhile, the Staatsoper unter den Linden was re-built in the middle of the war after bomb damage inflicted by the RAF. The *Berliner Illustrierte Zeitung* made a similar point with photographs: it contrasted ballet dancers in classical poses before an audience of German soldiers and Allied soldiers cheering chorus girls on a West End stage. And the paper concluded that the British government was quite right: this war was indeed about the defence of Western civilisation.[39]

The theme of 'the land without music', in other words, could be extended: for instance, to the graphic arts. It was common knowledge, after all, that Britain's greatest painters were Holbein, Rubens and Van Dyck. (What graced British museums had often simply been looted, like the Elgin Marbles.)[40] Neither the reference to Holbein nor to Grecian marble was an accident. An article in the journal *Die Musik* demonstrates what was involved.[41] The piece was a comprehensive assault on Britain's cultural credentials, carried out with verve and a degree of knowledge. It identified Purcell as a composer of genius and acknowledged the lesser but 'undoubted' abilities of other, named Elizabethan musicians. Yet it noted that 'never in their history' had the British 'initiated major innovation in music'. And so it had been in architecture and the graphic arts: pleasant minor talents recurred but figures of international stature were lacking. Even literature revealed a decline: neither in poetry nor in drama had Shakespeare or Milton found worthy successors. How to account for this? The explanation lay in the differing histories of Britain and continental Europe. From the age of Shakespeare or Purcell onwards, Britain had channelled all her national energies into empire and foreign conquest. The result was, in its way, undeniably impressive. No continental power could match it. Yet it had come at the price of artistic sterility. The difference, then, was between nations, like Germany or Italy, that had patiently added to the store of Western culture, and an island race which for the last three centuries had plundered and enslaved under palm and pine.

In the scale of anti-British propaganda, the concept of 'the land without music' was a relatively minor affair. The theme was always overshadowed by the regime's anti-plutocratic and anti-imperialist rhetoric. Culture, as we have seen, was not originally an area where the Nazis had wished to attack Britain. The Third Reich's earlier claims of kinship and its appreciation of English literature made such attacks extremely problematic. Indeed cultural arguments were notably absent in the shorter propaganda campaigns before the outbreak of war. This is in contrast to the situation elsewhere – notably in Poland, or later in Russia – where the supposed absence of any indigenous culture was central to Nazi racial and political arguments. It was in contrast also to anti-semitic and anti-American propaganda, which both emphasised cultural 'degeneracy'. In extending the attack to British culture, the Third Reich was essentially reacting to Britain's own agenda. The claims of British politicians in the autumn of 1939 that the war with Germany was about the defence of Western civilisation itself required a response. The 'land without music' was the answer.

It follows that the denigration of Britain's cultural record was intended as a transient measure. And indeed, British culture, or the supposed lack of it, soon ceased to occupy the Reich's media. Yet the matter did not end there. Events, rather than mere propaganda, revived the topic. As the fighting went on, the initiative passed increasingly from the Reich to the Allied side. For the Propaganda Ministry, this meant that it now had to react to developments rather than prepare the ground for them. The most obvious instance in the case of Britain was the steady escalation of the RAF's bombing campaign, and this would resurrect the cultural theme in the regime's propaganda.

In the second half of 1943, the scale of the damage inflicted on Germany's cities could no longer be ignored. A response from the regime to reassure the public, or at least to channel its anger, was overdue. Yet Hitler refused absolutely to visit the affected towns and regions. Reality was not allowed in the Führer's presence. It thus fell to Goebbels to formulate a suitable media strategy. It was decided to try and turn the devastation to the regime's advantage. Crucial to this plan was the fact that the RAF was clearly not focusing on military targets. What was being attacked were civilian areas, and in particular the historic centres of German cities. Herein lay a glimmer of hope for Nazi propagandists. By late 1943 the Third Reich had demonised the British for years without much success, as the SD reports regularly revealed. Now the Royal Air Force was coming to the regime's rescue. *Das Reich* duly reported that Commander Harris was gloating publicly about 'the picture post card stuff' that was being destroyed.[42]

Das Schwarze Korps, often at the vanguard of Nazi propaganda, had featured a cartoon in 1942 of a British airman in conversation with a female admirer. Asked whether he had also been in action over Japan, his interest is immediately kindled: 'Are there ancient churches in Japan?'[43] The focus then was not simply on the destruction, but on British motives and underlying British attitudes. After the destruction of Hamburg in 1943, *Das Schwarze Korps* published an article purporting to be by a survivor from that city. Predictably enough, it was an exercise in cold rage. Central to the article, however, was the issue of culture (the title of the piece – a vision of the fall of Troy – was the same quotation that had inspired Victor Klemperer some twenty years earlier).[44] This occasioned the following train of thought: what if Britain had never existed? The question was all the more significant since the people of Hamburg had been stereotypically known in Germany for their anglophilia and their sometimes comic aping of British custom. Now, the article suggested, Hamburg was having to think again about its beloved 'English cousins'. Without them, German culture, clearly, would be richer; and in the wider scales of Western civilisation, Britain's absence would scarcely have been perceptible.

The SS newspaper had deliberately selected a North German perspective to fit the occasion. (Even without Britain, it explained, there would have been a Reformation, based, moreover, on theological argument not royal fiat 'from the bed chamber'.)[45] However, the Catholics, too, were soon provided for: the destruction by Allied armies of the monastery at Monte Casino – the cradle of Western monasticism – was again widely covered in the Reich's press. It was not just that the *Wehrmacht* had specifically evacuated the area to save Monte Casino, and had communicated as much to the Allies, it was the methodical destruction of the monastery by the Anglo-Saxon powers that was highlighted. Here was evidence of the fate awaiting Europe at the hands of the barbarian hordes – British and American – that were threatening it.[46] Again and again, a connection was being drawn between what the British were doing to Germany (and to other countries in Europe) and their supposed cultural failings at home. One of the most striking instances occurred in the magazine of the Hitler Youth in the spring of 1944. The article is so remarkable that it deserves to be examined at length.

It began from the premise that Britain 'was envious' of a culture she had been unable to equal. The name of Händel was once more invoked to illustrate the point. This led to a rhetorical question, addressed to the readers: 'Do any of you know a single . . . British composer or musician?' The article then proceeded to explain why Britain had failed to make an impact on Western civilisation. 'The British are complete materialists', driven by the desire 'to trade, to loot, to expand territorially, and to lord it over others'. 'This has led them to neglect all that is of true value in life.' It had also left them with a 'fanatical hatred for all things German' and the desire to subdue 'the spirit of Germany with bombs'. But that strategy would fail. Germany's monuments were being destroyed, it was true: but in their very destruction they became 'even more immortal', 'like the Acropolis'. That 'ancient, beautiful and unique buildings' were being 'reduced to rubble' was undeniably tragic: but it also linked Germany more firmly than ever with Ancient Greece. 'For posterity knows *Hellas* only in fragments.' 'Early sculpture from Olympia' and those of Bamberg Cathedral, 'the Parthenon' and the great buildings 'of our own age at Nuremberg': all would be linked, all would reveal to the world 'a spiritual kinship' between Greece and the Reich. And there was this further consolation. The example of Greece demonstrated that noble ruins 'bore witness' for ever to the genius of those that had created them; but they were also a mute but 'powerful rebuke to the forces of destruction'.[47]

There can be few documents that reveal more clearly the boundless cynicism of Nazi propaganda. And the comparison of the Parthenon with the arena of the Nazi rallies at Nuremberg is by no means the most brazen aspect of this piece. To assess it accurately, it must be remembered to whom it was addressed: the so-called *Pimpfe*, the youngest age group in the Hitler Youth – boys of twelve or thirteen in other words, who were frequently taught classics at school and who read in their spare time German retellings of Homer and Greek myth. The boys who read this article, it should be noted, had no memory of life before the Third Reich. Of the world outside Nazi Europe they knew only what the regime had chosen to tell them. And what it was telling them about Britain in 1944 will have become clear.

But there is also another point, scarcely less uncomfortable: such Nazi propaganda depended for its credibility on Britain's own actions. The regime had only intermittently succeeded in modifying German perceptions about Britain. Now, the systematic destruction of Germany's cities seemed to bear out all the Nazis' most outrageous assertions. And this was having an effect on the views of ordinary Germans. Some of the most revealing glimpses of attitudes at the time reach us once again via the pages of Viktor Klemperer's diary. Throughout 1943, he had been encouraged by signs of growing discontent with the regime. In July of that year, he recorded a risqué joke about the Führer and the party; his interlocutor, a munitions worker, had used it to illustrate the prevailing mood of cynicism in the factory where he worked. Yet the same man had added darkly, 'But Cologne, which they [i.e. the Nazis] are exploiting is gaining them new friends again.'[48] This is not Nazi propaganda or the sentiment of German apologists. These are the perceptions of confirmed enemies of the regime, who wished for its downfall as fervently as the people who had sent the bombers. And in 1943 they wished to God that the RAF had remained grounded.

For Klemperer, the moral issue was none the less clear-cut: morality, though perhaps flawed, was with the Allied arms. When the Third Reich started an appeal in July 1944 towards the rebuilding of the Goethe House in Frankfurt, he was outraged. He regarded it in the circumstances as contemptible cynicism on the part of the regime.[49] Yet his own diary suggests that others may not have shared his views. And these others were, once again, confirmed enemies of the Nazis. In January 1945, the very last remnants of Dresden Jewry – Klemperer among them – were discussing what had been happening in Poland: details of pogroms and of children's brains being dashed out. The conversation then turned to Nuremberg, which had been largely destroyed in a recent air raid. Nuremberg, of course, had been the city of the Nazi rallies. It had been the city where Germany's Jews had been publicly stripped of their civil rights. But it was also the city of Dürer, and its centre had retained the architectural perfection of Dürer's day. Allied bombing had levelled the medieval city. Hitler's arena on the outskirts was almost undamaged. This, then, was being discussed by the small group of Dresden Jews who were

35   *The Duke of Windsor inspecting a model of the Zwinger Palace in Dresden; the palace itself was destroyed by the RAF in February 1945*

still alive in 1945. And with news of Nazi killings in Poland still ringing in his ears, Klemperer heard a fellow Jew describe the bombing of Nuremberg quite simply as 'a crime'.[50] Ordinary – 'Aryan' – Germans, one imagines, would have agreed without any of Klemperer's misgivings.

A month later Dresden itself was obliterated. The city, known as the German Florence, was of no obvious strategic relevance. What was destroyed were not factories but churches, palaces and museums. The industrial town of Pirna nearby remained undamaged and contributed to the war effort right to the end; a large Luftwaffe base on the outskirts of Dresden was able to provide initial shelter to the survivors. It was in such perfect condition that a despairing Klemperer concluded – in February 1945 – that the Nazis were invincible.[51] Like Pirna, the base remained undisturbed by the RAF to the end. It was only the historic core of Dresden that had been obliterated. There, however, the destruction was so complete that for years after the war sheep grazed in what had been the city's centre.

That this must have had an effect on ordinary Germans, and must have shaped their perceptions of Britain, is obvious. Yet beyond these simple facts few definite conclusions can be drawn. For as the Third Reich began at last to disintegrate, most of the historians' meagre sources disintegrated with it. The link between Nazi propaganda and actual perceptions – always difficult to quantify exactly – vanishes in the dust of Germany's collapsing cities. Newspapers were still printed, and continued to be so almost to the end. But their distribution was increasingly erratic, and it is often an unwarranted assumption to think that a particular article would have been widely read. Goebbels still broadcast with demonic energy, but not every radio in Germany was in working order. And by the spring of 1945 not everyone was inclined to listen. In the little village in Saxony where Klemperer found refuge for a while, and where no one knew that he was Jewish, the noise of evening conversation completely drowned out the sound of the radio. When someone in the busy room noticed Klemperer straining to hear, he turned to reassure him, 'It's only Goebbels.'[52] Events had overtaken Nazi propaganda.

8 The decline of the West: German fears and illusions in the shadow of defeat

'The result of this war', Hitler declared in January 1942, 'will be the most enormous [political] transformation of the world, though not in the way we might have wished.'[1] Hitler was not talking about the Reich's problems. He was reacting to the news, half a world away, that the Japanese were advancing on Singapore and were likely to capture it. What filled him with increasing gloom as 1941 gave way to 1942 was the spectacle of the British Empire collapsing in the Far East. Strange though it may sound, he was as much shaken by the scale of the British rout as his great opponent in Downing Street.

This was no sudden whim, nor an isolated instance. It formed part of a recognisable pattern in the Führer's reactions. A few weeks earlier, Hitler had received the leader of the Dutch Nazis: the visit coincided with the news that Japanese forces were taking over the Dutch East Indies. The entries in the *Table Talk* for those days are among the rare occasions where Hitler displays genuine emotion: 'I never wished for this in the Far East!', he exclaimed. Mussert's dejection at three centuries of Dutch colonising effort being destroyed in a few days had been 'deeply moving'.[2] 'East Asia', Hitler suggested a few days later, 'might have been defended successfully if all white nations had stood together' instead of engaging in fratricidal war.[3] He had warned, he claimed, about the danger to the colonial empires should Britain unleash another war against Germany. 'But the gentlemen [in London] had been totally arrogant.'[4]

It will have become clear that the Nazi leadership's attitudes towards Britain, even during the war, were altogether less straightforward than they would have appeared to outsiders at the time. The Japanese, after all, were supposedly the Third Reich's esteemed allies; and Britain had been vilified for years as the main obstacle to peace in Europe. News of Britain's humiliation in the Far East one might have imagined to have caused jubilation among the Nazi leadership. Instead, the mood was sombre: Hitler declared that Germany 'lacked an emotional rapport' with the Japanese, and in the same breath began to look forward to the day when a joint Anglo-German army would go into action against the United States.[5] Even in 1942, then, Hitler still expected Britain to make peace: more than that, he expected her to become Germany's principal ally. It will be useful, therefore, to recall briefly the evolution over the years of Hitler's views on Britain.

Starting out from a position of hostility and envy of British power, Hitler had moved in the early twenties towards advocating an alliance with Britain. After the *Machtergreifung*, his government sought to bring this about. Initially, this policy appeared to bear fruit: Britain silently tolerated a revision of Versailles, and the Anglo-German naval agreement of 1935 seemed a harbinger of wider co-operation. Yet these hopes were never realised. Britain, it seemed, was not prepared to enter a genuine partnership with the Reich: this suspicion became more pronounced as the thirties wore on. Allied to this was an increasing awareness of the limitations of British power and of the various challenges facing Britain from within her empire and from without.[6] This, clearly, transformed the situation, and the more aggressive policies of the year 1938 were its direct result.

None of this meant, however, that Hitler had wholly abandoned the idea of Anglo-German partnership even after 1938. To understand how this was possible, one needs to remember what he thought constituted the basis of any alliance. His unpublished *Second Book* could not be clearer about this. 'Alliances must be based not on liking but utilitarian considerations.'[7] More specifically, Britain would only enter into a pact with Germany 'in the furtherance of British interests'.[8] It had become clear by 1937, however, and perhaps even earlier, that Britain detected no advantage in closer ties with a peaceful Germany. Perhaps, then, she would think again if she was faced by a potentially threatening Germany. After all, previous British conduct suggested that Britain did indeed conciliate credible rivals (provided they did not seek to acquire actual British territory). At Fashoda in 1898, for instance, Britain and France had stood at the brink of war. Less than a decade later they were allies. France had accepted British control over the Sudan, but Britain had allowed France to expand in other directions, notably Morocco. This had not been done out of any ancient British love of France but for simple utilitarian considerations: the defence of the Empire's colonial frontiers was much easier with France as an ally. Similarly, Britain had since the mid-nineteenth century consistently appeased the United States (over the southern borders of British Columbia, and later with Alaska, over the Pacific, and more recently over naval parity). This was the best way to protect the exposed borders of British North America. On one occasion, in 1846, the United States had threatened war: Britain had promptly given in to Washington's demands. Hitler may not have been familiar with the detail, but he recognised the pattern of behaviour. In the Second Book he notes that Britain was prepared to accept provocations by the United States which, had they emanated from Liberia, would have resulted 'in bloody retribution'.[9]

What had worked for America and France would now work for Germany also. It is worth bearing in mind that Hitler had not merely evoked the American example but, in his Munich days, also that of France.[10] And of course Fashoda, as we have seen, was discussed in the German press in 1936. There is, in other words, an internal logic to Nazi reasoning, however doubtful its initial assumptions. At some stage, however, Hitler concluded that war with Britain was probably unavoidable. It is difficult to time this exactly, and this is not the place to rehearse again familiar arguments. The evidence is notoriously ambiguous. It is simply not clear whether Hitler thought either during the Sudeten crisis, or even a year later over Poland, that Britain would intervene.[11] Yet what is beyond question is that he expected war sooner or later. He said as much to Goebbels shortly after the Munich agreement. To quote Goebbels, the Führer 'foresees a very great conflict in the future; very likely with Britain, which is systematically preparing for it'.[12] This conflict, Hitler added, would decide 'European hegemony'.

It is perhaps understandable that this is usually regarded as a definitive break. Hitler, it is suggested, had abandoned the idea of an alliance and was now openly seeking conflict. Yet does this really fit the evidence? Only ten days earlier, Hitler had intimated to Goebbels his continued preference for an understanding with Britain.[13] He added, however, that Britain was 'blocking Germany's progress'. Are the two positions, then, quite as incompatible as they seem? Once again, the Second Book may furnish the answer: 'Just as for the last three hundred years Britain's allies could become enemies and enemies allies, so it will be in the future.'[14]

War, in other words, might be inevitable but need not be the final word. There was in Hitler's mind no fundamental conflict of interest with Britain, at least as far as the Third Reich was concerned. Germany would expand *eastwards*. This need not affect Britain. An alliance was therefore possible, and remained so at every stage of the Reich's initial expansion. There might, of course, be conflict with Britain at a later date. One could never exclude this in politics. But for the foreseeable future, Anglo-German relations would essentially be determined by Britain: war or peace was her choice alone. The aim of German hegemony over the continent to balance Britain's maritime Empire was non-negotiable. (Britain had not sought Germany's permission either in creating her Empire.) She could concede Nazi demands gracefully and enter an alliance, which by 1938 seemed unlikely; or she could choose war, in which case her armies would swiftly be defeated, as indeed they were. The result would still be continental hegemony for Germany. With the Wehrmacht massing on the Channel coasts, and the Luftwaffe ready to strike, Britain would again be offered partnership. And this time she would doubtless accept, since she would now detect obvious advantages in it.

This view is not only consistent with Hitler's earlier pronouncements about the nature of alliances but is also supported by his peace offers after September 1939, and by numerous entries in the *Table Talk* from 1941 onwards. The result of this war, Hitler thus declared in July 1941, will be 'permanent friendship with Britain'.[15] (It was not for nothing that the new British embassy was being built in Berlin at that time.) First, however, it would be necessary to deliver a 'knock-out blow' which was the 'precondition' for earning Britain's respect.[16] That, after all, was how Britain herself had traditionally treated potential rivals. Defeat would thus mark a new beginning for Britain; it would not signify the end of national sovereignty as was to be the case with France.

This is borne out by Hitler's wider arguments. Hitler, we know, admired British imperialism, British 'ruthlessness' and Britain's political acumen. All of these he suggested the Third Reich needed to emulate. And Hitler highlighted also Britain's record of reconciliation with (defeated) former enemies. Why should this item alone not have formed part of Hitler's plans? The fact that partnership was not offered to any other nation is essentially irrelevant. Britain had always enjoyed special status in Hitler's political plans. She alone was both racially and politically a worthy partner of the Reich. The occupied countries of Europe, on the other hand, were either too small to be genuine equals or they lacked the necessary racial qualities.

There is further evidence supporting this view. And that evidence is particularly revealing: Hitler repeatedly made comparisons between the British Empire and the old Austrian Empire. 'Anglo-German relations', he observed in September 1941, 'were reminiscent of Austro-Prussian relations in 1866.'The Austrians, like the British, had been 'similarly obsessed' with an 'imperial ideal' (*Reichsidee*).[17] Force had been necessary to reconcile them to changed political realities. In January 1942, Hitler returned to this thought. It was difficult, he knew, to accept imperial decline. The Austrians had found it hard, and so now did the British.[18] Nor was it only Hitler, it should be noted, who was struck by apparent Austro-British similarities. The travel writer Colin Ross, whose judgement Hitler praises elsewhere in the *Table Talk*, was also struck by the parallels.[19] Ross, like Hitler, was Austrian, and therefore perhaps particularly alive to the idea. But the thought also occurred to non-Austrians, like Hans Grimm, the author of *Volk ohne Raum*: a figure, it may be noted, of some influence among German conservatives and the far right throughout the Weimar years, and beyond.[20]

The implications are obvious. The old Austrian Empire had for over a century countered with dogged resistance Prussian expansionism. In much the same way Britain had sought to arrest German growth since Bismarck's day. Austria had accepted a Prussian-led Germany only after her armies had been decisively beaten in 1866. It would be no different with Britain. And there was this further thought: Austria could perhaps have fought on – her armies had simultaneously defeated Italy. She was thus not entirely defenceless. Had she decided to hold out, other powers might have become involved and Prussia would have been forced on the defensive. But the price of that decision would have been Austria's utter exhaustion. Habsburg armies might have ended up technically victorious but the Empire, in victory, would have been even closer to collapse, and more dependent than ever on outside support. Wisely, thought Hitler, and presumably most of Germany too, it chose partnership with Prussia instead.

The relevance of all this in 1940 and beyond hardly needs spelling out. 'There is only one country in this war which has nothing to gain and everything to lose' by fighting on, as Hitler put in at the beginning of 1942.[21] Should Singapore be lost, India itself would be threatened. All recent wars in which Britain had been involved had been fought on other nations' soil. This time it was British territory itself that was at stake. The First World War had been 'a pyrrhic victory' for Britain. Since then the Empire had been further weakened; its only hope of survival now was an end of hostilities in Europe and the active support of 'a strong continental power'.[22] It follows from this that Hitler did not envisage a partnership of equals after 1940. Austria had been the junior partner among the Central Powers. So it would be with Britain. She had, after all, elected to dissipate her energies and treasure rather than give way gracefully. For the first time in her history she would thus be the junior partner in whichever alliance she now entered: in an Anglo-American or Anglo-Soviet alliance as much as in an Anglo-German one.

Anglo-German relations had moved on from the days of Richthofen's *Brito-Germania*. The world had changed in spite of Britain. Germany might not have won the war yet, but assuredly, Hitler thought, Britain had already lost it.[23] By the summer of 1942, with the Wehrmacht in control of Europe from the Atlantic in the west to the Volga and the Caucasus in the east, he envisaged Britain as 'a pilot fish' to the Third Reich's whale.[24] But at least in an alliance with Germany she would keep her Empire and be allowed to manage its inevitable decline, rather than having to surrender it abruptly and ignominiously.

What will have become clear is that there was a strong internal logic to Hitler's argument. It of course failed utterly to anticipate Britain's actual response; Nazi policy towards Britain had been mistaken but it was not irrational, as it is sometimes claimed. Hitler, it seems, never appreciated that his own policies in the later thirties had made an agreement exceedingly unlikely: the Third Reich had been rather too successful in projecting a threatening image. Its emulation of supposed British 'ruthlessness' had led to a solid anti-Nazi consensus in London, which survived even the darkest days of 1940–42. Britain was thus essentially unfathomable to Hitler after 1939. The prolonged periods of German inaction, after the conquest of Poland and after the fall of France, and the wild oscillation in official pronouncements between intemperate outbursts and conciliatory speeches demonstrate all too clearly that no one in Berlin really knew how to end the war which they had started. Since Britain would not be moved either by generosity or threats, the regime had the double task of explaining events to itself and to the German people.

Hitler entertained various explanations, and inevitably shadowy Jewish machinations featured in most of them. 'How the British had become embroiled in this war was an odd story': Churchill had been 'used by the Jews', and the fact that the War Minister, Hoare-Belisha, was Jewish was surely no accident.[25] Alternatively, it had been the fault of Baldwin and Chamberlain, who had both been 'connected with the armaments industry'.[26] The Royal Navy, *per contra*, had been anxious for an understanding with Germany: should war break out overseas, the 'German Navy would assume duties in European waters' and the entire British fleet would be free to act elsewhere. An alliance had been a distinct possibility, but the Jews had put a stop to it.[27] Now that war had gone on for so long Hitler thought there were additional factors: it was difficult for Churchill and his ministers to make peace without exposing the folly of their previous policy. 'The problem is that . . . the leading men fear a criminal tribunal once the game is up.' For, once the people of Britain were told how generous the Reich's terms had been, there would be 'the most tremendous uproar'.[28] The Tower loomed for the government in London.[29] Yet, for all that, peace would occur eventually because Britain's current military commitments were economically unsustainable.[30]

Hitler's wartime views were thus a mixture of the grotesque and the shrewd. He was, it seems, genuinely unable to appreciate how the people of Britain – and not merely their government – perceived the Third Reich. At the same time, he was able to deliver an undeniably astute assessment of Britain's predicament. In fact, it might be said that he was more percipient about the ultimate cost of the war to Britain than most people in Britain were at the time. It is often suggested that the Anglo-German conflict at the heart of the Second World War was one between a wholly unrealistic Nazi leadership and a consistently sober government in London. This is, however, an oversimplification. There was a mixture of realism and extraordinary misjudgement on *both* sides. In particular, both combatants failed utterly to foresee the inevitable consequences for their own country of a prolonged war; and both failed also to appreciate the psychological impact of their words and deeds on the other nation. This is important because instances of obvious misjudgement by the respective enemy reinforced the credibility of both Churchill and Hitler and obscured their own blunders. The degree of illusion overall (and of blundering) was obviously greater on the Nazi side, but there was sufficient evidence of shrewdness to allow the fantastical to go unchallenged.

Compared to Hitler, Goebbels was more consistently clear-sighted. He too had succumbed to premature euphoria after the fall of France but, famously, soon grew to appreciate Churchill's true stature as a leader. In July 1940 he had still looked upon Churchill as 'a fool'.[31] Six months later, he was deeply impressed: Churchill was *ein toller Bursche*, a colloquial phrase which might translate in modern terms as 'Quite a guy'.[32] Goebbels was particularly impressed by the way Churchill had rallied the support of his nation in adversity. Churchill, as Goebbels put it in an article for *Das Reich*, was 'undeniably' 'a demagogue of rare talent'.[33] This was probably as close as Goebbels could get to praising Churchill in public.

It will have become clear from all this that the regime faced a real dilemma after 1940 in explaining why Britain was still fighting. It was, after all, impossible to admit that this had been entirely unforeseen. The solution was to suggest a fundamental fault line between Britain and the continent of Europe. In one of his most well-known pieces of wartime journalism – 'Of the semi-divinity of the British' – Goebbels emphasised the gap in perceptions. He spoke of the difficulty 'not only for a German but for any normal European' to appreciate fully the British mentality. They were an island race, Goebbels suggested, and looked on Europe as something 'alien and incomprehensible'; what is more, they did not even seek to comprehend it.[34] This was undeniably a shrewd manoeuvre. The article was ostensibly concerned with British plutocrats. But the suggestion of a British inability to understand Europe was obviously of much wider use, and the readers might, with luck, apply that insight to other issues also.

Equally shrewd was the way Goebbels, almost imperceptibly, was widening the perspective from a purely German one to a supposedly pan-European one. This was soon done much more overtly. The Third Reich began to suggest that the Anglo-German conflict was really an Anglo-European conflict, in which Germany merely played the role of Europe's principal spokesman and champion. This imaginative interpretation of events did, none the less, connect with earlier Nazi views of British and European history.

From his earliest Munich days, Hitler had been struck by one feature of Britain's imperial expansion: British power had consistently benefited from European disunity. British diplomats, he suggested in 1919, had always contrived 'to sow discord among the nations', so as to profit from it.[35] This reflected wider German views at the time, even if the extent of the supposed British malice varied in individual assessments. What seemed undeniable was that Britain had flourished first as a maritime and then as an imperial power because the nations of continental Europe had concentrated on fighting each other rather than challenging Britain's relentless expansion overseas. Those European powers that might have stopped Britain – the Spanish, French, Dutch, Portuguese or, in 1914, the Germans – had invariably been defeated with the help of other European nations. Britain had, moreover, acquired many of her most precious colonies from other European powers. Continentals had planted the vines, the British had made off with the grapes. In some cases this had been achieved through conquest, in others – as in the case of the Cape Colony – Britain had used more imaginative routes. With the Netherlands occupied by Napoleon's forces, Britain had placed the Cape under her temporary protection and had then somehow forgotten to return it to its owners. Nazi accounts of British imperial expansion habitually quoted J. R. Seeley: the British Empire had been acquired 'in a fit of absentminded-ness'.

Such historical reminiscences were not without contemporary resonance in 1940–41.[36] The Royal Navy was bombarding the French fleet, and Allied forces were overthrowing Vichy officials in France's colonial empire. The Dutch West Indies and Danish possessions such as Iceland and the Faroes experienced protective occupation by Britain in 1940. Nazi propaganda pointed to Britain's past record and invited the public to draw their own conclusions. (Goebbels was also convinced, later in the war, that Sicily, Sardinia and Corsica, all of them already liberated by the Allies, would share the fate of Malta, Cyprus or Gibraltar.)[37] In France, in particular, Nazi propaganda could exploit existing anti-British sentiment, based on long French memories. Canada, India, the Leeward Islands, Mauritius, the Seychelles, Egypt and the Sudan – France's territorial loss to Germany was trifling compared to what she had lost to Britain. There was thus a wealth of anti-British literature, which the Propaganda Ministry found helpful even in its domestic campaigns: French drawings and cartoons of the Boer War, for instance, became a staple in the Reich's own propaganda. Observations by Stendhal, Victor Hugo and Napoleon about various British character defects were also useful.[38]

Malicious descriptions of how the French or the Dutch had suffered as a result of Britain's expansionism were, however, only one half of the Nazi strategy. The other highlighted the extent to which continental armies had been used for British purposes. In Germany's own case, there were the Hessians fighting for Britain in her North American wars. More generally, the Nazis were keen to suggest that most European conflicts had followed a recognisable pattern: continentals had fought and died; Britain had reaped the rewards. This, unsurprisingly, became the central theme of Nazi interpretations of the Second World War.

First there had been 'Britain's Game with Poland', to quote the title of a 1940 book.[39] Poland, the Nazis suggested, had been given a meaningless guarantee. As events had demonstrated, Britain was always going to be unable to safeguard Poland's borders. After the war, A. J. P. Taylor famously contrasted the fates of Czechoslovakia and Poland. The Czechs had supposedly been betrayed by Britain: as a result, they had survived the war almost unscathed, with their cities practically the only ones on the entire continent of Europe to remain undamaged. Poland had received Britain's support: as a result, the country was utterly devastated, its cities rased to ground, millions of its nationals killed, half of its territory annexed by the Soviets, and the reminder handed to Stalin at Yalta. Nazi propaganda used almost identical arguments as Poland's fate gradually unfolded. When, towards the end of the war, Stalin refused to relinquish the eastern part of Poland, and Britain forced the Polish government in exile to accept this, the Nazi press revisited the arguments of September 1939.[40] And the articles displayed a grim satisfaction that Britain's cynicism was at last revealed to the world: Danzig, as the Third Reich had always suggested, had been a mere pretext for Britain, and Poland no more than a tool to be discarded after use.[41]

The strategy of Nazi propaganda in this regard emerges most clearly in an article with the eloquent title: 'Entente perfide'. Poland, it suggested, 'had bled to death', abandoned to her fate. That had been no accident. 'Britain had wanted to win the war the easy way'. This meant encouraging her allies and the neutral countries to fight and, as soon as they had exhausted their strengths, deserting them.[42] The theme of British armies retreating beyond a watery horizon at the first sight of trouble recurred in the early years of the war. Norway, Dunkirk, and later Greece, all seemed to conform to a recognisable pattern. By November 1940 *Das Reich* was able to produce a cartoon of a Greek landlady offering her English visitors rooms 'with a view of the sea'.[43] The message was so obvious that no further comment was required. In occupied Belgium, meanwhile, a newspaper produced a cruel cartoon contrasting the valour of the ancient Hellenes at Thermopylae with the speedy retreat to the foreshore by modern Britons. For all its French captions, this was unmistakably Nazi propaganda. (The cartoon was subsequently published in Germany as supposed evidence of how others nations saw the British.)[44]

Such propaganda concentrated particularly on the fate of France. Throughout the Phoney War, the Reich's media had repeated the thought that 'Britain would fight to the last Frenchman'.[45] This was intended to sow discord, if possible, in the Allied camp. But domestically it was to reassure a still anxious German public. These, it was suggested, were no longer the Tommies of the Great War but the effete British youth of recent

36   'Thermopylae, 1941'

Nazi propaganda. Britain's conduct after Dunkirk therefore required a review of propaganda tactics. The answer came in the guise of Britain's attack, after the armistice, on France's fleet at Oran and later at Dakar. This would ultimately prove the turning point not merely in Nazi propaganda but in the regime's own perceptions of Britain: the moment when the notion of a peculiar British 'ruthlessness' began to re-emerge after being in abeyance for several years.

The British attack on the French fleet had a profound effect on the regime and the German public alike. It seemed a textbook example of the perfidy of Albion. France, which had been noticeably unenthusiastic about going to war, but had done so trusting in Britain's support, had been betrayed at every stage. RAF air cover had proved elusive: the German media analysed in detail the Anglo-French disagreement over the role of the Royal Air Force.[46] While France was still fighting, moreover, the British were already heading for their ships. But Dunkirk was not to be the final insult. The very planes which had been withheld from France in her hour of need now returned to attack her unsuspecting ships. It was, in a sense, the perfect illustration of the amoral 'ruthlessness' which Hitler had always regarded as the essence of the British character.

During the First World War a British cartoon had famously portrayed as swine German soldiers surrounding the dead body of Edith

Cavell. Goebbels was probably unfamiliar with it. But in his diary he arrived at a strikingly similar image after the events of Oran. 'The British press', he noted, 'were practically grunting with delight over their cowardly attack on the French fleet.'[47] It is perhaps no accident that in the week of Oran the SD report noted a hardening of opinion among ordinary Germans.[48] Himmler's agents had reported a mood hostile to compromise. One of the most frequent sentiments was that Britain would have to be 'smashed': Oran had exceeded everything one had considered credible. Mussolini's attack on France – 'kicking a man when down' in the famous phrase – had inspired contempt in Germany. Yet, in retrospect, that outrage seemed trifling compared to the actions of the Royal Navy and the RAF. Indeed, Britain's 'cowardly attack' – the phrase recurs again and again – was identified by the SD as a significant factor in German public opinion.

All of this made it possible for Nazi propaganda to suggest that this was no longer simply an Anglo-German conflict. It was now Europe against the *Störenfried England* – 'Britain, the Meddler' or 'Britain, the Disturber of Peace'. In a speech in Danzig – the location was symbolic – Rosenberg had already proclaimed that Germany was no longer 'merely acting out of self-interest' but had become 'the guardian of Europe'. She was now trying to end the continent's 'unhappy division' into 'dozens of small states' which had traditionally been manipulated by Britain. The aim was to free Europe once and for all from the constant threat of a '*Hungerblockade* by a piratical island'.[49] 'There must be an end' to Britain's 'causing trouble on the continent': 'we owe it to the generations who built up Europe' (and the article used the emotionally coloured term *das Abendland*).[50] What was needed was a 'Monroe doctrine for the continent of Europe': the aim must be 'Europe for Europeans'.[51] For two centuries and more, nothing had been allowed to happen in Europe without Britain's express permission: the current conflict was thus nothing less than 'the European War of Independence'.[52]

It is no accident that memories of the Great War and of Versailles had been systematically revived since the spring of 1939. Just as important, however, was the memory of twenty years of fruitless attempts to win Britain's friendship. Here perhaps – in a combination of all these factors – lie the roots of the extraordinary self-deception that allowed some Germans to believe right to the end in their country's peacefulness. In February 1945 Viktor Klemperer noted in his diary what he called *vox populi* – the voice of the public: 'Our poor Führer, and to think how much he had always desired peace.'[53]

Un régiment albano-gréco-abysso-polono-tchéco- norvégo-hollando-belgo-franco-roumano-austro-juif
ı été formé à Londres.

37   'Un régiment albano-gréco'

Nazi propaganda might occasionally have satirised Britain's attempt to fight on by any means, but even that, of course, highlighted the British determination 'to cause trouble in Europe'. A Belgian newspaper produced a cartoon, later also published in Germany, of Churchill inspecting a regiment of exiles: Albanians, Greeks, Abyssinians, Poles, Czechs, Dutchmen, Belgians, Frenchmen, Rumanians, Austrians and, of course, Jews of every nationality.[54] Yet, in a sense, this daring enumeration of the victims of the Axis demonstrates the extent of Nazi confidence: the leadership was certain that even a defeated and occupied continental Europe desired peace above all else in 1940–41, and preferred the Wehrmacht to the RAF.

The ground was thus prepared for the unlikely inflation of Nazi altruism that characterised the regime's propaganda as war progressed. Britain effectively provided the foil for supposed German idealism. If, in September 1939, Germany had fought 'for her right', she was soon fighting for Europe, and before long she had even drawn the sword for the enslaved multitudes under the brutal yoke of the British Empire. From 1942 onwards, the German media frequently focused on India. Articles abounded, books were published, and even two lush pre-war films without detectable political message – *Das indische Grabmal* and *Der Tiger von Eschnapur* – were re-issued. Nor was support for India limited to propaganda. At this time, the Third Reich sought to assist radical Indian nationalists and their leader Subhas Chandra Bose in creating an Indian army.

This was evidence of the regime's desperation. Hitler, it will be remembered, had been unhappy to see the Far East fall to the Japanese, essentially on racial grounds. This made him an unlikely champion of Indian independence. Twenty years earlier, in *Mein Kampf*, he had suggested that a man of *völkisch* convictions would naturally prefer to see India remain under British rule.[55] Alfred Rosenberg had warned in 1930 that Nazi policy must steer clear of all 'sentimentality' about the 'oppressed nations'. He also urged Nazis to remember that Gandhi had supported the British cause in the Great War: '*he* had been free of sentimentality' towards Germany; the Reich needed to be equally unsentimental about India. Support of Indian nationalism would only ever be warranted 'if Britain had burnt all her boats' *vis-à-vis* Germany.[56]

Rosenberg had further observed in 1930 that there was a division of labour between Britain and the Reich: Britain's 'task' was that of 'safeguarding the white race in Africa and Western Asia'; that of Germany was protecting Europe from 'Mongol' chaos.[57] By 1943, with the Wehrmacht in steady retreat in the East, 'Mongol' chaos had become a real threat: hence the readiness to support a free India. The British Empire now had to be sacrificed to save Europe. British actions had left no alternative. It had been 'the tragedy of the Germanic race that its people had never felt a sense of family ties'.[58]

'Tragedy' is indeed the unspoken word dominating Nazi views in the final years of the war. Hitler's prophecy that the world would be changed utterly was coming true beyond even his expectations. And the implications, the Nazis felt, not just for Germany, which was confronting defeat, but for Europe, and for Britain herself, were all equally grim. The catastrophic German losses in the East, and Britain's visibly diminishing stature in the Allied war effort, thus provide the background to the final Nazi reassessment of Britain.

Nazi observers had noted, even before the war, a steady erosion of British power and a concomitant strengthening of the United States. Naval parity and Britain's financial debt were regarded as the price Britain had paid for her wilful declaration of war in 1914.[59] It had also been noted that even in the Great War Britain's strength had been insufficient to defeat Germany. American help had been necessary. Germany had lost the war in 1918, but so in a sense had Britain. The damage to the British Empire had been so severe that it never fully recovered. The events of the inter-war years had demonstrated this beyond all doubt, though Britain's leaders, it seemed, never appreciated this fully. From the vantage point of 1942, the Reich's press could thus make two connected observations. 'People who win wars, do not have to fight the same war again' a quarter of a century later. Secondly, in the circumstances, it was 'pure madness' (*nackter Wahnsinn*) to 'engineer' another war in September 1939.[60] It may perhaps have been slightly premature to entitle the article 'So much for Britain' but the arguments about the country's underlying weakness are not so easily dismissed. And they point once again to the view that the Third Reich's attitudes to Britain contained a rational core sufficiently large to sustain, for some time, Nazi self-delusion.

Events after September 1939 had merely accelerated Britain's decline. After the fall of France, and once the Reich had abandoned its invasion plans as unrealistic, two things seemed obvious to the Nazi leadership. The armies facing each other across the Channel had this in common: neither was able to land unaided on the other shore. Dunkirk had not been a temporary retreat, it marked the end of British power in Europe. (Only geography had saved Britain from France's fate.) The second thought was connected with this. Britain could only hope to re-establish a presence on the continent by relying, more heavily than ever, on outside help. Nazi predictions were borne out by events. When the British Army returned to France, almost four years after its precipitate evacuation, it did so as the junior partner of the US Army. Britain was no longer master of her own destiny;[61] or as Hitler put it to his inner circle, one was witnessing Britain's 'reduction, with dizzying rapidity, to a second rank power'.[62] This thought, it should be stressed again, did not fill him with cheer.

The German media occasionally satirised Britain's dependence on the United States. *Das Reich* marked the Lend-Lease Act with a cartoon about life in Buckingham Palace. This centred on a troubled night in which the King expressed his fear that 'Churchill might trade me in' for a ship or two.[63] But the leadership itself viewed the matter with the utmost gravity. In October 1941 – before Japan had entered the war – Hitler had made the following gloomy observation: 'Were the Empire to break apart now it would have been due to our arms.' Yet the Reich would not stand to gain. 'Russia would seize India, the Japanese the Far East, the Americans Canada, and I would be unable even to prevent them from establishing themselves in the South [i.e. the Mediterranean].' It was a disagreeable prospect. On the other hand, should the Empire survive – and perhaps founder at a later date – then the Third Reich might conceivably take part in the eventual 'bankruptcy auction'.[64] (Those who suggest even today that Britain ought to have made peace in 1940 to preserve the Empire for all time might care to reflect on that last thought.)

But it was not simply the prospect of a premature division of the spoils among foreign powers that alarmed the Nazi leadership. What was particularly objectionable was that the United States should have become 'the heir presumptive of the British Empire'.[65] It is well known that Hitler and most of his paladins felt a lively distaste for America. (This was, moreover, shared by substantial numbers of their subjects, and was further reinforced, it seems, by actual encounters with Americans. When injured prisoners of war were exchanged in 1943, there was high praise from the returnees for the British, who had been 'honourable and solicitous' about their captives' welfare; there was later also conspicuous praise for Canada; yet the Americans were described by those who had encountered them as *roh* – 'brutal' and 'rude'.)[66]

The thought that Britain was in the process of becoming an American colony – 'a Heligoland of the United States' – was thus able to provoke genuine outrage in the Nazi leaders.[67] What is indeed striking about the coverage of Anglo-American news in the later years of the war is how little gloating there was about Britain's diminishing stature. The Third Reich might have been expected to take comfort in the thought that, amid its general failure, it had at least succeeded in destroying the empire of its oldest enemy. There is no evidence of this. There were jibes about the relatively minor role the British Army had so far played in the war in Europe – it was described in 1943 as 'perhaps more rested than we are' – but the characteristic Nazi gleefulness that had accompanied other nations' misfortunes was largely absent.[68]

Instead, there was barely disguised bafflement. How could the people of Britain not notice what was happening? Did they not see through American machinations, which were so shamelessly transparent? Britain would not be permitted to keep India: every American pronouncement from the President to individual generals in the East pointed that way. The American special envoy Phillips, according to *Das Reich*, had described the Raj as 'immoral'.[69] Yet, the paper noted, American revulsion for colonialism did not apparently extend to the Pacific, where the US was planning to expand its sphere of dominance; nor did it preclude US involvement in the Middle East, where it was seeking to control the region's oil wells, thus supplanting Britain in that region.[70] American ideals, in other words, were linked with American self-interest. Did

Britain not notice the palpable hypocrisy of its main ally? (In a sense, however, the Nazi press admitted, the United States was indeed Britain's natural heir: America was as adept as the British Empire at disguising national aggrandisement with moral rhetoric.)

These articles throughout 1944 and 1945 about potential Anglo-American conflict remain in part a mystery. Were they intended to persuade the German people that they should not abandon hope yet because their enemies were not united? If so, they failed noticeably in their purpose. Already in 1943 the SD had reported that the public did not 'take kindly' to articles about the US threat to the British Empire. The wish to deflect attention from domestic worries seemed too transparent.[71] Goebbels was usually careful not to ignore the conclusions of the weekly SD reports. Yet the offending articles persisted. They must, then, have reflected above all the preoccupations of the leadership. In January 1945, on the day the Third Reich celebrated for the last time the anniversary of the Seizure of Power, Goebbels noted that the enemy coalition was 'bound to fracture': the Führer was right about that. The clash of interests between the three allies was simply too pronounced. The aim therefore was 'to hold firm' – literally, 'to remain on our legs' – until that day arrived.[72] Perhaps, then, Goebbels hoped that by explaining the American threat to the British, he might speed up that process. After all, he himself had written, in his weekly column for *Das Reich*, that 'the war must somehow reach a turning point, and must do so soon, if it is not to be lost . . . by all combatants'. This barely disguised invitation in 1944 to some of the protagonists to change sides had moreover concluded with the observation, 'We are not merely talking to our own people but the world, and we know the enemy hears us too.'[73]

This leaves a final point to be considered: what of the German public during the war? How did they perceive their most stubborn opponent? That there was little enthusiasm for the war will have become clear. By October 1939 a mood of stoic determination had taken hold. There seemed be no alternative but to fight. During that period there was a closing of ranks and a clear identification of Britain as the enemy. And yet the widespread affection for Britain had not completely disappeared. There is sufficient anecdotal evidence to warrant that conclusion. The Princess Vassiltchikov, for instance, records in her diary in March 1940, 'In the streets and restaurants we usually speak English, but nobody here ever objects.'[74] In the summer of 1943, she did receive hostile stares for speaking French; but, significantly, she adds 'This sort of thing used not to happen, but the bombings are making people more bitter.'[75] Later that year, in November 1943, she shared a train journey with German friends, 'who just would not abandon their habit of speaking all the time in loud English . . . the other passengers did not seem to mind'.[76] It was, by contrast, less advisable to speak German in Britain at the time: German émigrés – both Jewish and 'Aryan' refugees from Nazi terror – were interned on Churchill's orders. This allows the significance of Marie Vassiltchikov's observations to emerge more clearly. The only indication she gives in her entire diary of anti-British sentiment is an outburst by a teacher who in July 1940 described the British as *Schweine*.[77] Yet, significantly, that was in the aftermath of Oran, when Germany did indeed feel that Britain ought to pay for this her most outrageous misdeed.

The tenor of these observations is also supported by Himmler's security services. The SD reports about popular attitudes towards Britain often made uncomfortable reading for the leadership. Schoolmasters were a particular concern in the early years. The teaching of English was frequently being 'conducted in a manner incompatible with our being at war'.[78] This was partly due to 'stubborn adherence to old teaching practice' but in some cases also undeniably the effect of 'personal admiration' for Britain. The teaching of history suffered from similar defects. The problem was particularly pronounced in Catholic schools, where additional provocations occurred.[79] In the weeks before Christmas of 1939, nuns at Aachen had rehearsed their charges in the English version of 'Silent Night'. Given the pronounced emotional overtones to German speakers of that particular carol, the SD was probably right to detect a political intention.

In a separate report in 1940, Catholic laymen were quoted as saying that one was living through a dark age: German victory would probably herald the end of the Church.[80] Therefore, 'the bitterest peace would be preferable'. Yet such sentiments often revealed how limited German knowledge of Britain was. Should the Wehrmacht conquer the island, it was thus observed, 'the crucifixes would disappear from schools and offices' in Britain too.[81] A Protestant clergyman from Hamburg, meanwhile, declared the British 'would win the war because they attended church more frequently'. Britain, in other words, had become for the enemies of the regime the antithesis of the Third Reich and the repository of their hopes for change.[82] And with the Nazi regime's typically brutal reaction to such dissent, many of these reports end with the stereotypical phrase, 'the Gestapo have been informed'.

Yet there were limitations in enforcing Nazi conformity. Goebbels himself was outraged to discover the activities of a press connected with the shrine of Our Lady of Bavaria. In 1940 it was sending out pamphlets to Catholic soldiers urging them to pray for the conversion of England.[83] Here, in other words, was a rival view of the world, barely touched by Nazi ideology. The regime's attempts to emphasise the supposed inhumanity of the British encountered different problems: they were undermined by elderly men who reminisced volubly about their own experiences as prisoners of war in the Great War, and loudly proclaimed, 'Grant God that my son is in British captivity.'[84] The SD reported that such sentiments were extremely widespread.

There was also, in the early years of the war at least, a notable readiness on the part of many Germans not to let the bombing raids of the RAF distort their judgement about Britain. There was much anger and distress certainly, but again the detail is revealing. When a Berlin hospital was hit in June 1940, prompting predictable propaganda coverage, Berliners contradicted in public the assertion that there had been no military targets in the vicinity. The Arado (aircraft) works were frequently cited.[85] A few months later the same issue re-emerged. The public are 'frequently dubious' about reports of the RAF deliberately targeting civilian areas; the view is that the British do 'target military installations but that their aim is abysmal'.[86] No less revealing are the reactions to the cynical attempt by Goebbels to exploit the RAF attack on Berlin's Bethel Mental Hospital. The newsreel comment provoked barely disguised merriment in the cinemas: the SD recorded comments to the effect of how touching it was to see such concern for the 'hereditarily diseased'.[87] (The same account, moreover, mentioned that the public claimed to be discerning patterns in the reporting of British air raids.)

It is therefore worth taking seriously Goebbels' complaints, in September 1942, about the German 'mania for objectivity', and his insistence that the Germans would have to 'learn how to hate'.[88] Equally significant, perhaps, is the remark in the SS newspaper, in the midst of the war, about what it called *Objektivitätsspießer*. This spontaneous and untranslatable term of abuse combines 'objectivity' and the word for a 'narrow-minded utterly conventional bourgeois'. Such *Objektivitätsspießer*, observed the SS journalists, looked upon Britain as their 'ardently admired exemplar'.[89]

The escalation of the RAF's attacks did, however, put such feelings under some strain. The scale of the destruction was horrific: the loss of life overwhelming. The victims were, most commonly, women and children; all able-bodied men (and older boys in the Hitler Youth) were at the front. Goebbels' propaganda probably mattered less here than the actions of the Royal Air Force itself. Evidence of this comes, again, from familiar wartime diaries. Princess Vassiltchikov – Russian, not German – records on Christmas Eve 1943 that she was making this entry after a British raid. 'I find this disgraceful; even in the First World War (which was bad enough) both sides suspended hostilities that night.'[90] By the end of the war, her diary suggests that she had almost been numbed into silence by the raids. In Dresden, meanwhile, Viktor Klemperer was wondering in September 1944 who would kill him in the end: 'the British [or] the Gestapo?'[91] (Klemperer thought he would prefer to be killed by the British.) This was no isolated thought. Other Jewish survivors in Dresden were also reminded of the worst days of the Gestapo terror: 'These days, one sits and waits for the British as one used to do . . . for the bloodhounds of the Gestapo.'[92]

The most revealing document, however, is an SD report in February 1944 about the effect of the bombing. It is worth quoting at length.[93] In its preamble it notes that there was still evidence of 'characteristic' German objectivity and 'the attempt even now to do the enemy justice'. Yet there was also, 'for the first time', evidence of genuine hatred. But what 'predominated were feelings of revulsion, contempt and bitterness'. Yet different parts of the Reich reacted differently, and hatred was limited to the most affected areas and tended, after a while, to abate. The SD quoted as representative from the letter of a survivor: 'As you walk through the smoke and the debris, you are filled by a single thought: "how can we avenge this?" I have never in my whole life known what it is to hate. I do now. How can there be a God who allows murder on such a scale? For this is murder.'

The fact that this was being said in Germany, where murder had much earlier made its home, does not totally destroy the import of this outburst. But the significance lies not in the rage or the cry for revenge. These are hardly surprising. What follows is significant. Another victim is quoted as mourning her possessions, yet she asserts, 'I have nothing against the British'. Indeed she suggests that some of them might be 'worthy of emulation' by her own countrymen. 'This ambiguity', notes the SD, 'pervades all sections of society'. While some demanded 'an eye for an eye', others warned that this would only result in 'British women and children' suffering the same fate. 'We were German, after all . . . and could not use methods we deplored in others.' 'The people to blame for this war', the source added, 'were the leaders, who would contrive to vanish in the end.' The SD notes in conclusion that, while there was often anger against the RAF pilots, 'there was no evidence of hatred against the British people as a whole'. As for Churchill, he was frequently regarded as 'a man of ability'.

Judging by such reports, the Nazis would seem to have failed. But as a basis for a new Germany after the war, and for earning that long-desired friendship of the British, this was perhaps not bad.

Conclusion

When the Nazis came to power in 1933, they regarded the establishment of a partnership with Britain as their central policy objective. This was consistent with wider German aspirations. After the First World War, there had been a gradual waning of anti-British sentiment. Political events in the 1920s, such as the French occupation of the Ruhr, had accelerated that process. Cultural influences, notably the spread of English literature, and indeed of the English language, had assisted it. This transformation touched most sections of German society. The political right were particularly affected: Britain's apparent conservatism in politics, manners and the arts exerted a powerful attraction and softened older enmities. The Nazi aim of Anglo-German partnership was thus not incompatible with wider German thought. There were parallels also between the Nazis and ordinary Germans in their extremely circumscribed factual knowledge of Britain: Germany's economic problems had restricted her people's contacts with the wider world. This would become a crucial political factor after 1933: a limited understanding of Britain provided the basis for the regime's foreign policy.

Anglo-German friendship, moreover, meant different things to different people. For most Germans, it implied a guarantee of peace and British help in achieving a revision of Versailles. To the Nazis it meant more: it would lead to an eventual division of the world into spheres of influence. Hitler had long regarded the British Empire as the exemplar for the Third Reich's hoped-for expansion. A central role in this was played by the notion of a peculiar British 'ruthlessness' in war and peace. This concept provided a vital connection between Hitler's imperial aspirations and Nazi racial science, which had been developing separately. Together they formed the core of the Third Reich's perceptions of Britain, and the foundation also for the Nazis' persistent misjudgement of likely British reactions to their policies.

Hitler's views spread quickly within the party. Beyond its confines, however, it was necessary to exercise caution. The initially precarious position of the Third Reich made it necessary to disguise the regime's intentions. This also affected public perceptions of Britain. The precise basis of the regime's admiration of Britain was at first partly hidden, though it began gradually to emerge in articles in the press about imperial history, in school books and, most clearly of all, in educational guidelines. What was advocated was that Germany should learn from British history and should seek to emulate Britain's apparent lack of scruples in dealing with non-Britons. Here Nazi intentions and the views of ordinary Germans began to diverge. Indirect proof comes in the shape of the regime's later propaganda about Britain's imperial atrocities. Its effectiveness as propaganda relied on appealing to the same moral values which the regime had earlier sought to destroy.

Differences between the leaders and the led also emerged in other ways during the late thirties. Following repeated rebuffs by Britain, the regime began to move towards confrontation. The German public did not necessarily do likewise, as the reception of prominent Britons on the eve of war suggests. The leadership, moreover, began to detect evidence of British weakness and imperial decline. This led to a complete reappraisal by the leaders of their attitudes towards Britain. It also set the tone for official Nazi propaganda as peace gave way to war.

Central to the attempt at re-educating the German public about Britain was the notion of British senescence. This was rooted partly in the Nazis' own youthfulness, and in part was prompted by encounters with Britain's more elderly political class. The abdication crisis in 1937 greatly strengthened these perceptions. Views of Britain's decline thus had at their core a biological and racial element. The perspective was, however, widened to include governance and, most crucially, Britain's supposed technological backwardness. If Nazi *Rassenkunde* achieved only limited impact on perceptions of Britain, as the tone of the party's own newspapers suggests, the idea of technological backwardness was more successful. It appealed to Germany's own self-image as a leader in science and engineering. It connected also with the image of a more traditional Britain which emerged from British literature.

After the outbreak of war, this theme was joined by the conception of British social backwardness, with which it was linked in the person of the Duke of Windsor. Memories of the Duke's interest in the social question provided the background against which Goebbels unfolded his anti-plutocratic campaign. This appealed not only to the Third Reich's self-image of social innovation but deliberately revived German memories of the Depression. It played a significant role in justifying domestically the war with Britain. The regime's supposed social concern thus helped deflect attention from its aggressive foreign policy and put responsibility for war on British 'plutocrats' fearful of social justice.

The third theme of Nazi propaganda in the initial stages of the war was Britain's imperial record. This had already been sounded on the eve of war. In response to foreign criticism, the Third Reich resorted systematically to the 'atrocity story', using the darker chapters in British history to justify its policies. The examples of Palestine or India were used to legitimise the regime's breach of treaty obligations. Particular attention was also paid to the fate of white victims of British colonialism: the Irish, the Boers, the Acadians of North America. Parallels were drawn with Germany's own fate, as famine was highlighted as a supposedly preferred weapon of British policy. The Third Reich thus hypocritically castigated what it had secretly admired and sought to put into practice itself. Increasing Nazi brutality in fact soon began to undermine the effect of anti-imperial rhetoric. Propaganda films about Ireland revealed this clearly. Their message of resistance against injustice and despotism acquired unwelcome political overtones. The gradual disappearance of such propaganda after the invasion of Russia highlights once more the limits of domestic acceptability of amoral 'ruthlessness' among ordinary Germans, and the Propaganda Ministry's recognition of the fact.

Nazi determination to denigrate a Britain that had spurned their offers of partnership also extended to the cultural sphere. Britain was described as a soulless, philistine nation wholly in thrall to commercial gain. The fact that British literature, and particularly British drama, had achieved extraordinary popularity in Germany before 1939 makes culture an unlikely propaganda weapon. Indeed, Nazi efforts here would appear to have been mainly in response to British challenges. The topic was never given the prominence that British 'plutocracy' or Britain's imperial record received. Yet the RAF's methodical destruction of Germany's architectural heritage, while leaving undamaged nearby industrial plant or military installations, unexpectedly revived the theme and gave it, for the first time, real resonance.

Britain's unwavering determination to fight on also led to a re-adjustment in the private opinions of the leadership. Essentially, Hitler, and those closest to him, simply reverted to their earlier notion of British 'ruthlessness'. Hopes of a change of heart in Britain continued even after the Battle of Britain. There is, however, clear evidence of mounting desperation as the war ran its course. The determination to target the British Empire both in propaganda terms and by supporting Indian nationalists is eloquent proof of this. The Nazis were thus forced to harm what they genuinely valued most.

The picture that emerges is therefore of dramatic changes in Nazi perception in the mid-thirties and during the Battle of Britain. Of crucial importance on both occasions was the extraordinarily limited factual knowledge upon which the regime attempted to base its policies. This had been inherited from Weimar Germany but had been greatly exacerbated by Nazi policies. The Nazis' anti-intellectual instincts and political, racial and religious intolerance had systematically closed off the regime's domestic sources of information. Imposition of conformity had, more-over, encouraged the country's experts to highlight aspects of Britain which the regime might find congenial while ignoring or deliberately under-estimating features inimical to National Socialism. Hitler's govern-ment was thus caught, domestically and internationally, in a trap of its own making.

In this the German public were the regime's largely unenthusias-tic servants. There was a closing of ranks in the autumn of 1939, but as the rumours about the Duke of Windsor's restoration demonstrate the longing for peace remained. There was also, with the exception of the *annus mirabilis* of 1940, an unmistakable reluctance to accept the more extreme claims of Nazi propaganda – at least in the case of Britain. Individual memories and independent thought counteracted to a substantial degree Goebbels' efforts. The hatred which the regime sought to inspire remained largely absent. Against the dramatic fluctuations in the regime's views during the twelve years of Nazi rule must be set the opinions of ordinary Germans which, in their core of admiration for Britain, remained essen-tially unchanged. The failure of the Third Reich to modify these percep-tions substantially may explain in part why the post-war West Germany could be anchored much more easily in the Western democratic commu-nity than most Allied experts had considered likely in 1945.

Notes

Notes to introduction

1   Viktor Klemperer, *Ich will Zeugnis ablegen bis zum Letzten, Tagebücher 1933–1945* (Berlin 1995), 29 April 1943.

1   The view from Weimar: German perceptions of Britain before 1933

1   See Eberhard Jäckel and Axel Kuhn (eds.), *Hitler: Sämtliche Aufzeichnungen 1905–1924* (Stuttgart 1980).

2   Adolf Hitler, *Mein Kampf*, trans. Ralph Mannheim (London 1969), pp. 564–6, 579–10, 606–7.

3   Elke Fröhlich (ed.), *Die Tagebücher von Joseph Goebbels: Sämtliche Fragmente* (Munich 1987), 13 and 15 February 1926 and 16 April 1926.

4   Alfred Rosenberg, 'Gedanken über das Wesen englischer Politik', *Völkischer Beobachter*, 20 February 1926; reprinted in Alfred Rosenberg, *Der Kampf um die Macht* (Munich 1937).

5   See Josef Henke, *England in Hitlers außenpolitischem Kalkül 1935–1939* (Boppard 1973) and his 'Hitlers England-Konzeption: Formulierungen und Realisierungskonzepte', in Manfred Funke (ed.), *Hitler, Deutschland und die Mächte* (Kronberg 1978), pp. 584–603. Robert Ingrim, *Hitlers glücklichster Tag: London am 18.6.35* (Stuttgart 1951). Axel Kuhn, *Hitlers außenpolitisches Programm: Entstehung und Entwicklung 1919–1939* (Stuttgart 1970). A fine recent account in English, which also glances beyond Hitler, is G. T. Waddington, 'Haßgegner: German Views of Great Britain in the Later 1930s', History 81 (1996), 22–39. Finally, there is Gerhard Weinberg's forceful rebuttal of most German research on the topic: 'Hitler and England, 1933–1945: Pretense and Reality', in Weinberg, *Germany, Hitler and World War* II (Cambridge 1998), pp. 85–94.

6   Hugh Trevor-Roper (ed.), *Hitler's Table Talk 1941–1944* (London 1953). The original text has since become available: Werner Jochmann (ed.), *Monologe im Führerhauptquartier 1941–1944: Die Aufzeichnungen von Heinrich Heims* (Hamburg 1980). Subsequent quotations are based on the original German. (A point about translation: Germans habitually speak of 'England' even where they are referring to Britain. Unless a reference is thus clearly limited to England, 'Britain' has been chosen here as the more appropriate term.)

7   Postage stamps celebrating the alliance in 1941 simply featured a double portrait of the leaders.

8   See, for instance, the SD report of 29 July 1943. Heinz Boberach (ed.), *Meldungen aus dem Reich: Die geheimen Lageberichte des Sicherheitsdienstes der SS 1938–1945* (Herrsching 1984), p. 5540.

9   See Weinberg, *Germany, Hitler and World War II*, pp. 109–20 for a succinct account of Hitler's attitude towards Britain after 1937.

10   Hugh Trevor-Roper, *The Testament of Adolf Hitler: The Hitler–Bormann Documents February–April 1945* (London 1961), p. 84. See also Weinberg, *Germany, Hitler and World War II*, p. 119.

11   Ernst Kris and Hans Speyer, *German Radio Propaganda: Report on Home Broadcasts during the War* (New York 1944), pp. 215–17.

12   Cf. Boberach, *Meldungen*: 8 August 1940, p. 1452, or 20 January 1941, p. 1916.

13   Viktor Klemperer, *Leben sammeln, nicht fragen wozu und warum: Tagebücher 1918–1932* (Berlin 1996). See particularly the entries for 7 February, 23 September and 17 October 1919; 15 January, 1 April, and 9 July 1920; and 17 May 1921.

14   Klemperer, *Diaries*, 14 February 1920.

15   Ibid., 24 November 1918.

16   See for instance, ibid., 19 July 1921.

17   See ibid., 8 July 1920.

18   Jäckel and Kuhn, *Hitler*, p. 346: 'Hätte er [i.e. Lloyd George] sie mit den Stiefeln getreten, man würde uns am nächsten Tag gemeldet haben, daß der Tritt noch erträglich war, denn er sei nicht genagelt gewesen.'

19   Ibid., 17 February 1922, p. 577; 6 March 1921, p. 332; 22 May 1921, pp. 403–4; 20 July 1921, p. 444; 29 May 1921, p. 418. See also Konrad Haiden's early account of those years: *Geschichte des Nationalsozialismus* (Berlin 1932), p. 48.

20   Colin Ross, *Die Welt auf der Wage: Ein Querschnitt von zwanzig Jahren Weltreise* (Leipzig 1929), p. 84.

21   The apparently strident demands for their return in the late thirties were intended mainly as a way of embarrassing the British and extracting concessions from them in Europe (see Klaus Hildebrand, *Vom Reich zum*

Weltreich: Hitler, NSDAP, und koloniale Frage 1919–1945 (Munich 1969), pp. 452ff, or Andrew Crozier, *Appeasement and Germany's Last Bid for Colonies* (Basingstoke 1988).

22 *Table Talk*, 2 February 1942.

23 Goebbels, *Diaries*, 6 February 1938. Ribbentrop's Leipzig speech eleven months earlier had produced an angrily dismissive diary entry – though whether this was provoked by the gaucherie of the speech or its subject is not entirely clear (see 3 March 1937).

24 Cf. Johann Elßler's letter of 30 June 1809. For a translation, see H. C. Robbins Landon and David Wyn Jones, *Haydn: His Life and Music* (London 1988), p. 314.

25 Johann Froembgen, *Marlborough: Englands Fahnen im deutschen Wind* (Leipzig, n.d.). The book is advertised in these terms in: Anon., *England ohne Maske* (Leipzig 1939). The author's other output, it should be noted, included a life of Franco.

26 For an account of growing British exasperation with France's machinations in the Rhineland, see David G. Williamson, *The British in the Rhineland 1918–1930* (Oxford 1991), pp. 258–9.

27 For the more problematic side of the occupation see David G. Williamson's article, 'Cologne and the British', *History Today* 27:11 (1977), 695–702.

28 See 'Erinnerungsblätter 1919', in Ralf-Georg Reuth (ed.), *Joseph Goebbels Tagebücher* (5 vols., Munich 1992), vol. I, p. 68. (The Fröhlich edition does not include these.)

29 Williamson, 'Cologne and the British'.

30 Ibid.

31 Williamson, for one, is struck by the similarity (ibid., 702).

32 Education was the preserve of the individual states: the change of policy was therefore gradual.

33 Klemperer, *Diaries*, 11 November 1921.

34 The connection is explicit in the introduction by Otto Baumgarten to his *Religiöses und kirchliches Leben in England* (Leipzig 1922), p. 1.

35 See also Klemperer's diary entry about a meeting of German and Austrian linguists in Vienna, 26 May 1929: '"Englisch" ist "praktischer" "und wir haben keinen Grund auf französische Kultur zu sehen".'

36 By the 1930s, he concluded, none of the younger generation understood that language (Klemperer, *Diaries*, 14 October 1936).

37 Ibid., 10 October 1920.

38 The ratio of British and American topics in the philological journals of the period proves the point.

39 Cf. for instance the entry for 'Englische Sprache' in *Der Große Brockhaus*, 15th edition (Leipzig 1930).

40   Goebbels, *Diaries*, 9 April 1931.

41   *Der Türmer: Monatsschrift für Gemüt und Geist*, April 1927.

42   Erich Mühsam, 'Franz Bieberkopf und der Rundfunk', in Irmela Schneider (ed.), *Radiokultur der Weimarer Republik* (Tübingen 1984), p. 133.

43   Cf. Boberach, *Meldungen*, 18 December 1939. See also 'Liste der für Jugendliche und Büchereien ungeeigneten Druckschriften, Oct. 1940', in Jan-Pieter Barbian, *Literaturpolitik im 'Dritten Reich'* (Munich 1995), pp. 530–1.

44   Boberach, *Meldungen*, 18 December 1939.

45   *Das Schwarze Korps*, 5 January 1939.

46   Ernst Schultze, *Die Blutspur Englands* (Berlin 1940) or H. Wanderscheck, *Höllenmaschinen aus England* (Berlin 1940). The imitation is explicitly acknowledged in the SD report above.

47   *Das Schwarze Korps*, 6 April 1944.

48   Shaw's critical reputation has in fact held up consistently better in Germany than in Britain.

49   The only exception being Ben Jonson's *Volpone*, in a version by Stefan Zweig.

50   *Mein Kampf*, p. 236.

51   Goebbels, *Diaries*, 22 December 1937.

52   For Hitler's views on syphilis and the arts, see *Mein Kampf*, pp. 231–4.

53   On Shaw as an Irish author, see chapter 6 below.

54   See *Die Pause* 4:11 (1938).

55   Goebbels, *Diaries*, 21 July 1941.

56   The crossword puzzle was itself a recent Anglo-Saxon import.

57   Klemperer, *Diaries*, 5 August 1929.

58   Paul Cohen-Portheim, *England: Die unbekannte Insel* (Berlin 1931). W. Kellinghusen, *England: Das unbekannte Land* (Berlin 1937). Rudolf Kircher, *Wie's die Engländer machen: Politik, Gesellschaft und Kultur im demokratisierten England* (Frankfurt am Main 1929). Karl Silex, *John Bull zu Hause: Der Engländer im täglichen Leben. Wie er wohnt, sich amüsiert, sich anzieht, was er lernt, wird, treibt, verdient, ausgiebt* (Leipzig 1930).

59   See Walter Apelt, *Die kulturkundliche Bewegung im Unterricht der neueren Sprachen in Deutschland in den Jahren 1886–1945: Ein Irrweg deutscher Philologen* (East Berlin 1967).

60   See the relative lack of contemporary British literature in *Die neueren Sprachen* or *Archiv für das Studium der neueren Sprachen*.

61   *Table Talk*, 3 September 1942.

62   *Das Schwarze Korps*, 9 January 1936.

63   Wilhelm Dibelius, *England* (2 vols., Leipzig 1923), vol. II, p. 205. For Rosenberg's comments see 'Gedanken'.

64   *Der Türmer*, September 1925. Cf. also Jäckel and Kuhn, *Hitler*, 13 April 1923, p. 892.

65 Wilhelm von Richthofen, Brito-Germania: Die Erlösung Europas (Berlin 1926).

66 As for Germany's Protestants, Britain's Reformation offered them an emotional link in much the same way that the House of Hanover did. Hans Grimm makes both points explicitly in 'Englisch-deutsche Probleme im Wandel unserer Zeit', Inneres Reich 4:1 (1937), 277.

67 Der Türmer, March 1927.

68 Günther Hellmann, Ideen und Kräfte der englischen Nachkriegsjugend (nach literarischen Selbstzeugnissen) (Breslau 1939), p. 23.

69 Berliner Illustrierte Zeitung, 30 January 1936.

70 On conformity and social cohesion, see Dibelius and his influential thoughts on the British and German concepts of freedom in England, vol. II, pp. 205–29.

71 Reinhard Spitzy, How We Squandered the Reich (Norwich 1997).

72 Ibid., p. 107.

73 See Berliner Illustrierte, 5 November 1936.

74 Country Life, March 1936.

75 Klemperer, Diaries, 16 September 1935.

76 Cf. ibid., 12 February 1919.

77 Ross, Die Welt auf der Wage, p. 87.

78 See 'Deutschfeindliches aus England', Der Türmer, August 1927.

79 Inevitably, one wonders whether that Irish maid might not simply have been a literary device to point the lesson and adorn the tale. It is worth noting, therefore, that the woman's sentiments are largely echoed by de Valera in an interview for Alfred Rosenberg's Nationalsozialistische Monatshefte 30 (September 1932), 428.

80 Mein Kampf, pp. 131–2.

2   'The Germanic isle': Britain and Nazi racial science

1   'Die rassische Bedingtheit der Außenpolitik', in Alfred Rosenberg, Blut und Ehre: Ein Kampf für deutsche Wiedergeburt (Munich 1936), p. 337.

2   See, for instance, Mein Kampf, pp. 602–3.

3   Das Schwarze Korps, 16 January 1936: 'Sightseeing Sir?'

4   Grimm specifically invokes these links in his 'Englisch-deutsche Probleme'.

5   Even the leading journal, the Zeitschrift für vergleichende Sprachforschung, was German.

6   In the case of English, the first decades of the twentieth century were marked by the publication of the definitive Austro-German accounts of Old and Middle English. See Carl Luick, Historische Grammatik der englischen Sprache (Leipzig 1914); Carl Brunner, Abriß der mittelenglischen Grammatik (Halle 1938).

7   Cf. the preoccupation with Germanic *Lehnwörter* in the Romance languages.

8   The craze for 'authentic' Germanic names to replace the Graeco-Roman imports of Christianity (to say nothing of the even more suspect Old Testament variety) was a connected phenomenon.

9   See August, Count von Platen, 'Das Grab im Busento' (1828); Felix Dahn, *Ein Kampf um Rom* (1876–8).

10   See F. Braun, *Die letzten Schicksale der Krimgoten* (St Petersburg 1890) and Richard Löwe, *Die Reste der Germanen am Schwarzen Meer: Eine ethnologische Untersuchung* (Halle 1896).

11   Cf. Karl Heinz Roth, '"Generalplan Ost" – "Gesamtplan Ost": Forschungsstand, Quellenprobleme, neue Ergebnisse', in Mechthild Rössler et al. (eds.), *Der 'Generalplan Ost': Hauptlinien der nationalsozialistischen Planungs- und Vernichtungspolitik* (Berlin 1993), pp. 25–117.

12   Werner Sombart, *Händler und Helden: Patriotische Besinnungen* (Leipzig 1915).

13   Baumgarten, *Religiöses und kirchliches Leben*, p. 1.

14   Ibid.

15   Jäckel and Kuhn, *Hitler*, p. 1217.

16   *Mein Kampf*, p. 133.

17   The actual cartoon does not survive (see Jäckel and Kuhn, *Hitler*, p. 1256).

18   Baumgarten, *Religiöses*, p. 1.

19   The title does not translate easily: *Gesittung* has no real equivalent in English. 'Moral Principles' should not be taken to mean Christian morality: Gustav Hübener, *England und die Gesittungsgrundlagen der europäischen Frühgeschichte* (Frankfurt am Main 1930). When Hübener's book was reissued in 1940, the reviews revealed the change that had taken place in German hopes during the later 1930s: 'The book demonstrates . . . how close the ties with Continental culture once were' (*Die neueren Sprachen* 48: 7, 8 (1940), supplementary page).

20   See *Beowulf*, l.455. Beowulf apart, the similarity with the German epics is greatest in *Widsith*, *Deor*, *Waldere* and the *Finnsburg Fragment*.

21   For the connection with the *Ring*'s Siegmund theme, see *Beowulf*, 874ff.

22   It is as if the war had somehow become linked in right-wing minds with the famous football match played between the trenches. The naval blockade simply did not constitute a recognised part of football rules. While the German Army stuck to the rules, the British had switched to rugby, simply picked up the ball and scored a goal. The goal was real enough, but in a sense it did not count. Continuing nationalist self-delusion could thus coexist with at least a minimum of political realism.

23   The quotation, drawn from an article on Shakespeare, is paradigmatic of what the Nazis most admired in English literature. Cf. Paul

Borgwardt, 'Shakespeare und seine Behandlung im heutigen Klassen-unterricht', *Die neueren Sprachen* 44 (1936), 208. For the wider resonance of this Teutonic heroism, see, *inter alia*, Levin Ludwig Schücking, *Heldenstolz und Würde im Angelsächsischen* (Leipzig 1933).

24   See Hans F. K. Günther, *Rassenkunde des deutschen Volkes*, 12th (revised) edition (Munich 1928), pp. 40–1.

25   Hans F. K. Günther, *Ritter, Tod und Teufel: Der heldische Gedanke*, (Munich 1920), p. 94.

26   *Völkischer Beobachter*, 13 September 1935.

27   'Rücksichtslose Willenstat': Günther, *Ritter*, p. 96.

28   For Günther's own version of events see his post-war account, *Mein Eindruck von Adolf Hitler* (Pähl 1969).

29   See *Die Bewegung*, 29 July 1930.

30   Cf. Viktor Klemperer, *LTI: Aus dem Notizbuch eines Philologen* (Leipzig 1996).

31   Jäckel and Kuhn, *Hitler*, p. 1217.

32   *Mein Kampf*, p. 132, again p. 132, and p. 167 respectively.

33   Cf., *inter alia*, *Das Reich*, 19 July 1942: 'Die sogenannte russische Seele', or the radio broadcasts reporting the fall of Stalingrad. For the latter, see Kris and Speyer, *German Radio Propaganda*, pp. 431–2.

34   *Table Talk*, 6 September 1942.

35   Ibid., 31 August 1942.

36   Hitler repaid such chivalry with characteristic crassness: he insisted on having the bodies disinterred and transferred to Germany.

37   See Jäckel and Kuhn, *Hitler*, 17 June 1920, p. 147.

38   Ibid., 17 February 1922, p. 577.

39   Gerhard L. Weinberg (ed.), *Hitlers Zweites Buch: Ein Dokument aus dem Jahre 1928* (Stuttgart 1961), p. 167 (hereafter, *Zweites Buch* (Second Book)).

40   Kircher, *Wie's die Engländer machen*, p. 89.

41   Grimm, 'Englisch-deutsche', 277.

42   Ibid.

43   W. Schulz, 'Englisch als erste Fremdsprache', *Zeitschrift für den französischen und englischen Unterricht* 24 (1925), 334. See also Dibelius, *England*, vol. II, p. 204, or M. Kuttner, *Westeuropäische und deutsche Kultur* (Leipzig 1927), pp. 28–9.

44   *Table Talk*, 8 August 1941.

45   Klemperer, *Diaries*, 21 April 1922.

46   Ibid., 4 February 1921.

47   Cf. Jäckel and Kuhn, *Hitler*, 20 July 1921, p. 444.

48   Ibid., 2 February 1921, p. 309.

49   Ibid.

50   Jäckel and Kuhn, *Hitler*, p. 1217.

51   See *Zweites Buch*, p. 164.

52   Ibid.

53   *Table Talk*, 8 August 1941.

54   This is a point made over many years by Gerhard Weinberg.

55   Weinberg is, however, entirely right about one thing: the Nazis never grasped that their systematic breaches of treaties and verbal undertakings effectively precluded an Anglo-German settlement after 1939 as far as Britain was concerned.

56   *Zweites Buch*, p. 28.

57   See, *inter alia*, Jäckel and Kuhn, *Hitler*, 20 March 1923, p. 846.

58   *Table Talk*, 6 September 1942.

59   See Hans Günther, *Rassenkunde des deutschen Volkes*, 16th edition (Munich 1935), p. 494.

60   *Table Talk*, 24 August 1942.

61   *Zweites Buch*, p. 166.

62   For the reactions of Germany's *Anglisten* to Günther: see Gerwin Strobl, 'The Bard of Eugenics: Shakespeare and Racial Activism in the Third Reich', *Journal of Contemporary History* (July 1999), 323–36.

63   Friedrich Merkenschlager, the author of *Götter, Helden und Günther: Eine Abwehr des Güntherschen Rassengedankens* (Nuremberg 1926), was sacked from his research post at the Pflanzenbiologische Anstalt Berlin in September 1933. See also the related fate of another academic 'old fighter', Karl Saller, who was removed from Göttingen University in January 1935. For the background to both cases see Cornelia Essner, 'Im "Irrgarten der Rassenlogik" oder nordische Rassenlehre und nationale Frage', *Historische Mitteilungen* 7 (1994), 90ff.

64   Voßler's repeated championship of Jewish academics did not help either. For details, see Helmut Heiber (ed.), *Universität unterm Hakenkreuz: Der Professor im Dritten Reich: Bilder aus der akademischen Provinz* (Munich 1991), p. 224.

65   Hans Peter Lütjen, 'Das Seminar für Englische Sprache und Kultur 1933 bis 1945', in Eckart Krause, Ludwig Huber and Holger Fischer (eds.), *Hochschulalltag im Dritten Reich: Die Hamburger Universität 1933–1945* (Berlin 1991), p. 750.

66   Ibid., p. 740.

67   Ibid, p. 744.

68   See *Table Talk*, 2 February 1942.

69   Ludwig Alsdorf, *Indien* (Berlin 1940). Cf. *Table Talk*, 22 August 1942.

70   See Goebbels' Diaries, 5 March 1940; and Willi A. Boelcke (ed.), *Kriegspropaganda 1939–41: Geheime Ministerkonferenzen im Reichspropaganda-ministerium* (Stuttgart 1966), 2 November 1939.

71   Rosenberg, 'Gedanken'.

72   See Hermann Weber, 'Die politische Verantwortung der Wissenschaft:

Friedrich Berber in den Jahren 1937 bis 1945', in Krause et al., *Hochschulalltag*, p. 939.

73   *Mein Kampf*, pp. 380ff.

74   Günther, *Rassenkunde des deutschen Volkes*, p. 494.

75   Günther, *Ritter*, pp. 137–8.

76   The senate of Jena University had done its utmost to prevent Günther's appointment, and protested formally after the decision had been forced through by Frick, the minister responsible for higher education in the state of Thuringia. Since the episode occurred in 1930, when the Nazis were still kept from power elsewhere, the protests were forceful in tone, and the whole affair became a *cause célèbre*.

77   Wilhelm Langenbeck, *Englands Weltmacht in ihrer Entwicklung vom 17. Jahrhundert bis auf unsere Tage* (Leipzig 1919), p. 26; and Dibelius, *England*, vol. I, pp. 161–2.

78   Walter Scheidt, 'Rassenkunde der britischen Inseln', in Paul Hartig and Wilhelm Schellberg, *Handbuch der Englandkunde* (2 vols., Frankfurt am Main 1929), vol. II, p. 88.

79   Kircher, *Wie's die Engländer*, pp. 199–204.

80   Baumgarten, *Religiöses*, p. 4.

81   'Das richtungs- und gesinnungslose Vielwissen': Hans Günther, *Der Nordische Gedanke unter den Deutschen* (Munich 1925), p. 121.

82   Jäckel and Kuhn, *Hitler*, p. 1217.

83   Günther elaborated on the dangers of urbanisation in a tract dedicated to Rosenberg: *Die Verstädterung: Ihre Gefahren für Volk und Staat vom Standpunkt der Lebensforschung und Gesellschaftswissenschaft* (Leipzig 1934).

84   Hans Günther, *Kleine Rassenkunde Europas* (Munich 1925), p. 181.

85   For the enduring appeal of this anecdote, see, for instance, Grimm, 'Englisch-deutsche'.

86   Alfred Rosenberg, 'Englands Schicksalsstunden', *Nationalsozialistische Monatshefte* 4 (July 1930), 160.

87   See Bernhard Pier, *Rassenbiologische Betrachtungsweise der Geschichte Englands* (Frankfurt am Main 1935), pp. 17–19, which is based on Günther's work. See also Scheidt, 'Rassenkunde der britischen Inseln', p. 65.

88   This piece of propaganda was actually broadcast by the English Language Service of German radio five weeks into the war. For details, see Horst J. P. Bergmaier and Rainer E. Lotz, *Hitler's Airwaves: The Inside Story of Nazi Broadcasting and Propaganda Swing* (New Haven 1997), pp. 293–4.

89   *Zweites Buch*, p. 223.

90   *Table Talk*, 5 November 1941.

91   Ibid., 2 September 1942.

92   Volker Raddatz, *Englandkunde im Wandel deutscher Erziehungsideale* (Kronberg 1977), p. 141.

93   *Table Talk*, 27 January and 25 June 1942, respectively.

94   For an account of the tangled web of Nazi racial thought, see Cornelia Essner's excellent article 'Im "Irrgarten der Rassenlogik"', or G. Field's older but still useful 'Nordic Racism', *Journal of the History of Ideas* 38 (1977), 523–40.

95   For Günther's career after 1933, see Gisela Bock, *Zwangssterilisation im Nationalsozialismus* (Opladen 1986), pp. 68ff.

96   Günther, *Mein Eindruck von Adolf Hitler*, pp. 13ff and 62ff.

97   See Madison Grant, *The Passing of the Great Race: Or the Racial Basis of European History* (New York 1917), and Theodore Lothrop Stoddard, *The Revolt against Civilisation: The Menace of the Under-man* (New York 1922).

98   William Inge, *England* (London 1926).

99   Günther, *Rassenkunde Europas*, p. 16.

100   Ibid., p. 189.

101   Ibid., p. 190 (that count had proved alarmingly low).

102   See *Jenaische Zeitung*, 4 June 1930.

103   Some academics, like the art historian Dagobert Frey, were reluctant to identify individual characters by their alleged racial background. They preferred instead to ascribe the artistic vision that produced them to 'Celtic influence' – or, as in Frey's case, 'possibly Celtic influence'. Political dues were thus paid without too much professional loss of face. See Frey, *Englisches Wesen in der bildenden Kunst* (Stuttgart 1942), p. 421.

104   For the interplay of academic research and Nazi policy in the East, see Michael Burleigh, *Germany Turns Eastward* (Cambridge 1988).

3   *Empire builders: Britain as a paradigm for Nazi expansion*

1   *Zweites Buch*, p. 165.

2   See, for instance, 'Politische Auswirkungen der Londoner Seeabrüstungs-konferenz', *Die Bewegung*, 10 June 1930, or 'Die deutsche Kriegsmarine und die Flottenvereinbarungen der 5 Seemächte', ibid., 10 March 1931; Rosenberg, 'Englands Schicksalsstunden'; 'Irland und Großbritannien', *Die deutsche Zukunft: Organ der NS-Jugend* (July 1932); or 'Das Ergebnis von Ottawa', ibid. (October 1932).

3   See C. G. Harke, 'Des britischen Reiches Schicksalsstunde', *Der Angriff* 20 May 1929. The title of the piece – 'The British Empire's Moment of Destiny' – was itself something of a recurring theme in Nazi journalism (see below).

4   Cf. a series of articles in the *Berliner Illustrierte* in September and October 1936: Karl Bartz, 'Schicksalsstunden eines Weltreiches'. These were based on Bartz's book *Englands Weg nach Indien: Schicksalsstunden des britischen Weltreiches* (Berlin 1936).

5   In the case of Italy, coverage did expand in the late thirties, but the perspective was strictly contemporary.

6   *Berliner Illustrierte*, 1 October 1936.

7   Goebbels would later choose this as a title for a collection of his journalism: *Die Zeit ohne Beispiel: Reden und Aufsätze aus den Jahren 1939/40/41* (Munich 1941).

8   Austrian history, of possible relevance in the case of Bohemia, also offered no precedent: the Austro-Hungarian administration of Bosnia-Herzegovina, prior to 1908, was hardly an obvious parallel, since it did not replace an existing government; moreover, Habsburg rule was established within the framework of a wider international settlement.

9   The identification of the Czechs as a *Kolonialvolk* was quite overt within Nazi government. See, for instance, Boelcke, *Kriegspropaganda*, 29 January 1940.

10 This stratagem clearly owed more to the advisers of the leadership than to its principal exponents. Rosenberg, for instance, failed to spot the significance of Protectorate status entirely. Hence the comparison between a German Bohemia and a British Ireland in *Völkischer Beobachter*, 23 March 1939: 'Europa und England' (reprinted in Rosenberg, *Tradition und Gegenwart* (Munich 1941), p. 248.

11 Goebbels, *Diaries*, 19–24 March 1939.

12 *Westdeutscher Beobachter*, 31 March 1939.

13 The alarm of many of the Reich's generals and senior civil servants, as Hitler's plans unfolded, is too familiar to require retelling here. As for the German public, their response during the Sudeten crisis speaks for itself.

14 The fact that France's humiliation did not preclude a later Anglo-French alliance must also have seemed relevant as Germany's relations were coming under greater strain. As the *Second Book* makes clear, conflict with Britain was, in Hitler's mind, not necessarily permanent – a point often missed.

15 *Das Schwarze Korps*, 5 January 1939: 'Das ungeschriebene Gesetz'.

16 *Berliner Illustrierte*, 24 September 1936.

17 Kircher, *Wie's die Engländer*.

18 Klemperer, *Diaries*, 13 October 1920: 'Er [i.e. Klemperer's namesake the banker Victor von Klemperer] redete auch sehr gut über englische und deutsche Kolonisationsmethoden, ausgezeichnet ergänzend, was Dibelius neulich vortrug. Die Engländer haben die Eingeborenen überall verdienen und nach eigener Façon selig werden lassen und Anhänglichkeiten geerntet. Wir schreckten durch preußische Disciplin ab.'

19 See Lothar Kühne, *Das Kolonialverbrechen von Versailles* (Graz 1939).

20   Dibelius, *England*, vol. II, pp. 220 and 214 respectively.

21   See Phillip Aronstein, 'Die Kulturkunde im englischen Unterricht', *Monatsschrift für Höhere Schulen* 25 (1926), 266–7.

22   *Zweites Buch*, p. 165: 'Wenn die Erde heute ein englisches Weltreich besitzt, dann gibt es aber auch zur Zeit kein Volk, das auf Grund seiner allgemeinen staatspolitischen Eigenschaften sowie seiner durchschnittlichen politischen Klugheit mehr dazu befähigt wäre'. (Hitler's German here is characteristically vague and 'staatspolitische Eigenschaften' is practically untranslatable.)

23   Cf., *inter alia*, Dibelius, vol. II, p. 202; Kircher, *Wie's die Engländer*, p. 17, and the substantial list of quotations from various educational sources quoted in Raddatz, *Englandkunde*, pp. 125–6.

24   See Dibelius, vol. I, p. 188.

25   See Baumgarten, *Religiöses*, p. 116: 'Da dem Engländer sehr starke Triebe der Machtbehauptung und Machterweiterung, der Weltbeherrschung . . . eignen'.

26   Cf., *inter alia*, F. Brie, 'Der englische Nationalcharakter', *Lebensfragen des britischen Weltreiches* (Berlin 1921), pp. 54 and 68; Dibelius, *England*, vol. I, pp. 201–6; or W. Zorn, 'Kulturkunde im neusprachlichen Unterricht', *Monatsschrift für Höhere Schulen* 27 (1928), p. 52.

27   See, particularly, the magazines *L'Assiette au Beurre* and *Le Rire*.

28   Kircher, *Wie's die Engländer*, p. 96.

29   See Rosenberg, 'Gedanken'.

30   Klemperer, *Diaries*, 1 October 1924. Note also Klemperer's post-war bitterness about the role of his profession in undermining the Weimar Republic: cf. *Und so ist alles schwankend: Tagebücher Juni bis Dezember 1945* (Berlin 1995).

31   Dibelius, vol. I, p. 182. See also Hans Richert, *Die deutsche Bildungseinheit und die höhere Schule: Ein Buch von deutscher Nationalerziehung* (Tübingen 1920), p. 71.

32   See the substantial number of quotations on this topic in Raddatz, *Englandkunde*, pp. 122–4.

33   Dibelius, *England*, vol. II, p. 168.

34   Langenbeck, *Englands Weltmacht*, p. 28.

35   Dibelius, *England*, vol. II, pp. 216–18 (eagerly echoed by Rosenberg, 'Gedanken').

36   Klemperer, *Diaries*, 24 November 1936.

37   Baumgarten, *Religiöses*, p. 70.

38   Cf. Karl Arns, 'Zum Thema: Carlyle als Mittelpunkt des englischen Unterrichts in Prima', *Zeitschrift für den französischen und englischen Unterricht* 19 (1920), pp. 164–72. See also his *Der religiöse britische Imperialismus* (Bochum 1919).

39 Arns, 'Zum Thema', p. 171.

40 Klemperer, *Diaries*, 2 March 1921: 'Und man hat jetzt Sinn für den Aufstand eines unterdrückten Volkes, für die Wildheit eines Siegers.' (These thoughts were prompted by a film set in Spain at the time of the 1808 rising against the French.)

41 Klemperer, *Diaries*, 13 October 1920.

42 Dibelius, *England*, vol. I, pp. 107–9.

43 *Mein Kampf*, p. 133.

44 *Zweites Buch*, p. 164.

45 Cf. Baumgarten, *Religiöses*, pp. 70ff.

46 See Michael Freund, *Oliver Cromwell* (Leipzig 1933); Johannes Tralow, *Gewalt aus der Erde* (Berlin 1933); Mirko Jelusich, *Oliver Cromwell* (Vienna 1933) (Jelusich, who was briefly director of Vienna's Burgtheater after the *Anschluß*, also produced a stage version of his novel in 1934); Max Schweigel, *Oliver Cromwell* (Leipzig 1935) (written in English for use in schools). Finally, Cromwell was the focus of interest of a professional historian: Wilhelm Oncken, *Vier Essays über die Führung einer Nation* (Berlin 1935).

47 Heinrich Bauer, *Oliver Cromwell, Ein Kampf um Freiheit und Diktatur* (Munich 1932).

48 Heinrich Bauer, 'Cromwell und die deutsche Revolution', *National-sozialistische Monatshefte* 39 (June 1933), 255–62.

49 Ibid., 256.

50 Ibid, 261.

51 Ibid., 256.

52 Ibid., 259: 'Wir erkennen klar die zwingende Gleichartigkeit dieser uns vorausgehenden, aus den Tiefen der germanischen Seele aufbrechenden, nationalen Revolution, die vorwärts getragen und zum Sieg geführt wird durch die übermenschliche Schöpferkraft eines Einzelnen, zu dem überwältigenden Geschehen unserer Tage.'

53 Goebbels is an apparent exception: see his assessment of the Schleicher cabinet that there was 'no obvious Cromwell' among them (13 August 1932: 'Ein Cromwell sitzt nicht in diesem Kabinett'). Goebbels' knowledge, however, may have been both recent and superficial. It may not be unconnected with a tract by one Weygand von Miltenberg entitled *Schleicher, Hitler? – Cromwell!* (Leipzig 1932). Yet see also Hitler's observations to the Bulgarian Honorary Consul of December 1922 about his plans for a dictatorship, to be succeeded by 'a form of government similar to the Commonwealth' (*ähnlich dem Lordprotektorat*) (Jäckel and Kuhn, *Hitler*, late December 1922, p. 773); or, twenty years later, a remark in the *Table Talk* (26 February 1942) that Britain could only be saved by another Cromwell. How much Hitler actually knew about Cromwell is difficult to establish.

54   Cf. Raddatz, *Englandkunde*, p. 144, who lists as examples R. Fränkel, *Der fremdsprachliche Unterricht und die neue Erziehung* (Leipzig 1933), p. 15; A. Krüper, 'Englisch als Lehrfach der nationalsozialistischen höheren Schule', *Die neueren Sprachen* 43 (1935), 94; and Krüper, 'Das geschichtliche und politische Schrifttum in der englischen Schullektüre', *Neuphilologische Monatsschrift* 6 (1935), 242.

55   Bauer, 'Cromwell', 255.

56   See the reference to a play by one W. Frerichs, published in Bielefeld 1938, in *Archiv für das Studium der neueren Sprachen* 93 (173) (1938), 270.

57   Goebbels, *Diaries*, 18 November 1935.

58   See the BBC interview with Hitler's majordomo at the Berghof, Hermann Döring, in Laurence Rees, *The Nazis: A Warning from History* (BBC Films 1997).

59   Cf. *Das Schwarze Korps*, 16 January 1936: 'Sightseeing, Sir: A Handful of Soldiers'.

60   Ibid., 10 April 1935: 'Eine Handvoll Soldaten beherrscht ein 300 Millionen Volk': 'Man muß gestehen die Engländer waren ausgezeichnete Kaufleute, aber vielleicht noch bessere Menschenkenner, Menschenbehandler und Soldaten. Ja, Soldaten! . . . Dieser Film hat vom Anfang bis zum Ende den Geist und die Haltung, die in unserem neuen Deutschland dem ganzen Volk eigen ist: Treue und Pflichterfüllung bis zum Letzten, Kameradschaft und Sorge um den Anderen, der vielleicht schwächer ist. Da ziehen sie nun im Ausland über unser neues Deutschland her, sie machen aus uns ihren Behauptungen nach eine einzige Kaserne, in dem Drill und – um ihren blöden Ausdruck zu gebrauchen – 'Kadavergehorsam' jedes Menschentum unterdrücken und ersticken, und dann kommt aus diesem selben Ausland ein Film zu uns, ein Ausschnitt aus dem Leben eines großen und mächtigen Volkes, der genau das betont, was diese räudigen Zungen bei uns . . . an den Pranger stellen wollen.'

61   Cf. ibid., 16 January 1936.

62   Wolfgang Greiser, *Raleigh* (Burmeisters Abenteuer Serie, Bremen 1935); W. Freiburger, *Nelson's Life and Deeds*. (n.p. 1937) (written in English for use in German schools); see also the translation from the Italian original of Ettore Bravetta's account of Nelson's life, *Der große Admiral* (Berlin 1936); Theodor Lücke, *Wellington: Der eiserne Herzog* (Berlin 1938); Froembgen, *Marlborough*.

63   Cf. Emil Bode, *Der Eroberer Südafrikas* (Lübeck 1932), which anticipates the Third Reich's interest in Rhodes. Bernhard Voigt's *Fürs größere Vaterland: Der Lebenstraum des Rhodes* (Hamburg 1933) was later re-issued with the less emotive title *Cecil Rhodes: Der Lebenstraum eines Briten* (Potsdam 1939) – a reflection of the deteriorating relations with Britain. Finally there is

Dagobert von Mikusch, author of an encomium of General Franco *Rhodes: Der Traum einer Weltherrschaft* (Berlin 1936).

64   Hans Franke, *Das Ende des Kapitän Cook* (Saarlautern 1937). The book is recommended in those terms by a reviewer in *Der Pimpf: NS-Jungenblätter* 11 (November 1937).

65   Cf. Stephan Bohr, *Afrikaforscher und Missionar Dr. Livingstone* (Jugendglocken 6, Bremen 1934); 'Dr. Livingstone', *Der Pimpf* 1 (January 1939).

66   Cf. Alfred Ehrentreich, '"Lawrence of Arabia" im Lichte seiner Freunde', *Archiv für das Studium der neueren Sprachen* 93 (173) (1938), 81–4; Fritz Steuben, *Emir Dynamit: Bilder aus dem Leben des Obersten Lawrence* (Stuttgart 1933).

67   Max Spatzier (ed.), *Heralds of British Imperialism* (Teubners Neusprachliche Lesestoffe im Dienste nationalpolitischer Erziehung, vol. II, Leipzig 1935).

68   Margaret von Seydewitz and Alwin Paul, *Eminent Englishmen*, vol. 1 (Leipzig 1934); vols. II and III (1935); all three published in English for use in schools.

69   Cf. *Erziehung und Unterricht in der Höheren Schule: Amtliche Ausgabe des Reichs- und Preußischen Ministeriums für Wissenschaft, Erziehung und Volksbildung* (Berlin 1938), p. 216: 'Stoffe . . . welche für die Denkart, den Volkscharakter, für die Artverwandtheit oder das Anderssein des fremden Volkes kennzeichnend sind, und Werke, welche die großen geschichtlichen Leistungen in den fremden Führerpersönlichkeiten, ihre Kraftquellen und Ideale aufdecken . . . Dabei darf auch das Heldentum des Forschers und Entdeckers nicht vergessen werden': (quoted in Kurt-Ingo Flessau, *Schule der Diktatur: Lehrpläne und Schulbücher des Nationalsozialismus* (Munich 1977), p. 86).

70   Walter Hübner, 'Englisches Schrifttum und deutsche Erziehung', *Neuphilologische Monatsschrift* 5 (1934), 197 (quoted in Raddatz, *Englandkunde*, p. 57): 'Politische Schulung will die völlige Neuprägung des Menschen zu einer Gesinnungs- und Willensbereitschaft, zu einer Bejahung der Opfer heischenden Zukunft des Volkes.'

71   A recognisable echo of Wilhelm Frick, the first Nazi Minister of Education. See Frick, *Kampfziel der deutschen Schule* (Langensalza 1933).

72   Alwin Paul, 'Übung – Lektüre, Übersetzung und Besprechung von englischen und amerikanischen Werken über den Weltkrieg (mit besonderer Berücksichtigung der Kriegsschuldfrage)', *Die höhere Schule* 2 (5) (1935), 129–34: 'weil "gerade das englische Schrift- und Volkstum" "charakterbildende Themen" bilde und "aus einer uns artverwandten Seele entspringe"', quoted in Reiner Lehberger, *'Collect all the English inscriptions you can find in our city': Englischunterricht an Hamburger Volksschulen 1870–1945* (Hamburg 1990), p. 743.

73   '. . . Das fremde Volkstum [ist] in allen seinen Äußerungen zu erfassen

als Ausdruck des Rassischen, als bedingt durch seine blutmäßige Zusammensetzung . . . Hier kann die Betrachtung des artverwandten englischen Volkes und seiner Kultur und Geschichte immer wieder beispielhaft wirken, wenn gezeigt wird, wie hier durch die Jahrhunderte hindurch ein überwiegend nordisches Volk um seine völkische Form ringt, und wie gerade bei den großen Führergestalten das instinktsichere Überwinden artfremder Hemmungen besonders sinnfällig wird' (Erich Kirsch, 'Englisch', in Rudolf Benze und Alfred Pudelko (eds.), *Rassische Erziehung als Unterrichtsgrundsatz der Fachgebiete* (Frankfurt am Main 1937), p. 164 and quoted in Reiner Lehberger, 'Neusprachlicher Unterricht in der NS-Zeit', in Reinhard Dithmar (ed.), *Schule und Unterricht im Dritten Reich* (Neuwied 1989), p. 119.

74   Heinrich Bauer, 'Shakespeare', *Nationalsozialistische Monatshefte* (1933), 372–7.

75   Hans Günther, 'Shakespeares Frauen und Mädchen aus lebenskundlicher Sicht', *Jahrbuch der deutschen Shakespeare-Gesellschaft* 73, Neue Folge 14 (Weimar 1937), p. 95. (For a discussion of this, see Strobl, 'Shakespeare and Racial Activism'.)

76   Dibelius, *England*, vol. II, p. 171. Cf. also the echoes of Dibelius in the remarks about public schools in the entry for '*England*' in *Meyers Konversationslexikon*, 8th edn (Leipzig 1936): 'Es kommt aber weniger auf die intellektuelle Ausbildung an als auf die Erziehung zum Gentleman, auf die Schulung des Willens, der Selbstzucht und der Führereigenschaften im Sport.'

77   Cf. ibid., vol. II, p. 168.

78   It is surely no accident that the single most famous cry for freedom in the German language is that of the Marquis de Posa in Schiller's *Don Carlos*, 'Sire, grant us freedom of thought.'

79   It is perhaps worth noting, for instance, that in the ever popular paintings of Spitzweg, created during the intense political repression of the Restoration, nearly all the characters depicted are also characters in the secondary sense of the term. (Much the same could be said of the characters of Nestroy in the Austria of Metternich.)

80   Fränkel, *Der fremdsprachliche Unterricht und die neue Erziehung*, quoted in Raddatz, p. 147.

81   A line of argument echoed enthusiastically by Rosenberg ('Gedanken').

82   *Mein Kampf*, pp. 230–1.

83   Klemperer, *LTI*, p. 245.

84   See, for instance, Bruno Dreßler, 'Die Entwicklung der körperlichen Ertüchtigung in der englischen Erziehung', *Die neueren Sprachen* 44 (1936), 359.

85 See, for instance, Reinhold Hoops, 'England und sein Weltreich', *Die neueren Sprachen* 43 (1935), 48.

86 Waldemar Schmidt, 'Neuphilologie als Auslandswissenschaft', *Die neueren Sprachen* 43 (1935), 496.

87 See Raddatz, *Englandkunde*, p. 147.

88 Hermann Heuer, 'Englische und deutsche Jugenderziehung', *Zeitschrift für neusprachlichen Unterricht* 36 (1937), 221, quoted in Raddatz, *Englandkunde*, p. 146.

89 See, for instance, Ernst Barts, 'Wesen und Ziele der englischen Boy Scout Movement', *Die neueren Sprachen* 45 (12) (1937), 489: 'In der Erziehungsarbeit des Dritten Reichs spielt die Charakterschulung eine ebenso große Rolle wie bereits seit langer Zeit in dem uns durch Sprache und Rasse eng verwandten Großbritannien.'

90 'Vormilitärische Jugenderziehung in England', *Morgen: NS-Jugendblätter* 11 (November 1935).

91 'Vormilitärische Jugenderziehung in England part 2', *Morgen* 12 (December 1935).

92 See 'Jungvolk auf Englandfahrt', *Morgen* 2 (February 1936).

93 Hermann Fenger, *England und Friesland in ihren kulturellen und wirtschaftlichen Beziehungen* (Bonn 1935); Karl-Hermann Jacob-Friesen, 'Steinzeitliche Beziehungen zwischen Niedersachsen und England', *Die neueren Sprachen* 47 (1939)), 260–7.

94 Erhard Riemann, *Germanen erobern Britannien: Ergebnisse der Vorgeschichte und der Sprachwissenschaft über die Einwanderung der Sachsen, Angeln und Jüten nach England* (Königsberg 1939).

95 Rolf Roeingh, *Ein Schwert hieb über den Kanal: Die siegreiche Englandfahrt Wilhelms des Eroberers nach den Bildberichten des Teppichs von Bayeux* (Berlin 1941).

96 Herbert Beer, *Führen und Folgen, Herrschen und Beherrschtwerden im Sprachgut der Angelsachsen: Ein Beitrag zur Erforschung von Führertum und Gefolgschaft in der germanischen Welt.* (Sprache und Kultur der germanischen und romanischen Völker: Anglistische Reihe vol. xxxi (Breslau 1939)).

97 Cf. the review in *Archiv für das Studium der neueren Sprachen* 95 (177) (1940), 119: 'mit großem Fleiß . . . Empfehlenswert wäre es allerdings gewesen, wenn er gesondert . . . dargelegt hätte, zu welchen neuen Erkenntnissen seine Untersuchung geführt hat.' As a response to a piece funded by the SS, this is splendidly phrased.

98 Cf. also Hitler's dismissal of ethnic 'kinship' in international affairs (*Zweites Buch*, p. 28).

99 In Jäckel and Kuhn, *Hitler*, 17 April 1920, p. 123.

100 Günther, *Rassenkunde des deutschen Volkes*, p. 145 and *Kleine Rassenkunde Europas*, p. 181. Günther based his conclusions on the data of Grant and of a Victorian study, John Beddoe's *The Races of Great Britain* (London 1885).

101   See Robert S. Wistrich, *Weekend in Munich: Art, Propaganda and Terror in the Third Reich* (London 1995).

102   Kirsch, 'Englisch', in Benze and Pudelko (eds.), *Rassische Erziehung*, p. 164.

103   *Das Schwarze Korps*, 5 January 1939: 'Das ungeschriebene Gesetz: Ein Weg zur Weltmacht'.

104   Ibid.

105   Ibid.

106   Rosenberg, 'Die rassische Bedingtheit', pp. 339–40.

107   Cf. the telltale wording in the review of Peter Aldag's *Juden erobern England* and *Juden beherrschen England* in *Das Reich*, 18 August 1940: 'Am verblüffendsten und interessantesten ist das . . . Kapitel, in welchem Aldag die judenfreundliche Einstellung Cromwells schildert.'

108   *Berliner Illustrierte*, 25 November 1937: 'Der Weg zum vollkommenen Menschen: Sir Francis Galton, der Vater der bewußten Rassenpflege'.

109   See, for instance, Günther, *Kleine Rassenkunde Europas*, pp. 412ff.

110   Günther, 'Shakespeares Frauen', pp. 86–8.

111   *Das Schwarze Korps*, 12 January 1939: 'Das ungeschriebene Gesetz: Der Weg zur Weltmacht'.

112   *Das Schwarze Korps*, 22 May 1935: 'Widernatürliche Unzucht ist todeswürdig'.

113   Ibid.

114   Jäckel and Kuhn, *Hitler*, 17 April 1920, p. 122.

115   See *Table Talk*, 17 September 1941, 3 March 1942 and 22 August 1942.

116   Yet to read Curzon's anxious viceregal correspondence with the India Office on the subject of maharajas visiting Britain and impressionable Englishwomen (particularly of the lower orders) is to see that Hitler may have had a point after all. For details, and related issues, see Ronald Hyam, *Empire and Sexuality: The British Experience* (Manchester 1990).

117   *Table Talk*, 22 August 1942. (See also its unmistakable echoes in Goebbels' 'Seid nicht allzu gerecht', *Das Reich*, 6 September 1942.)

118   See n. 100.

119   Rosenberg 'Englands Schicksalsstunden', 165. That such thoughts were connected with the presence of black French soldiers in Germany during the Allied occupation of the Rhine is an obvious point.

120   Richthofen, *Brito-Germania*, p. 105.

121   For proof of the mental link between the British and Habsburg Empires, see *Table Talk*, 31 January 1942, or authors as different as Colin Ross (*Die Welt*, p. 76) and Hans Grimm ('Englisch-deutsche Probleme', p. 276).

122   Rosenberg, 'Die rassische Bedingtheit', p. 340.

123   Ibid.

124   *Das Schwarze Korps*, 10 April 1935.

125   *Table Talk*, 22 January 1942.

126   *Das Schwarze Korps*, 10 February 1940.

127   *Ausstellung 'Raubstaat England'* (Munich 1941).

4   *'Their aged bones are rattling': Britain and the Nazi concept of modernity*

1   This seemed clear even to some member of the leadership itself: cf. Gobbels' diary entry of 24 November 1937 expressing concern about 'one-sided information' reaching the Führer; a concern, he notes, shared by Neurath.

2   Cf. Michael Bloch, *Ribbentrop* (London 1992), pp. 96ff.

3   On Göring's ambiguous role, see Richard Overy, *Göring: 'The Iron Man'* (London 1984), especially pp. 77 and 90–3.

4   Yet, even at this stage, Hitler's preference may have been an understanding with Britain. See Goebbels, *Diaries*, 21 August 1938.

5   Cf. Goebbels' entry of 13 July 1937 on the subject of Hitler's current views about the British Empire: 'Der Führer erörtert Englands Stellung in der Welt. Sieht sie als sehr geschwächt an. Das Imperium ist im Stillstand, wenn nicht im Rückgang.'

6   The details of this supposed instinct are set out most clearly in an early speech at Rosenheim on 17 June 1920: 'Macht geht vor Recht' (Jäckel and Kuhn, *Hitler*, p. 147). Cf. also Goebbels' remarks about 'democratic brutality' (*Diaries*, 20 October 1937).

7   That events in Palestine also provided ample scope for anti-semitic propaganda goes without saying.

8   Goebbels, *Diaries*, 21 August 1938.

9   Ibid., 3 September 1937

10   Ibid., 4 April 1937.

11   Ibid., 30 December 1937.

12   Ibid., 31 December 1937.

13   *Table Talk*, 7 January 1942.

14   *Table Talk*, 2 February 1942.

15   See, for instance, Gobbels' diary entry for 21 October 1936. Yet there appears to have been a degree of vacillation: cf. the sharply contradictory diary entries for 10 April and 14 August 1937. (That the embers of past hopes still glowed a little is demonstrated by Hitler's own remarks in the *Table Talk*: see 26 February and 2 September 1942).

16   Karl Maßmann, *Die alten Männer wollten Krieg* (Berlin 1939).

17   *Das Schwarze Korps*, 26 October 1939.

18   Maßmann, *Die alten Männer*, p. 7.

19   Ibid., p. 26.

20   See the newly nazified *Wiener Zeitung*, 18 May 1938 (i.e. about two months after the *Anschluß*); there had been no suggestion in that paper of

Chamberlain's health being in any way compromised before the annexation.

21   Goebbels, *Diaries*, 7 August 1936.

22   Ibid., 7 February 1938.

23   Ibid., 19 March 1939 (Goebbels actually uses the English words here).

24   Ibid., 18 March 1939.

25   Ibid., 13 October 1939.

26   Ibid., 26 February 1940.

27   Ibid., 12 April 1940.

28   Ibid., 9 May 1940.

29   Ibid., 28 January 1937.

30   Ibid., 24 March 1939.

31   See Speer's reminiscence to this effect about Goebbels and Göring: *Erinnerungen* (Berlin 1969), p. 177.

32   Goebbels, *Diaries*, 1 December 1937.

33   See ibid., 9 May 1932: 'Ein vergreistes Haus'. Neither 'old', nor 'senescent' capture adequately the dismissive flavour of *vergreist*. The colloquial misuse of 'geriatric' comes closest.

34   Ernest Bramsted, *Goebbels and National Socialist Propaganda, 1925–1945* (Michigan 1965), pp. 436ff.

35   Goebbels, *Diaries*, 26 April 1940. (See also Goebbels, 'Der neue Stil', in *Die Zeit ohne Beispiel*, p. 168.)

36   Though there is perhaps an element of steadying the nerves of his followers in it.

37   Klemperer, *Diaries*, 27 March 1941.

38   W. Schmidt, 'Junges Deutschland – altes England'. *Die neueren Sprachen* 41 (1933), 409–10 (see Raddatz, *Englandkunde*, p. 142).

39   Even a book such as Adolf Halfeld's *England: Verfall oder Aufstieg* (Jena 1933) proves that point. In the words of an anonymous reviewer, Halfeld emphasised the 'unverbrauchte Lebenskraft des Engländers' (*Hamburger Monatshefte für auswärtige Politik* 6 (December 1934), p. 14).

40   The point had been made explicitly to German newspaper readers on the occasion of Chamberlain's earlier visit in September. See, for instance, the detailed coverage, with photographs, in the *Berliner Illustrierte*, 22 September 1938.

41   Goebbels, *Diaries*, 12 October 1937 (see also *Table Talk*, 31 August 1942).

42   Ibid.: 'der Herzog ist wunderbar. Ein netter, sympathischer Junge, offen, klar, mit gesundem Menschenverstand, Blick für modernes Leben und soziale Fragen. Welch ein Genuß, sich mit ihm zu unterhalten. Er springt gleich auf alles an, interessiert sich für jedes Problem, ist gar nicht snobistisch. Wir unterhalten uns über tausenderlei. Parlamentarismus, soziale und Arbeiterprobleme, nationale und internationale Fragen.

Schade, daß er nicht mehr König ist. Mit ihm wären wir zu einem Bündnis gekommen ... Den Herzog hat man gestürzt, weil er das Zeug hatte, ein richtiger König zu werden. Das ist mir nun klarer denn je. Ich habe ihn in diesen 3 Stunden richtig liebgewonnen. Ein sehr genußreicher Nachmittag. Eine Persönlichkeit. Schade, jammerschade!'

43 The literal translation – 'a personality' – fails adequately to convey the admiration inherent in the German word.

44 See *Berliner Illustrierte*, 2 December 1937.

45 See ibid., 5 March 1933: 'Beim Prinzen von Wales'.

46 The paper used the Prince's choice of clothing, a brown suit, for the observation, 'Brown is the fashion these days.' (The *Berliner Illustrierte* tried to keep its distance from the regime longer than most: as late as the Sudeten crisis, it insisted on referring to Hitler as the 'Reich Chancellor' rather than as the Führer: cf. 22 September 1938).

47 Cf. *Berliner Illustrierte*, 26 November 1936.

48 Ibid., 12 November 1936: 'Hallo! Hier Eduard! Anekdoten um den englischen König'.

49 His actual words, 'dem Volk aufs Maul schauen', demonstrate graphically his approach.

50 See *Table Talk*, 24 August 1942.

51 Hans Grimm, 'Baldwin – oder vom schweren Verstehen', *Inneres Reich* 4 : 2 (1937), 433: 'Wer ... die Baldwin-Rede *englisch* hörte oder las, dem wird sie wie mir weder seltsam noch wunderlich geklungen haben, sondern als eine ehrlich gemeinte und nicht unbedeutende Erklärung. Erst, als ich die Rede mir in die deutsche Sprache herüberholte und mit deutschen Ohren deutsch hörte, wurde sie mir fremd und beinahe ärgerlich und sank nicht wenig an Wert; und ich war doch ein Hörer guter Vorbereitung und besonders guten Willens ... Und es mag sein, daß die Engländer vielmehr durch die "anders verstandenen" Sprachmittel aus einander gerieten, als solches von Seelen auch sein mußte.'

52 Spitzy, *How We Squandered the Reich*, pp. 289–90. Spitzy puts particular emphasis on the appearance of British weakness, which is discussed below.

53 Goebbels, *Diaries*, 27 March 1937: 'Die Engländer machen augenblicklich eine kreuzdumme Politik. Reißen das Maul auf, legen sich mit jedem an, aber sind zu feige und zu schwach zum Handeln ... Eden ist ein seltener Dummkopf.'

54 Cf. Hitler's reaction to Britain's collapse in the Far East in *Table Talk*, 18 December 1941: 'Jahrelang habe ich jedem Engländer gesagt: Sie werden Ostasien verlieren, wenn sie in Europa einen Konflikt beginnen! Da waren die Herren ganz hochnäsig.'

55 *Zweites Buch*, p. 167.

56   See, for instance, Goebbels, 'Die verpaßten Gelegenheiten', in *Die Zeit ohne Beispiel*, p. 296. This specifically links the themes of Allied incompetence and unthinking arrogance.

57   The sweeping powers accorded to the Reich President under the Weimar constitution, so fatefully exploited by the *Ersatz-Kaiser* Hindenburg, can only have deepened such misconceptions.

58   See Goebbels' account of Hitler's views on the subject: *Diaries*, 4 December 1936.

59   *Table Talk*, 14 October 1941.

60   See, for instance, the retrospective account in *Table Talk*, 31 August 1942: 'Die Rede des Windsors vor den Frontkämpfern, er betrachte die Einigung mit Deutschland als die größte Aufgabe seines Lebens, hat ihm das Genick gebrochen.' Whether Hitler had actually believed this at the time of the abdication is less clear.

61   See, for instance, Goebbels, *Diaries*, 4 December 1936.

62   See ibid., 12 October 1937.

63   See also Goebbels' description of Halifax as 'sterile' (*Diaries*, 10 January 1940) and Hitler's comments in *Table Talk* of 22 July 1941 that none of the Englishmen with whom he had official dealings had been 'men'.

64   See ibid., 4 December 1937.

65   Ibid., 28 October 1937.

66   *Das Reich*, 11 August 1940: 'Alte und junge Völker'.

67   Cf. *Berliner Illustrierte*, 8 July 1940: 'England aber bereitet sich vor'.

68   Ibid., 28 April 1937: 'The English Character'.

69   Cf. Kris and Speyer, *German Radio Propaganda*, pp. 215–17.

70   Maßmann, *Die alten Männer*, p. 35.

71   Klemperer, *Diaries*, 24 October 1944.

72   See Goebbels, *Diaries*, 23 June 1940. (See also Boelke, *Kriegspropaganda*, for that day.)

73   See *Das Reich*, 11 August 1940: 'Alte und junge Völker'.

74   Ironically, the Third Reich saw off the top hats: the perceived need to wear gas masks led to a reluctant compromise with the twentieth century.

75   See *Junge Welt: Reichszeitschrift der Hitler-Jugend* 8 (August 1942).

76   See, for instance, Anon., *Die verlorene Insel: Das Gesicht des heutigen England* (Berlin 1941), pp. 24–5.

77   Cf. *Das Reich*, 20 October 1940: 'Die englische Oberschicht'.

78   *Das Schwarze Korps*, 26 October 1939 (italics in original): '... *das britische Volk straft sich mit der Führung, die es sich gegeben hat, es wird zugrunde gehen an der Verkennung der eigenen Aufgabe. Daß wir diese Vollendung eines Volksschicksals beschleunigen, auch das ist durch England veranlaßt. Unser Glaube war es von jeher, daß wir sehr wohl neben England leben ... könnten ... Es gibt viele*

unter uns, die Englands sich vollziehendes Schicksal bedauern . . . Sie meinen . . . das drohende Ende von Englands "Mission" müsse dem nordischen Führertum innerhalb der gesamten Menschheit den schwersten Stoß versetzen . . . In dieser Rechnung stimmt eines nicht: in ihr erscheint das . . . nordische Blut für alle Zeiten als feststehende, unverrückbare Größe . . . *Nicht Krieger, nicht idealistische Volksführer und Denker behielten im britischen Adel die Oberhand, sondern Börsenschieber, Schafzüchter, Kohlenbarone, Baumwollkönige und politisierende Advokaten.* Das nordische Element . . . ging verbittert in die Kolonien . . . *aus altem Mist können nicht neue Blüten treiben* . . . So wie ein in der Üppigkeit gemästeter Saurier die Eiszeit nicht überleben konnte . . . so wird auch das . . . britische Weltreich nicht in die neue Zeit eingehen . . . Nicht wir haben dieses Ende beschlossen . . . Der Saurier starb nicht, weil andere Geschöpfe ihm nach dem Leben trachteten. Er starb, weil er unzeitgemäß war. Die neuen Lebensbedingungen waren dem tatenlosen Vielfraß nicht günstig.'

79   *Das Schwarze Korps*, 10 October 1940: 'Weltanschauung und Rassebegriff'.
80   See ibid.
81   Ibid.
82   Ibid., 26 December 1935: 'Sightseeing, Sir?'
83   Ibid.
84   Boberach, *Meldungen*, 113 (8 August 1940), p. 1452: italics in the original.
85   Goebbels, *Diaries*, 6 July 1940.
86   Marie Vassiltchikov, *Berlin Diaries 1940–1945* (New York 1987), 2 May 1940.
87   Ibid., 26 January 1941.
88   See Goebbels, *Diaries*, 11 November 1939.
89   Boberach, *Meldungen*, 104 (11 July 1940), pp. 1362–3.

5   *'The class struggle of the nations': Britain and Nazi anti-capitalism*

1   Goebbels, *Diaries*, 16 April 1925.
2   See H. Rosenberg, 'J. R. Seeley's "The Expansion of England" im Rahmen des nationalpolitischen Unterrichts', *Neuphilologische Monatsschrift* 10 (1939), 75, quoted by Raddatz as a sentiment not untypical even at this late date; note also Raddatz's observation: 'Ausgesprochen kritische Stellungnahmen, die England und Deutschland scharf von einander abgrenzten, gab es vor 1939 kaum' (Raddatz, *Englandkunde*, p. 142).
3   See *inter alia*, 123 (June 1940): 'Krieg der Weltanschauungen'; 132 (March 1941): 'Freimaurerei in England'; 162 (2nd double vol. 1944): 'Die Freimaurerei in England'; 116 (November 1939): 'Empire und Judentum'; 149 (August 1942): 'Die jüdische Macht über England'.

4   See the *Schriften des Deutschen Instituts für außenpolitische Forschung*, notably the series Das britische Reich in der Weltpolitik.

5   Zsg. 102/3/175/56 (7), 19 November 1936, Bundesarchiv, Koblenz. Quoted in Hans Bohrmann (ed.), *NS-Presseanweisungen der Vorkriegszeit* (5 vols., Munich 1984–99), vol. IV: iii, p. 1404.

6   Zsg. 110/5/48, 27 May 1937; quoted in NS-Presseanweisungen, vol. V: ii, p. 1243.

7   The slogan adorned Nazi publications such as *Der Angriff*. For its specific link to the war against Britain see, for instance, *Das Schwarze Korps*, 28 December 1939: 'Das böse Beispiel'.

8   Wilhelm Ziegler's compilation of relevant material later formed the basis for the Propaganda Ministry's campaign (cf. Goebbels, *Diaries*, 5 March 1940).

9   *Berliner Illustrierte*, 2 December 1937: 'Trotz Kohlen und Erz arbeitslos'.

10 To see the parallel at its clearest, see *Das Reich*, 24 November 1940: 'Das deutsche Geheimnis': 'Denn wir betrachten das Recht auf Arbeit als allerwichtigstes und notwendigstes Freiheitsrecht.'

11 *Deutschland-Berichte der Sozialdemokratischen Partei Deutschlands (Sopade) 1934–1940* (7 vols., Salzhausen 1980), vol. VII (1940), 7 February 1940, p. 110.

12 *Das Reich*, 1 December 1940. (On Ley himself, see Robert Smelser, *Robert Ley: Hitler's Labor Front Leader* (Oxford 1988).)

13 *Das Schwarze Korps*, 27 March 1935: 'Jugend und Sozialismus'.

14 *Table Talk*, 18 October 1941.

15 *Das Schwarze Korps*, 14 January 1943: 'Einmal ganz objektiv'.

16 Cf. Boelke, *Kriegspropaganda*, 14 December 1939.

17 *Das Schwarze Korps*, 28 December 1939: 'Das böse Beispiel'.

18 See *Das Reich*, 26 May 1940: 'Englands verlorene Position'.

19 *Das Schwarze Korps*, 28 December 1939: 'Das böse Beispiel'.

20 Cf., for instance, Anon., *Englands Maske ist gefallen* (Düsseldorf 1939); Wolfgang Loeff, *England ohne Maske* (Leipzig 1939) (or the publications appearing collectively under that title in 1940); *Das 12 Uhr Blatt*, 22 March 1939: 'Maske ab, John Bull'; Adolf Rein, *Die Wahrheit über Hitler aus englischem Mund* (Berlin 1939).

21 *Das Schwarze Korps*, 26 February 1942: 'Antwort auf Soldatenfragen'.

22 Ibid., 9 November 1939: 'Es geht um's Geschäft'.

23 Ibid.

24 *Das Reich*, 24 November 1940: 'Eine Französin über die Engländer Anno 1937'.

25 Cf. *Das Schwarze Korps*, 9 November 1939: 'Es geht um's Geschäft' and 13 February 1941: 'Das ist Sozialismus, Mister Churchill!'; or Hitler's speech to munitions workers, 10 December 1940, printed, significantly, as an introduction to *Die verlorene Insel*.

26 *Das Schwarze Korps*, 28 December 1939: 'Das böse Beispiel'.

27 *Das Reich*, 29 December 1940: 'Neue Freiheit'.

28 *Das Schwarze Korps*, 9 November 1939: 'Es geht um's Geschäft'.

29 *Das Reich*, 21 July 1940: 'Das Ende der City'.

30 *Das Schwarze Korps*, 26 June 1941: 'Was ist Plutokratie'.

31 *Table Talk*, 16 August 1942. His 'source', he added, was 'the Lady Mitford'.

32 Ibid., 26 February 1942.

33 Goebbels, *Diaries*, 6 July 1940.

34 *Table Talk*, 3 September 1942. (See also related observations by Goebbels about Vansittart, who Goebbels thought would deserve 'a monument' for his contribution to the Nazi cause: *Diaries*, 24 April 1943.)

35 *Das Schwarze Korps*, 10 October 1940: 'Freie Bahn dem Tüchtigen'.

36 See, for instance, *Die verlorene Insel*, p. 70.

37 *Das Schwarze Korps*, 6 July 1939: 'deren sanft und melancholisch gebogene Nase die Schlittenkufe darstellt, auf der sie nach erreichen eines gewissen Bankkontos mit Sicherheit ins Oberhaus rutschen'.

38 F. O. H. Schulz, *Komödie der Freiheit: Die Sozialpolitik der großen Demokratien* (Vienna 1940), p. 129.

39 See ibid., p. 32.

40 See, for instance, H. Krieger, 'Der Rassengedanke im englischen Unterricht', in G. Gräfer (ed.), *Handbuch des englischen Unterrichts* (2 vols., Leipzig 1939), vol. I, pp. 248–64.

41 *Das Reich*, 26 May 1940.

42 Again, the article uses a linguistic trick here: the word chosen for 'values' – *Güter* – can also mean material goods.

43 *Das Reich*, 1 April 1945: 'Unser großer Auftrag: Die weltgeschichtliche Bewährung der Gegenwart'.

44 *Die verlorene Insel*, p. 15.

45 See *Berliner Illustrierte*, 14 November 1940.

46 See Boelke, *Kriegspropaganda*, 3 June 1940.

47 Cf. *Berliner Illustrierte*, 8 August 1940.

48 Cf. ibid., 15 August 1940.

49 *Das Schwarze Korps*, 10 July 1941: 'Verleugnen vor dem Feind'.

50 See Goebbels, *Diaries*, 19 September 1940.

51 See Boberach, *Meldungen* 124 (16 September 1940), p. 1574.

52 See ibid. 112 (5 August 1940), pp. 1443–4.

53 *Das Reich*, 4 August 1940: 'The Lower Middle Class: Ein Stand ohne Gesicht'.

54 Ibid. and 9 January 1941: 'London – sterbende Metropole'.

55 Ibid., 4 August 1940.

56 *Das Schwarze Korps*, 26 December 1935: 'Sightseeing, Sir?'

57 See the pre-screening publicity in the *Berliner Illustrierte*, 21 May 1942.

58   *Das Reich*, 7 April 1940: 'Armes und reiches England'.

59   *Das Reich*, 9 January 1941: 'London – sterbende Metropole'.

60   See Boguslaw Drewniak, *Der deutsche Film 1938–1945: Ein Gesamtüberblick* (Düsseldorf 1987).

61   See, for instance, Anna Kottenhoff, *Frauen- und Kinderarbeit in England: Eine sozialpolitische Kritik* (England ohne Maske 29) (Berlin 1940) or F. M. Rentorff, *Slums – EnglischesWohnungselend* (England ohne Maske 15) (Berlin 1940).

62   See Michael Grüttner, *Studenten im Dritten Reich* (Paderborn 1995), p. 376.

63   Ibid., p. 377.

64   Bericht über die ANSt-Arbeit des Gaues Berlin im II. Trimester 1940, 5 August 1940, p. 3. In: StA WÜ RSF/NSDStB II 533 α 432 (quoted in Grüttner, *Studenten*, p. 377).

65   Kottenhoff, *Frauen- und Kinderarbeit* (the book specifically thanks the 'Leaders of the Student League').

66   Ibid., p. 28.

67   *Westdeutscher Beobachter*, 4 December 1938, quoted in W. G. Knop, *Beware of the English!* (London 1939), p. 42.

68   *Das Reich*, 7 July 1940: 'Armes und reiches England'.

69   See Rentorff, *Slums*.

70   *Westdeutscher Beobachter*, 25 December 1938, quoted in Knop, *Beware*, p. 73.

71   *Das Reich*, 22 December 1940: 'Eine andere Welt'.

72   Cf. Klemperer, 4 April 1944. (See also *Das Schwarze Korps*, 10 February 1944: 'Die britische Verzweiflung'.)

73   See, for instance, *Die verlorene Insel*.

74   *Das Reich*, 24 November 1940: 'Das deutsche Geheimnis'.

75   Schulz, *Komödie*.

76   *Das Reich*, 25 August 1940: 'Warum verliert England?'

77   *Das Schwarze Korps*, 9 November 1939: 'Es geht ums Geschäft'.

78   *Das Reich*, 8 October 1944: 'Der verwässerte Beveridge'.

79   Boelke, *Kriegspropaganda*, 12 December 1940. (See also *Das Reich*, 19 January 1941: 'Auf den Pfaden des Nationalsozialismus' and 'Pseudosozialisten'.)

80   Ibid., 1 December 1940: 'Wie geht es weiter'.

81   Ibid.

82   *Table Talk*, 26 February 1942. (But see also Goebbels' more sober assessment in: Boelke, *Kriegspropaganda*, 'Tagesparole': 4 December 1940.)

83   Boberach, *Meldungen* 147 (5 December 1940), p. 1834.

84   Ibid. 155 (20 January 1941), p. 1916.

85   Cf. Klemperer, *Diaries*, 29 June 1940. (See also Goebbels' remark about the need to 'explain' the meaning of plutocracy to the public: Boelke, *Kriegspropaganda*, 2 February 1940.)

86   Cf. Ebhart Dünten, *England der Reaktionär* (Berlin 1940), and Bruno

Rauecker, *Die soziale Rückständigkeit Großbritanniens* (Berlin 1940). 'Das Land ohne Sozialismus' was a chapter heading in Carl Brinkmann, *Der wirtschaftliche Liberalismus als System der britischen Weltanschauung* (Berlin 1940).

87 Boberach, *Meldungen* 84 (3 May 1940), p. 1093.

88 *Deutschland-Berichte (Sopade)*, vol. VI (1939), p. 843.

89 Klemperer, *Diaries*, 19 March 1944.

6 *'The chorus of hypocrites': history and propaganda*

1 Speech of 28 April 1939, quoted, significantly, in Loeff, *England ohne Maske*, p. 236.

2 Cf. speech of 28 April 1939, in Max Domarus, *Hitler: Reden und Proklamationen* (2 double vols., Wiesbaden 1973), vol II: i, pp. 1173–4.

3 Ibid.

4 See *Das Schwarze Korps*, 24 November 1938.

5 See Knop, *Beware*.

6 Max Everwien's *Bibel, Scheckbuch und Kanonen: Das Gesicht Englands* (Berlin 1939), for instance, acknowledges frankly its debt to Count Reventlow's earlier patriotic endeavours.

7 Cf. Loeff, *England*.

8 Fritz Reipert, *Das ist England: Weltherrschaft durch Blut und Gold* (Berlin 1939).

9 Cf. Jäckel and Kuhn, Hitler, 'Der Weltkrieg und seine Macher', 17 June 1920.

10 Everwien, *Bibel*.

11 Cf. Friedrich Hussong, *Englands politische Moral in Selbstzeugnissen* (Berlin 1940) and Ernst Schultze, *Die Blutspur Englands: Geschichte der englischen Kriegsgrausamkeiten* (Berlin 1940).

12 Loeff, *England*, p. 195. (See also, *Das Reich*, 3 November 1940: 'Diplomatische Offensive'.)

13 Reinhold Gadow, *Seeräuberstaat England* (Berlin 1940).

14 *Das 12 Uhr Blatt*, quoted by Knop, *Beware*, p. 147.

15 Hans Hartmann, *Cant: Die englische Art der Heuchelei* (Berlin 1940).

16 See also W. Franz, 'Die Legende von der englischen Heuchelei', *Neuphilologische Monatsschrift* 2 (1931), 574–5.

17 Cf. Dibelius, *England* vol. I, pp. 203–6 and vol. II, pp. 75–6.

18 *Das Schwarze Korps*, 6 July 1939: 'Burenkrieg – Krieg gegen die Deutschen'.

19 Hans Galinsky, 'Das Sendungsbewußtsein des heutigen Britentum', *Anglia: Zeitschrift für englische Philologie* 63 (1939), 296–336.

20 For a good survey of newspaper coverage, see Knop, *Beware*. The historical studies, quoted above, also refer to these policies. See also historical novels such as Rudolf Brunngraber, *Opiumkrieg* (Stuttgart 1939).

21 For an account of the affair, see Bramsted, *Goebbels*, pp. 409–14.

22   *Das Schwarze Korps*, 24 November 1938: 'Wer im Glashaus sitzt': 'denn
während hier die Empörung eines Volkes sich Luft machte und dennoch
Maß hielt, gibt es dort ein Übermaß an menschlichen Verirrungen'.

23   Cf. Boberach, *Meldungen* 47 (31 January 1940), p. 710.

24   See, for instance, Conrad Oehlrich, 'Die britischen Versprechungen an
die Araber: Zur McMahon–Hussein-Korrespondenz von 1915–1916',
Hamburger Monatshefte für auswärtige Politik 6 (April 1939), 336–40.

25   Loeff, *England*, p. 7.

26   Fritz Berber, *Prinzipien der englischen Außenpolitik* (Berlin 1939).

27   Robert Bauer, *Irland im Schatten Englands* (Berlin 1940), p. 6.

28   Loeff, *England*, p. 236. The argument is ubiquitous in 1939: see, for
instance, *Völkischer Beobachter*, 25 March 1939: 'Die Moral der Reichen'.

29   Domarus, *Hitler*, vol. I: ii, 9 October 1938.

30   *Table Talk*, 8 August 1941.

31   Erich Ziebarth, *Zypern: Griechen unter britischer Gewalt* (Berlin 1940).

32   See, for instance, Robert Bauer, *Irland im Schatten Englands* and his earlier
Irland: Insel der Heiligen und Rebellen (Leipzig 1938).

33   See the entry for 9 May 1940 in Hans-Günther Seraphim, *Das politische
Tagebuch Alfred Rosenbergs aus den Jahren 1934/35 und 1939/40* (Göttingen
1956), p. 115.

34   Boberach, *Meldungen*, 89 (20 May 1940), p. 1155.

35   Goebbels, *Diaries*, 10 December 1940.

36   Boberach, *Meldungen*, 104 (11 July 1940), p. 1363.

37   Goebbels, *Diaries*, 9 July 1940 (see also 6, 7 July).

38   *Schlesische Tageszeitung*, 26 March 1939 (quoted in Knop, *Beware*, pp. 157–8).

39   *Deutschlandberichte (Sopade)*, vol. VI, 6 July 1939, p. 840.

40   See, as a random example, the following articles in *Das Reich* in the
summer months of 1940: 26 May 1940: 'Englands verlorene Position'
and 'Armes und reiches England'; 15 September 1940: 'Dokumente von
Oran'; 20 October 1940: 'Lebenswertes Leben'.

41   See *Berliner Illustrierte*, 18 November 1943.

42   See Ernst A. Olbert, *England als Sklavenhändler und Sklavenhalter* (Berlin 1940).

43   *Table Talk*, 3 March 1942.

44   Ibid., 4 January 1942.

45   See Galinsky, 'Sendungsbewußtsein'.

46   Ibid., p. 326.

47   *Der Pimpf* 3 (March 1940): 'Taps geht unter die Parlamentarier'.

48   *Mein Kampf*, p. 162.

49   Cf. *Das Reich*, 6 September 1942: 'Seid nicht allzu gerecht', reprinted in
Goebbels, *Das eherne Herz* (Munich 1943), p. 451.

50   Ibid., p. 454.

7   'The land without music': culture and propaganda

1   Cf. Alfred Rosenberg, 'Georg Friedrich Händel' (22 February 1935), in *Gestaltung der Idee: Blut und Ehre* (Munich 1936), pp. 282–4.
2   Ibid., p. 282.
3   Ibid., p. 284.
4   *Blut und Ehre*: i.e. blood and honour.
5   *Mein Kampf*, pp. 231–4.
6   See Goebbels, *Diaries*, 15 November 1938.
7   See Gerwin Strobl, 'Shakespeare and the Nazis', *History Today* 47: 5 (1997), 20–5.
8   Boelke, *Kriegspropaganda*, 23 November 1939.
9   Lütjen, 'Das Seminar', p. 750.
10   Ibid.
11   Raddatz, *Englandkunde*, pp. 173–4.
12   For evidence of the leadership's high regard for Shaw, see Goebbels, *Diaries*, 20 January 1930; 22 December 1937; 1 February 1938; 11, 12 and 17 October 1939; and 6 September 1940.
13   Boelke, *Kriegspropaganda*, 23 November 1939.
14   Boberach, *Meldungen* 46 (29 January 1940), pp. 700–1.
15   For instance, Hussong, *Englands politische Moral*, pp. 44–6.
16   Klemperer, *Diaries*, 2 January 1939.
17   *Das Schwarze Korps*, 5 January 1939: 'Scotland Yard – längst überholt'.
18   Vassiltchikov, *Berlin Diaries*, 26 July 1940.
19   See Wolfgang Keller, 'Die 76. Hauptversammlung der deutschen Shakespeare-Gesellschaft zu Weimar', *Shakespeare Jahrbuch* 76 (1940), 4.
20   Klemperer, *Diaries*, 14 October 1939.
21   Ibid., 24 September 1942.
22   *Das Schwarze Korps*, 6 April 1944; 'Die englische Methode'.
23   Ibid.: 'der Engländer . . . [wird] vermenschlicht'.
24   Klemperer, *Diaries*, 18 April 1938.
25   *Berliner Illustrierte*, 10 July 1941: 'Aufblühender Lotus'.
26   Ibid., 17 August 1939.
27   Klemperer, *Diaries*, 18 September 1939.
28   Ibid., 14 May 1940.
29   Ibid., 21 May 1941.
30   See the statistics published annually by the German Shakespeare Society.
31   *Table Talk*, 22 July 1941.
32   *Berliner Illustrierte*, 27 December 1940: 'London – sterbende Metropole'.
33   See the related attempts to chart racial decline in music: *Die Musik* 32: 2 (November 1939), 37–41.
34   *Berliner Illustrierte*, 12 December 1940: 'London – sterbende Metropole'.
35   *Das Schwarze Korps*, 6 April 1944: 'Die englischen Methode'.

36   Intriguingly, Karajan had conducted the *Enigma Variations* at Aachen in October 1938, possibly as a gesture after Munich: *Die Musik* 31 : 1 (October 1938), appendix x.

37   *Table Talk*, 22 July 1941.

38   *Die Musik* 31 : 12 (September 1939), 827.

39   *Berliner Illustrierte*, 14 December 1939: 'Die andere Seite'.

40   See, for instance, *Das Reich*, 1 December 1940.

41   *Die Musik* 32 : 1 (October 1939), 7–8.

42   *Das Reich*, 24 February 1944: 'Das Ziel vor Augen'.

43   *Das Schwarze Korps*, 16 July 1942.

44   Ibid., 18 November 1943: 'Einst wird kommen'. (See also Klemperer, *Diaries*, 14 February 1920.)

45   Ibid.

46   See, for instance, *Berliner Illustrierte*, 6 July 1944: 'Dokument der Barbarei'.

47   *Der Pimpf* 5/6 (May/June 1944): 'Die Freiheit und das Himmelreich'.

48   Klemperer, 5 July 1943.

49   Ibid., 22 July 1944.

50   Ibid., 15 January 1945.

51   Ibid., 19 February 1945.

52   Klemperer, *LTI*, p. 391.

8   *The decline of the West: German fears and illusions in the shadow of defeat*

1   *Table Talk*, 6 January 1942.

2   Ibid., 18 December 1941.

3   Ibid., 31 December 1941.

4   Ibid., 18 December 1941.

5   Ibid., 7 January 1942.

6   Cf. Goebbels, *Diaries*, 13 July 1937.

7   *Zweites Buch*, p. 29.

8   Ibid., p. 167.

9   Ibid., p. 119.

10   See Jäckel and Kuhn, Hitler: 'Rede auf dem NSDAP-Sprechabend', 20 March 1923, p. 846.

11   See, for instance, Goebbels' diary entry for 1 September 1938, according to which Hitler expected continued British neutrality.

12   Goebbels, *Diaries*, 24 October 1938.

13   Ibid., 21 August 1938.

14   *Zweites Buch*, p. 173.

15   *Table Talk*, 22 July 1941.

16   Ibid.

17   Ibid., 28 September 1941.

18 See ibid., 31 January 1942.

19 Cf. ibid., 2 February 1942 and Ross, *Die Welt*, p. 76.

20 See Grimm, 'Englisch-deutsche Probleme', 276.

21 *Table Talk*, 7 January 1942.

22 See ibid., 9 October 1941.

23 Ibid., 15 January 1942.

24 Hitler uses a freshwater image: 'Die Engländer sind ein kleiner Stechling von uns' (ibid., 9 August 1942).

25 Ibid., 18 October 1941.

26 Ibid., 1 November 1941.

27 Ibid., 27 January 1942.

28 Ibid., 2 September 1942.

29 See ibid., 4 August 1942.

30 Ibid., 6 February 1942.

31 Goebbels, *Diaries*, 3 July 1940.

32 Ibid., 24 January 1941.

33 *Das Reich*, 6 September 1942: 'Seid nicht allzu gerecht'.

34 Ibid., 16 June 1940: 'Von der Gottähnlichkeit der Engländer'.

35 Jäckel and Kuhn, Hitler: 'Rede auf einer DAP-Versammlung', 10 December 1919, p. 98.

36 See, for instance, *Das Reich*, 30 June 1940, 'Keine Bundesgenossen mehr'.

37 Goebbels, *Diaries*, 10 September 1943.

38 See, for instance, Otto Weise, *Franzosen gegen England: Französische Äußerungen* (Berlin 1940).

39 Heinz Lehmann, *Englands Spiel mit Polen* (Berlin 1940).

40 See, for instance, *Das Schwarze Korps*, 20 January 1944: 'Die Grenzen der Vernunft' or *Das Reich*, 25 February 1945: 'Yalta'.

41 See, for instance, *Das Reich*, 15 October 1944: 'Der überlegene Freund'.

42 Ibid., 14 July 1940: 'Entente perfide: Geschicht eines Bündnisvertrages'.

43 See *Das Reich*, 17 November 1940.

44 *Berliner Illustrierte*, 8 May 1941.

45 See, for instance, *Das Schwarze Korps* which made this point even before the commencement of hostilities, 25 May 1939: 'Der politische Soldat'.

46 See, for instance, *Das Reich*, 14 July 1940: 'Entente perfide'.

47 Goebbels, *Diaries*, 6 July 1940.

48 Boberach, *Meldungen*, 103 (8 July 1940), p. 1353.

49 Alfred Rosenberg, *Tradition und Gegenwart* (Munich 1941), pp. 396–7. 'Die Überwindung des Versailler Diktates', 15 April 1940. For the role of Ribbentrop's Foreign Office in propagating the new 'European' line, see Peter Longerich, *Propagandisten im Krieg: Die Presseabteilung des auswärtigen Amtes unter Ribbentrop* (Studien zur Zeitgeschichte 33, Munich 1987), pp. 77–80.

50 *Das Schwarze Korps*, 18 November 1943: 'Einst wird kommen'.

51 Ibid., 6 October 1940: 'Das interkontinentale Zeitalter'.

52 Das Reich, 6 October 1940: 'Europäischer Unabhängigkeitskrieg'.

53 Klemperer, Diaries, 19 February 1945: 'vox populi: Unser guter Führer, der sooo den Frieden gewollt hat.'

54 The cartoon, taken from an unidentified Belgian paper, appeared in the Berliner Illustrierte, 8 May 1941.

55 Mein Kampf, p. 601.

56 Rosenberg, 'Englands Schicksalsstunden', 154.

57 Ibid.

58 Das Schwarze Korps, 18 March 1943: 'Die harte Auslese': 'Es ist ja die Tragik der germanischen Rasse, daß in ihren Völkern ein Bewußtsein der Zusammengehörigkeit nie lebendig war.'

59 See Rosenberg, 'Englands Schicksalsstunden', 153.

60 Das Schwarze Korps, 5 February 1942: 'Und das war England': 'Wer einen Krieg gewinnt, braucht ihn nicht ein zweites Mal zu führen . . . einen Krieg vom Zaum zu brechen . . . war nackter Wahnsinn.'

61 See ibid.

62 Table Talk, 4 August 1942.

63 Das Reich, 27 October 1940.

64 Table Talk, 26 October 1941. See also Goebbels' report about Hitler's views a year earlier: Diaries, 3 July 1940.

65 Das Reich, 6 October 1940: 'Das interkontinentale Zeitalter'.

66 Boberach, Meldungen, 15 November 1943, pp. 6003–5.

67 See Das Schwarze Korps, 22 January 1942: 'Härte ist alles'.

68 See ibid., 17 June 1943: 'Zeit und Raum'.

69 Das Reich, 1 October 1944: 'Interessenkampf um Indien'.

70 See also ibid., 8 October 1944: 'Bruderzwist um Öl'.

71 See Boberach, Meldungen, 19 August 1943, p. 5647

72 See Goebbels, Diaries, 30 January 1945.

73 Das Reich, 1 October 1944: 'Die Fahne des Glaubens': 'Die Völker haben das dumpfe Empfinden, daß der Krieg auf irgendeine Weise und bald eine entscheidende Wendung nehmen muß, wenn er nicht von allen daran beteiligten Ländern . . . überhaupt verloren werden soll. Aber wir sprechen nicht nur zum eigenen Volk, sondern zur Weltöffentlichkeit, und der Feind hört mit.'

74 Vassiltchikov, Berlin Diaries, 26 March 1940.

75 Ibid., 27 July 1943.

76 Ibid., 28 November 1943.

77 Ibid., 12 July 1940.

78 See Boberach, Meldungen, 46 (29 January 1940), pp. 702–3.

79 See also ibid., 100 (27 June 1940), p. 1308.

80 Ibid., 127 (26 September 1940), pp. 1607–14.

81 Ibid.

82 Ibid. 4 (16 October 1939), p. 357.

83 See Boelke, *Kriegspropaganda*, 3 September 1940.

84 See ibid., 385 (24 May 1943), p. 5278.

85 Ibid. 100 (27 June 1940), pp. 1307–8.

86 Ibid. 125 (19 September 1940), pp. 1582–4.

87 Ibid. 127 (26 September 1940), pp. 1607–14.

88 Goebbels, 'Seid nicht allzu gerecht'.

89 *Das Schwarze Korps*, 14 January 1943.

90 Vassiltchikov, *Berlin Diaries*, 24 December 1943.

91 Klemperer, *Diaries*, 27 September 1944.

92 Ibid., 11 October 1944.

93 Boberach, *Meldungen*, 7 February 1944, pp. 6302–4.

Bibliography

Newspapers and magazines

Berliner Illustrierte Zeitung

B.Z. am Mittag

Country Life

Das Reich

Das Schwarze Korps

Das 12 Uhr Blatt

Der Angriff

Der Pimpf: NS-Jungenblätter

Der SA-Mann

Der Türmer: Monatsschrift für Gemüt und Geist

Der Völkische Beobachter

Die Bewegung

Die deutsche Zukunft: Organ der NS-Jugend

Die Musik

Die Pause

Die Post

Jenaische Zeitung

Junge Welt: Reichszeitschrift der Hitler-Jugend

Kladderadatsch

Morgen: NS-Jugendblätter

Münchener Illustrierte Presse

N.S. Kurier

Schlesische Tageszeitung

Simplicissimus

Westdeutscher Beobachter

Wiener Zeitung.

Other primary sources

Aldag, Peter. *Juden beherrschen England*. Berlin 1940.
   Juden erobern England. Berlin 1940.
Alsdorf, Ludwig. *Indien*. Berlin 1940.
Anon. *Die verlorene Insel: Das Gesicht des heutigen England*. Berlin 1941.
Anon. *Englands Maske ist gefallen*. Düsseldorf 1939.
Arns, Karl. *Der religiöse britische Imperialismus*. Bochum 1919.
   'Zum Thema: Carlyle als Mittelpunkt des englischen Unterrichts in Prima'.
      Zeitschrift für den französischen und englischen Unterricht 19 (1920), 164–72.
Aronstein, Phillip. 'Die Kulturkunde im englischen Unterricht'. *Monatsschrift für*
      Höhere Schulen 25 (1926), 266–7.
Ausstellung 'Raubstaat England'. Munich 1941.
Bartz, Ernst. 'Wesen und Ziele der englischen Boy Scout Movement'. *Die neueren*
      Sprachen 45 (12) (1937), 489.
Bartz, Karl. *Englands Weg nach Indien: Schicksalsstunden des britischen Weltreiches*. Berlin 1936.
Bauer, Heinrich. 'Cromwell und die deutsche Revolution'. *Nationalsozialistische*
      Monatshefte 39 (June 1933), 255–62.
   Oliver Cromwell, Ein Kampf um Freiheit und Diktatur. Munich 1932.
   'Shakespeare – ein germanischer Dichter'. *Nationalsozialistische Monatshefte* 41
      (1933), 372–7.
Bauer, Robert. *Irland: Insel der Heiligen und Rebellen*. Leipzig 1938.
   Irland im Schatten Englands. Berlin 1940.
Baumgarten, Otto. *Religiöses und kirchliches Leben in England* (Handbuch der englisch-
      amerikanischen Kultur: Herausgegeben von Wilhelm Dibelius). Leipzig
      1922.
Beddoe, John. *The Races of Great Britain*. London 1885.
Beer, Herbert. *Führen und Folgen, Herrschen und Beherrschtwerden im Sprachgut der Angelsachsen:*
      Ein Beitrag zur Erforschung von Führertum und Gefolgschaft in der germanischen Welt
      (Sprache und Kultur der germanischen und romanischen Völker:
      Anglistische Reihe, vol. XXXI). Breslau 1939.
Berber, Fritz. *Prinzipien der englischen Außenpolitik*. Berlin 1939.
Boberach, Heinz (ed.). *Meldungen aus dem Reich: Die geheimen Lageberichte des*
      Sicherheitsdienstes der SS 1938–1945. Herrsching 1984.
Bode, Emil. *Der Eroberer Südafrikas*. Lübeck 1932.
Boelcke, Willi A. (ed.). *Kriegspropaganda 1939–41: Geheime Ministerkonferenzen im*
      Reichspropagandaministerium. Stuttgart 1966.
Bohr, Stephan. *Afrikaforscher und Missionar Dr. Livingstone*. (Jugendglocken 6). Bremen
      1934.
Bohrmann, Hans (ed.). *NS-Presseanweisungen der Vorkriegszeit*. Munich 1993.
Borgwardt, Paul. 'Shakespeare und seine Behandlung im heutigen
      Klassenunterricht'. *Die neueren Sprachen* 44 (1936).

Bravetta, Ettore: *Der große Admiral*. Berlin 1936.

Brie, F. 'Der englische Nationalcharakter'. *Lebensfragen des britischen Weltreiches* (Beirat für die Auslandsstudien an der Universität Berlin). Berlin 1921.

Brinkmann, Carl. *Der wirtschaftliche Liberalismus als System der britischen Weltanschauung.* Berlin 1940.

Brunngraber, Rudolf. *Opiumkrieg*. Stuttgart 1939.

Cohen-Portheim, Paul. *Die unbekannte Insel*. Berlin 1931.

Deutschland-Berichte der Sozialdemokratischen Partei Deutschlands (Sopade) 1934–1940. Salzhausen 1980.

Dibelius, Wilhelm. *England*, 2 vols. Leipzig 1923.

Domarus, Max. *Hitler: Reden und Proklamationen*, 2 double vols. Wiesbaden 1973.

Dreßler, Bruno. 'Die Entwicklung der körperlichen Ertüchtigung in der englischen Erziehung'. *Die neueren Sprachen* 44 (1936).

Dünten, Ebhart. *England der Reaktionär*. Berlin 1940.

Ehrentreich, Alfred. '"Lawrence of Arabia" im Lichte seiner Freunde'. *Archiv für das Studium der neueren Sprachen* 93 (173) (1938), 81–4.

Erziehung und Unterricht in der Höheren Schule: Amtliche Ausgabe des Reichs- und Preußischen Ministeriums für Wissenschaft, Erziehung und Volksbildung. Berlin 1938.

Everwien, Max. *Bibel, Scheckbuch und Kanonen: Das Gesicht Englands.* Berlin 1939.

Fenger, Hermann. *England und Friesland in ihren kulturellen und wirtschaftlichen Beziehungen.* Bonn 1935.

Franke, Hans. *Das Ende des Kapitän Cook*. Saarlautern 1937.

Fränkel, R. *Der fremdsprachliche Unterricht und die neue Erziehung*. Leipzig 1933.

Franz, W. 'Die Legende von der englischen Heuchelei'. *Neuphilologische Monatsschrift* 2 (1931), 574–5.

Freiburger, W. *Nelson's Life and Deeds*. N.p. 1937.

Freund, Michael. *Oliver Cromwell*. Lübeck 1933.

Frey, Dagobert. *Englisches Wesen in der bildenden Kunst*. Stuttgart 1942.

Frick, Wilhelm. *Kampfziel der deutschen Schule*. Langensalza 1933.

Froembgen, Johann. *Marlborough: Englands Fahnen im deutschen Wind*. Leipzig 1938.

Fröhlich, Elke (ed.). *Die Tagebücher von Joseph Goebbels: Sämtliche Fragmente*. Munich 1987.

Gadow, Reinhold. *Seeräuberstaat England*. Berlin 1940.

Galinsky, Hans. 'Das Sendungsbewußtsein des heutigen Britentum'. *Anglia: Zeitschrift für englische Philologie* 63 (1939), 296–336.

Goebbels, Joseph. *Das eherne Herz*. Munich 1943.

   Die Zeit ohne Beispiel: Reden und Aufsätze aus den Jahren 1939/40/41. Munich 1941.

Grant, Madison. *The Passing of the Great Race: Or the Racial Basis of European History*. New York 1917.

Greiser, Wolfgang. *Raleigh (Burmeisters Abenteuer Serie)*. Bremen 1935.

Grimm, Hans. 'Baldwin – oder vom schweren Verstehen'. *Inneres Reich* 4:2 (1937), 426–33.

'Englisch-deutsche Probleme im Wandel unserer Zeit'. *Inneres Reich* 4:1 (1937), 273–300.

Günther, Hans F. K. *Der Nordische Gedanke unter den Deutschen.* Munich 1925.

   Die Verstädterung: Ihre Gefahren für Volk und Staat vom Standpunkt der Lebensforschung und Gesellschaftswissenschaft. Leipzig 1934.

   Kleine Rassenkunde Europas. Munich 1925.

   Mein Eindruck von Adolf Hitler. Pähl 1969.

   Rassenkunde des deutschen Volkes, 12th (revised) edition. Munich 1928.

   Ritter, Tod und Teufel: Der heldische Gedanke. Munich 1920.

   'Shakespeares Frauen und Mädchen aus lebenskundlicher Sicht'. *Jahrbuch der deutschen Shakespeare-Gesellschaft* 73, Neue Folge 14. Weimar 1937, pp. 85–108.

Haiden, Konrad. *Geschichte des Nationalsozialismus.* Berlin 1932.

Halfeld, Adolf. *England: Verfall oder Aufstieg.* Jena 1933.

Hartmann, Hans. *Cant: Die englische Art der Heuchelei.* Berlin 1940.

Hellmann, Günther. *Ideen und Kräfte der englischen Nachkriegsjugend (nach literarischen Selbstzeugnissen)* (Sprache und Kultur der germanischen und romanischen Völker: Anglistische Reihe, vol. XXXII). Breslau 1939

Heuer, Hermann. 'Englische und deutsche Jugenderziehung'. *Zeitschrift für neusprachlichen Unterricht* 36 (1937), 221.

Hitler, Adolf. *Mein Kampf.* Munich 1927; transl. Ralph Mannheim, London 1969.

Hoops, Reinhold. 'England und sein Weltreich'. *Die neueren Sprachen* 43 (1935).

Hübener, Gustav. *England und die Gesittungsgrundlagen der europäischen Frühgeschichte.* Frankfurt am Main 1930.

Hübner, Walter. 'Englisches Schrifttum und deutsche Erziehung'. *Neuphilologische Monatsschrift* 5 (1934).

Hussong, Friedrich. *Englands politische Moral in Selbstzeugnissen.* Berlin 1940.

Inge, William. *England.* London 1926.

Jäckel, Eberhard and Axel Kuhn (eds.). *Hitler: Sämtliche Aufzeichnungen 1905–1924.* Stuttgart 1980.

Jacob-Friesen, Karl-Hermann. 'Steinzeitliche Beziehungen zwischen Niedersachsen und England'. *Die neueren Sprachen* 47 (1939), 260–7.

Jelusich, Mirko. *Oliver Cromwell.* Vienna 1933.

Jochmann, Werner (ed.). *Monologe im Führerhauptquartier 1941–1944: Die Aufzeichnungen von Heinrich Heims.* Hamburg 1980.

Keller, Wolfgang. 'Die 76. Hauptversammlung der deutschen Shakespeare-Gesellschaft zu Weimar'. *Shakespeare Jahrbuch* 76 (1940), p. 4.

Kellinghusen, W. *England: Das unbekannte Land.* Berlin 1937.

Kircher, Rudolf. *Wie's die Engländer machen: Politik, Gesellschaft und Kultur im demokratisierten England.* Frankfurt am Main 1929.

Kirsch, Erich. 'Englisch', in Rudolf Benze und Alfred Pudelko (eds.), *Rassische*

Erziehung als Unterrichtsgrundsatz der Fachgebiete. Frankfurt am Main 1937, p. 164.

Klemperer, Viktor. *Ich will Zeugnis ablegen bis zum Letzten: Tagebücher 1933–1945.* Berlin 1995.

    Leben sammeln, nicht fragen wozu und warum: Tagebücher 1918–1932. Berlin 1996.

    LTI: Aus dem Notizbuch eines Philologen. Leipzig 1996.

    Und so ist alles schwankend: Tagebücher Juni bis Dezember 1945. Berlin 1995.

Knop, W. G. *Beware of the English!* London 1939.

Kottenhoff, Anna. *Frauen- und Kinderarbeit in England: Eine sozialpolitische Kritik* (Deutsche Informationsstelle: England ohne Maske 29). Berlin 1940.

Krieger, H. 'Der Rassengedanke im englischen Unterricht', in G. Gräfer (ed.), *Handbuch des englischen Unterrichts.* Leipzig 1939, vol. I, pp. 248–64.

Krüper, A. 'Das geschichtliche und politische Schrifttum in der englischen Schullektüre'. *Neuphilologische Monatsschrift* 6 (1935), 242.

'Englisch als Lehrfach der nationalsozialistischen höheren Schule'. *Die neueren Sprachen* 43 (1935).

Kühne, Lothar. *Das Kolonialverbrechen von Versailles.* Graz 1939.

    Störenfried England. Berlin 1939.

Kuttner, M. *Westeuropäische und deutsche Kultur.* Leipzig 1927.

Langenbeck, Wilhelm. *Englands Weltmacht in ihrer Entwicklung vom 17. Jahrhundert bis auf unsere Tage.* Leipzig 1919.

Lehmann, Heinz. *Englands Spiel mit Polen.* Berlin 1940.

Loeff, Wolfgang. *England ohne Maske.* Leipzig 1939.

Lücke, Theodor. *Wellington: Der eiserne Herzog.* Berlin 1938.

Maßmann, Karl. *Die alten Männer wollten Krieg.* Berlin 1939.

Mikusch, Dagobert von. *Rhodes: Der Traum einer Weltherrschaft.* Berlin 1936.

Miltenberg, Weygand von. *Schleicher, Hitler? – Cromwell!* Leipzig 1932.

Mühsam, Erich. 'Franz Bieberkopf und der Rundfunk', in Irmela Schneider (ed.), *Radiokultur der Weimarer Republik.* Tübingen 1984, pp. 131–4.

Oehlrich, Conrad. 'Die britischen Versprechungen an die Araber: Zur McMahon–Hussein-Korrespondenz von 1915–1916'. *Hamburger Monatshefte für auswärtige Politik* 6 (April 1939), 336-40.

Olbert, Ernst A. *England als Sklavenhändler und Sklavenhalter.* Berlin 1940.

Oncken, Wilhelm. *Vier Essays über die Führung einer Nation.* Berlin 1935.

Paul, Alwin. 'Übung – Lektüre, Übersetzung und Besprechung von englischen und amerikanischen Werken über den Weltkrieg (mit besonderer Berücksichtigung der Kriegsschuldfrage)'. *Die höhere Schule* 2 (5) (1935), 129–34.

Pier, Bernhard. *Rassenbiologische Betrachtungsweise der Geschichte Englands.* Frankfurt am Main 1935.

Rauecker, Bruno. *Die soziale Rückständigkeit Großbritanniens.* Berlin 1940.

Rein, Adolf. *Die Wahrheit über Hitler aus englischem Mund.* Berlin 1939.

Reipert, Fritz. *Das ist England:Weltherrschaft durch Blut und Gold.* Berlin 1939.

Rentorff, F. M. *Slums – Englisches Wohnungselend* (England ohne Maske 15). Berlin 1940.

Reuth, Ralf-Georg (ed.). *Joseph Goebbels Tagebücher,* 5 vols. Munich 1992.

Richert, Hans. *Die deutsche Bildungseinheit und die höhere Schule: Ein Buch von deutscher Nationalerziehung.* Tübingen 1920.

Richthofen, Wilhelm von. *Brito-Germania: Die Erlösung Europas.* Berlin 1926.

Riemann, Erhard. *Germanen erobern Britannien: Ergebnisse der Vorgeschichte und der Sprachwissenschaft über die Einwanderung der Sachsen, Angeln und Jüten nach England.* Königsberg 1939.

Roeingh, Rolf. *Ein Schwert hieb über den Kanal: Die siegreiche Englandfahrt Wilhelms des Eroberers nach den Bildberichten des Teppichs von Bayeux.* Berlin 1941.

Rosenberg, Alfred. *Blut und Ehre: Ein Kampf für deutsche Wiedergeburt.* Munich 1936.

Der Kampf um die Macht. Munich 1937.

Der Mythos des Zwanzigsten Jahrhunderts. Munich 1930.

'Englands Schicksalsstunden'. *Nationalsozialistische Monatshefte* 4 (July 1930), 153–66.

Gestaltung der Idee: Blut und Ehre, vol. II. Munich 1936.

Tradition und Gegenwart. Munich 1941.

Rosenberg, H. 'J. R. Seeley's "The Expansion of England" im Rahmen des nationalpolitischen Unterrichts'. *Neuphilologische Monatsschrift* 10 (1939), 75.

Ross, Colin. *Die Welt auf der Wage: Ein Querschnitt von zwanzig Jahren Weltreise.* Leipzig 1929.

Scheidt, Walter: 'Rassenkunde der britischen Inseln', in Paul Hartig and Wilhelm Schellberg, *Handbuch der Englandkunde,* 2 vols. Frankfurt am Main 1929, p. 88.

Schmidt, Waldemar. 'Junges Deutschland – altes England'. *Die neueren Sprachen* 41 (1933), 409–10.

'Neuphilologie als Auslandswissenschaft'. *Die neueren Sprachen* 43 (1935), 496.

Schücking, Levin Ludwig. *Heldenstolz und Würde im Angelsächsischen.* Leipzig 1933.

Schulz, F. O. H. *Komödie der Freiheit: Die Sozialpolitik der großen Demokratien.* Vienna 1940.

Schulz, W. 'Englisch als erste Fremdsprache'. *Zeitschrift für den französischen und englischen Unterricht* 24 (1925), 334.

Schultze, Ernst. *Die Blutspur Englands.* Berlin 1940.

Schweigel, Max. *Oliver Cromwell.* Leipzig 1935.

Seraphim, Hans-Günther. *Das politische Tagebuch Alfred Rosenbergs aus den Jahren 1934/35 und 1939/40.* Göttingen 1956.

Seydewitz, Margaret von and Alwin Paul, *Eminent Englishmen.* Vol. I, Leipzig 1934; vols. II and III, 1935.

Silex, Karl. *John Bull zu Hause: Der Engländer im täglichen Leben. Wie er wohnt, sich amüsiert, sich anzieht, was er lernt, wird, treibt, verdient, ausgiebt.* Leipzig 1930.

Sombart, Werner. *Händler und Helden: Patriotische Besinnungen.* Leipzig 1915.

Spatzier, Max (ed.). *Heralds of British Imperialism* (Teubners Neusprachliche Lesestoffe im Dienste nationalpolitischer Erziehung, vol. II). Leipzig 1935.

Speer, Albert. *Erinnerungen*. Berlin 1969.

Steuben, Fritz. *Emir Dynamit: Bilder aus dem Leben des Obersten Lawrence*. Stuttgart 1933.

Stoddard, Theodore Lothrop. *The Revolt against Civilisation: The Menace of the Under-man*. New York 1922.

Tralow, Johannes. *Gewalt aus der Erde*. Berlin 1933.

Trevor-Roper, Hugh (ed.). *Hitler's Table Talk 1941–1944*. London 1953.

    The Testament of Adolf Hitler: The Hitler–Bormann Documents February–April 1945. London 1961.

Vassiltchikov, Marie. *Berlin Diaries 1940–1945*. New York 1987.

Voigt, Bernhard. *Fürs größere Vaterland: Der Lebenstraum des Rhodes*. Hamburg 1933. (Reissued as *Cecil Rhodes: Der Lebenstraum eines Briten*. Potsdam 1939.)

Wanderscheck, H. *Höllenmaschinen aus England*. Berlin 1940.

Weinberg, Gerhard L. (ed.). *Hitlers Zweites Buch: Ein Dokument aus dem Jahre 1928*. Stuttgart 1961.

Weise, Otto. *Franzosen gegen England: Französische Äußerungen*. Berlin 1940.

Ziebarth, Erich. *Zypern: Griechen unter britischer Gewalt*. Berlin 1940.

Secondary sources

Apelt, Walter. *Die kulturkundliche Bewegung im Unterricht der neueren Sprachen in Deutschland in den Jahren 1886–1945: Ein Irrweg deutscher Philologen*. East Berlin 1967.

Barbian, Jan-Pieter. *Literaturpolitik im 'Dritten Reich'*. Munich 1995.

Bergmaier, Horst J. P. and Rainer E. Lotz. *Hitler's Airwaves: The Inside Story of Nazi Broadcasting and Propaganda Swing*. New Haven 1997.

Bloch, Michael. *Ribbentrop*. London 1992.

Bock, Gisela. *Zwangssterilisation im Nationalsozialismus*. Opladen 1986.

Bramsted, Ernest. *Goebbels and National Socialist Propaganda, 1925–1945*. Michigan 1965.

Burleigh, Michael. *Germany Turns Eastward*. Cambridge 1988.

Crozier, Andrew. *Appeasement and Germany's Last Bid for Colonies*. Basingstoke 1988.

Drewniak, Boguslaw. *Der deutsche Film 1938–1945: Ein Gesamtüberblick*. Düsseldorf 1987.

Essner, Cornelia. 'Im "Irrgarten der Rassenlogik" oder nordische Rassenlehre und nationale Frage'. *Historische Mitteilungen* 7 (1994), 81–101.

Field, G. 'Nordic Racism'. *Journal of the History of Ideas* 38 (1977), 523–40.

Flessau, Kurt-Ingo. *Schule der Diktatur: Lehrpläne und Schulbücher des Nationalsozialismus*. Munich 1977.

Grüttner, Michael. *Studenten im Dritten Reich*. Paderborn 1995.

Heiber, Helmut (ed.). *Universität unterm Hakenkreuz: Der Professor im Dritten Reich: Bilder aus der akademischen Provinz*. Munich 1991.

Henke, Josef. *England in Hitlers außenpolitischem Kalkül 1935–1939*. Boppard 1973.

    'Hitlers England-Konzeption: Formulierungen und Realisierungskonzepte', in Manfred Funke (ed.), *Hitler, Deutschland und die Mächte*. Kronberg 1978, pp. 584–603.

Hildebrand, Klaus. *Vom Reich zum Weltreich: Hitler, NSDAP, und koloniale Frage 1919–1945*. Munich 1969.

Hyam, Ronald. *Empire and Sexuality: The British Experience*. Manchester 1990.

Ingrim, Robert. *Hitlers glücklichster Tag: London am 18.6.35*. Stuttgart 1951.

Kris, Ernst and Hans Speyer. *German Radio Propaganda: Report on Home Broadcasts during the War*. New York 1944.

Kuhn, Axel. *Hitlers außenpolitisches Programm: Entstehung und Entwicklung 1919–1939*. Stuttgart 1970.

Lehberger, Reiner. *'Collect all the English inscriptions you can find in our city': Englischunterricht an Hamburger Volksschulen 1870–1945*. Hamburg 1990.
'Neusprachlicher Unterricht in der NS-Zeit', in Reinhard Dithmar (ed.), *Schule und Unterricht im Dritten Reich*. Neuwied 1989, pp. 117–34.

Longerich, Peter. *Propagandisten im Krieg: Die Presseabteilung des auswärtigen Amtes unter Ribbentrop (Studien zur Zeitgeschichte 33)*. Munich 1987.

Lütjen, Hans Peter. 'Das Seminar für Englische Sprache und Kultur 1933 bis 1945', in Eckart Krause, Ludwig Huber and Holger Fischer (eds.), *Hochschulalltag im Dritten Reich: Die Hamburger Universität 1933–1945*. Berlin 1991, pp. 737–56.

Moeller, Felix. *Der Filmminister: Goebbels und der Film im Dritten Reich*. Berlin 1998.

Overy, Richard. *Göring: 'The Iron Man'*. London 1984.

Raddatz, Volker. *Englandkunde im Wandel deutscher Erziehungsideale*. Kronberg 1977.

Roth, Karl Heinz. '"Generalplan Ost" – "Gesamtplan Ost": Forschungsstand, Quellenprobleme, neue Ergebnisse', in Mechthild Rössler et al. (eds.), *Der 'Generalplan Ost': Hauptlinien der nationalsozialistischen Planungs- und Vernichtungspolitik*. Berlin 1993, pp. 25–117.

Smelser, Ronald. *Robert Ley: Hitler's Labor Front Leader*. Oxford 1984.

Spitzy, Reinhard. *How We Squandered the Reich*. Norwich 1997.

Strobl, Gerwin. 'The Bard of Eugenics: Shakespeare and Racial Activism in the Third Reich'. *Journal of Contemporary History* (July 1999), 323–36.
'Shakespeare and the Nazis'. *History Today* 47: 5 (1997), 20–5.

Waddington, G. T. 'Haßgegner: German Views of Great Britain in the Later 1930s'. *History* 81 (1996), 22–39.

Weber, Hermann. 'Die politische Verantwortung der Wissenschaft: Friedrich Berber in den Jahren 1937 bis 1945', in Eckart Krause, Ludwig Huber and Holger Fischer (eds.), *Hochschulalltag im Dritten Reich: Die Hamburger Universität 1933–1945*. Berlin 1991, p. 939.

Weinberg, Gerhard L. *Germany, Hitler and World War II*. Cambridge 1998.

Williamson, David G. *The British in the Rhineland 1918–1930*. Oxford 1991. 'Cologne and the British'. *History Today* 27: 11 (1977), 695–702.

Wistrich, Robert S. *Weekend in Munich: Art, Propaganda and Terror in the Third Reich*. London 1995.

Index